Herman Hoeksema:
A Theological Biography

By Patrick Baskwell

ISBN: 978-0-578-01195-0

© 2009 All rights reserved

Full Bible Publications
Clover * Manassas

Dedication

I dedicate this thesis to my precious wife, Joan. Without her help and encouragement it simply never would have been.

Dr. Baskell currently teaches theology at St. Petersburg Theological Seminary in St. Petersburg, FL.

Contents

Introduction 11
    Bibliographic Materials 14
    Status of Research 17
Part One 21
Herman Hoeksema: A Spiritual/Intellectual Biography 21
Chapter 1 21
    The Early Years in Holland 21
    1.1 The Provenance of Herman Hoeksema 22
    1.2 Stories of Youth 25
    1.3 The Origins of the Afscheiding 26
    1.4 Hendrik de Cock 31
    1.5 Various Assessments 33
    1.6 Abraham Kuyper and the Doleantie 36
    1.7 Dissent 38
    1.8 The Influence of Abraham Kuyper 42
    1.9 A Different Paradigm 45
    1.10 A Positive Influence 46
    1.11 A Negative Influence 48
    1.12 Kuyper's Further Influence 50
    1.13 Conclusion 51
Chapter 2 54
    The Seminarian and the Dutch Reformed Church 54
    2.1 A New Home 54
    2.2 The Reformed Church in America 57

2.3 The Seminarian 62

2.4 William Wijnand Heyns 63

2.5 The Origin of Professor Heyns's View of the Covenant 69

2.6 A Chance Encounter 74

2.7 Foppe Martin ten Hoor 75

2.8 The Lines of Influence 82

2.9 The Student and His Predilections 84

2.10 The Young Minister 87

2.11 The Man and the Minister 88

2.12 Conclusion 94

Chapter 3 95

The Origin and Development of Hoeksema's Theology 95

3.1 The First Pastorate 95

3.2 Reformed and Nationalistic 97

3.3 Growth and Development 101

3.4 Our Doctrine 102

3.5 Origins of a Methodology 105

3.6 Hoeksema's Own Thoughts on the Subject 112

3.7 The Banner Articles 116

3.8 The Bultema Case 120

3.9 Eastern Avenue Christian Reformed Church 125

3.10 Conclusion 126

Chapter 4 129

The Janssen Affair 129

4.1 Professor Janssen 129

4.2 Contextually Speaking 134

4.3 In the Pages of the Banner 136
4.4 The Rhetoric Escalates 139
4.5 The Exchange Continues 144
4.6 The Rationalist and the Irrationalist 148
4.7 Hoeksema's Response 152
4.8 Abraham and the Covenant of Grace 154
4.9 The Letter from A. Dykstra 155
4.10 Janssen Reenters the Fray 157
4.11 The Controversy Widens 160
4.12 Conclusion 166

Chapter 5 169
1924 and Beyond 169
5.1 The Synod of 1922 and its aftermath 169
5.2 The Beginning of the End 176
5.3 The Twenties and Thirties 181
5.4 Reunion? 187
5.5 Schilder and Hoeksema in the 1940s 190
5.6 The Stroke 192
5.7 Conclusion 195

Chapter 6 199
The Rationalist 199
6.1 J. K. van Baalen 199
6.2 A. Kuyper Jr. 199
6.3 The Clark Case 202
6.4 Conclusion 206

Part Two 207
The Three Points Of Common Grace 207

The Three Points of Common Grace 209
    Acts of Synod, 1924, pages 145-147 209
Chapter 7 213
    Point One: The Favor of God to the Unregenerate 213
    7.1 Grace 214
    7.2 Grace and the Covenant 218
    7.3 Conditional versus Unconditional 221
    7.4 Professor Heyns's Judgment 224
    7.5 De Jong's Criticisms 227
    7.6 Hyper-Calvinism and the Call of the Gospel 233
    7.7 Calvin and the Free Offer 237
    7.8 G. C. Berkouwer 246
    7.9 Raymond Blacketer's Assessment 250
    7.10 Conclusion 251
Chapter 8 253
Point Two: The Restraint of Sin in the Heart of Man 253
    8.1 The Image of God as a Point of Contact 254
    8.2 The Image of God in Man 257
    8.3 The Restraint of Sin 262
    8.4 Further Criticism of Point Two 264
    8.5 Organic Development 266
    8.6 Conclusion 273
Chapter 9 275
Point Three: The Development of Culture 275
    9.1 Synod's Confessional Proof 276
    9.2 Culture 278
    9.3 The Cultural Aspirations of Humanity 281

9.4 General Revelation 286
9.5 Anabaptism and the Antithesis 290
9.6 Was Van Baalen Correct? 295
9.7 Christ against Culture 296
9.8 Conclusion 301
Conclusion 303
Bibliography 309

Introduction

In 1924 Herman Hoeksema and a small, but loyal, band of followers found themselves at odds with their own denomination, the Christian Reformed Church. The Christian Reformed Church, at the time a small denomination consisting largely of Dutch immigrants to the United States and Canada and the descendents of Dutch immigrants, found Hoeksema and his followers guilty of denying the 'doctrine' of common grace; a 'doctrine' recently adopted in three points and elevated to confessional status. Hoeksema, aided by Henry Danhof and George Ophoff, fought the acceptance of this 'doctrine' of common grace by the Christian Reformed Church both from the pulpit and in print. In the end there was not room in the Christian Reformed Church for both; the Three Points of Common Grace were accepted while Hoeksema and company were summarily rejected.

The conflict surrounding Hoeksema had to do with burning issues and discussions in the Reformed world in the beginning of the twentieth-century. Hoeksema had very distinctive opinions, but due to the clash neither his opinions nor the development of his thought was ever analyzed unless by people who were themselves participants of the conflict. Now, after almost a century, it is time, with the required distance, to take up this work and to analyze Hoeksema's thought. This study, however, is not about common grace as a whole; rather, it is my attempt to understand one of the more characteristic persons of Reformed theology in the first half of the last century. And now, with more distance, to bring forth again his arguments in the discussion on common grace, and, in a broader perspective, to apply them to the relation of church and society.

What is this common grace that Hoeksema would receive the ultimate sanction a minister can get for having denied it? Actually, as the Three Points themselves show, common grace is not just a single concept, it is actually a rubric, or category, which contains several, rather disparate tenets. In saying this, I am following primarily the exposition of the 'doctrine' as it was given confessional status in the Christian Reformed Church in Hoeksema's day. Simply put, common grace allows non-Christians to be credited with doing a certain amount of good, especially in the civic realm and in other areas of culture. Common grace also maintains that one of the functions of the Holy Spirit is to restrain sin in the heart of non-Christians. Yet, another facet of common grace is the favorable attitude on the part of God towards the unbeliever in the free offer of the Gospel. There are indeed other things that make up common grace, but in the course of our study we will concern ourselves primarily with these three tenets because these are the ideas which were given confessional status in the Christian Reformed Church in 1924 and which Hoeksema resisted, even to his removal from the denomination. From this perspective, this thesis is not meant to be the definitive study of the 'doctrine' of common grace. It is rather the study of one man's encounter with these concepts and his rejection of them as seen through his eyes. There have indeed been many others since Hoeksema's time who have weighed in on the debate, but it would be beyond the scope of our study to deal with them all at any length.

I would also like to ask the question: Who was this man Herman Hoeksema? The Protestant Reformed Churches, which he founded after being released from his charge in the Christian Reformed Church, say that he was a remarkable man. The Christian Reformed Church and her historians portray Hoeksema as little more than a footnote to their history. In the course of time since 1924, Hoeksema has more often been ignored than grappled with, let alone refuted. Born into relative poverty in the Netherlands, Hoeksema learned at an early age to fight for what he wanted. It seems, however, he liked the fighting aspect a bit too much and this did not suit him well in his later ecclesiastical struggles. Yet, in spite of his rather inauspicious beginnings and some rather disagreeable personality traits, it is my belief that, as one of the most distinctive and consistent Reformed theologians of the twentieth-century, Herman Hoeksema is still a force that must be reckoned with.

In order to answer my questions about Herman Hoeksema and the 'doctrine' of common grace, I begin my thesis with a spiritual/intellectual biography of Herman Hoeksema (Chapters 1-6). The only work to cover the period in Herman Hoeksema's life prior to his immigration from Holland to the United States in any detail is a biography written by his daughter-in-law Gertrude

Hoeksema, and published in 1969, under the title *Therefore Have I Spoken*—this has been the only biography on Herman Hoeksema to date. I am greatly indebted to this work for much of the material in the following pages. Yet, for material on Hoeksema's parentage and early chronology, I am also indebted to Mr. M. S. Mulder who graciously supplied me with these particulars as they are recorded in the municipal offices of Hoogezand/Sappemeer. While the biography that follows may build on the work of Gertrude Hoeksema, they are indeed very different. Her concern was to chronicle the life of her father-in-law for readers in the denomination, which he founded. In a sense, she was introducing the younger generation in the Protestant Reformed Church to their spiritual grandfather. My intent, by comparison, is to analyze Hoeksema's intellectual and spiritual development. Hence, the spiritual/intellectual biography chronicles Hoeksema's spiritual and intellectual odyssey from his native Holland, through the early years in the pastorate in the United States, through the conflicts which continually seemed to beset him, and ending in the late 1940s following a debilitating stroke from which he never fully recovered. While it may be objected that Hoeksema lived until 1965 and that I am neglecting a large portion of his adult life, I feel justified in the parameters I have chosen. By the time of Hoeksema's debilitating stroke in 1947 his theology was already finished, and thus, for our purposes, his spiritual, intellectual development was essentially complete. Granted, his theological thinking did not cease with the stroke, but, at least to my mind, any further development in his theology did.

The second part of the following thesis (Chapters 7-9) will concentrate primarily on the 'doctrine' of common grace. I say primarily, because I will only include those distinctives of Hoeksema's theology, which in some way relate to, or hinge upon his evaluation of common grace. In this part of the thesis I intend to examine in some detail the doctrine of common grace as it was contained in the Three Points adopted by the Synod of the Christian Reformed Church in 1924, devoting a chapter to each of the Three Points. In examining the Three Points we will be, if you will, looking through Hoeksema's eyes in both our understanding and evaluation of these important concepts and their applications, both intended and unintended.

The analysis that follows, therefore, is intended to demonstrate both the significance and coherence of Hoeksema's theology by way of his denial of common grace and his own distinctive developments. It is not a pleasant thing to be immersed in the sorry affairs of church struggle and strife, bitterness and hatred, as happened in the Christian Reformed Church and in Hoeksema's life, but I think it is beneficial in the long run to see the power that sin had in these institutions of benevolence, and the rank unwillingness among members of the clergy for any brotherly discussion of differences. Hence, I intend to present this conflict with all its hatreds, contradictions and absurdities. Additionally, by means of the framework and divisions I have chosen, i.e. beginning with a spiritual/intellectual biography of Hoeksema and then proceeding to analyze through Hoeksema's eyes the Three Points of Common Grace of 1924, I believe we will gain a better view of the life of the mind that indeed characterized the man Herman Hoeksema.

Bibliographic Materials

Much of the material used here relating to Hoeksema's development and the common grace struggle has not been used before. *The Banner* articles in particular are almost completely forgotten by the Christian Reformed Church and even the Protestant Reformed Churches in their continued treatment of the subject. It is my contention that these articles, four years worth, are crucial for understanding Hoeksema's developing thought, and I have endeavored to demonstrate this throughout. All editions of *The Banner*, extending back to its inception in 1866, can be found in the Archives at the Heckman Library on the campus of Calvin College and Seminary in Grand Rapids, Michigan. The Archives at Calvin College and Seminary also contain Hoeksema's senior paper entitled 'Rousseau and Education,' which he wrote in 1912, his last year in the preparatory division of Calvin Seminary, which later became Calvin College. Also available in the Archives are a complete set of the *Acts of Synod* for the Christian Reformed Church. For my purposes, only the years 1922, 1924, 1926 and 1928 were of significance. In addition to its holdings, the Archives at the

Heckman Library produces a historical magazine entitled *Origins*, which I have found especially helpful in bringing to light the lesser known aspects of the history of the Christian Reformed Church, immigration issues particularly as they bear on the Christian Reformed Church in Canada and significant people connected in some way with the development of Dutch Reformed theology both in the United States and abroad.

With regard to archives, I have already mentioned the birth and population records held in the municipal offices in Hoogezand-Sappemeer. These were supplied to me by M. S. Mulder, who is curator of these records, and who was very timely in responding to my requests for information. The final archive that I made use of was the Public Records Office in the Cook County Health Department, Chicago, Illinois. It was here that I obtained the death certificate for Johanna Bakema, nee Hoeksema, Hoeksema's mother.

Another source I have employed in the thesis are the many interviews I conducted with members of the Hoeksema family, as well as any surviving associates. Not surprisingly a high percentage of those 'associates,' many advanced in years at the time of the interview, are now deceased. Not all the interviews were helpful, some were downright hostile, but a complete list of those I used can be found in the bibliography.

Hoeksema's shorter writings can be found in both *The Banner* and *The Standard Bearer*. *The Banner*, discussed above, is the official organ of the Christian Reformed Church, and Hoeksema's contributions to the rubric 'Our Doctrine' in *The Banner* span the years 1918-1922, with the last article dated 31 August 1922. With his dismissal from the ministry of the Christian Reformed Church, Hoeksema proceeded to found the Protestant Reformed Churches in 1924. At the same time he also established a new periodical, *The Standard Bearer*, both as his outlet in the Protestant Reformed Churches and as a rival to *The Banner* in the Christian Reformed Church. The many volumes of *The Standard Bearer*, the first issue bearing the date October 1924, are more readily available than those of *The Banner*. Several years ago the Protestant Reformed Churches committed all past issues of *The Standard Bearer* to CD, complete with its own search engine. Their stated plan at the time was to update the set every ten years and it has been updated once since it's unveiling. The complete set is available from the Reformed Free Publishing Association, 4949 Ivanrest Avenue SW, Grandville, MI 49418-9709.

In addition to the many hundreds of articles contained in both *The Banner* and *The Standard Bearer*, the Hoeksema corpus also includes hundreds of unpublished sermons still in manuscript. A word about these sermons is in order because of their unusual provenance. As David Engelsma of the Protestant Reformed Churches has written regarding these sermons:

> The explanation of the existence of these sermons in written form is a story in itself. So far as I have been able to determine, Hoeksema's own outlines…no longer exist. But as Calvin had his scribes in Geneva, to whom we are indebted for the sermons by Calvin that we posses, Hoeksema had his scribe. He was Martin Swart (1891-1977), a member of the First Protestant Reformed Church in Grand Rapids, Michigan from its beginning in 1924 to his death in 1977. For many of those years, Mr. Swart took down Hoeksema's sermons by his own system of shorthand. Older members of First Church remember seeing Mr. Swart absorbed in his writing, service after service, as Hoeksema preached. Those were the days before tape recordings. Immediately upon returning home, Swart would write out the sermon in full with a pencil. Later, he transcribed the sermon into spiral notebooks with a pen. (Engelsma 2000b:293.)

Swart, who worked his whole life 'as a wood cutter in furniture factories in Grand Rapids' (Engelsma 2002:xxiv), produced 'some 70 notebooks' (Engelsma 2000b:293) of Hoeksema's sermons in this manner. The notebooks to this day remain in the Swart family although they have been copied several times over the years with at least one copy residing in the Heckman Library, Calvin College and Seminary in Grand Rapids, Michigan. I have my own copy of all the Swart transcriptions.

As amply demonstrated by the above sources, the Hoeksema corpus is simply enormous. His industry as a pastor, teacher, author and polemicist was seemingly inexhaustible. Hence, the time and effort expended in sifting through this veritable mountain of material in order to understand the man and his thought has been considerable.

Status of Research

Aside from the many articles written in the denominational magazines of the Christian Reformed Church and the Protestant Reformed Churches, there is relatively little said elsewhere concerning Herman Hoeksema. Even the Christian Reformed Church has had little to say as of late. This situation began to change somewhat in 2000 when both the April and November issues of the *Calvin Theological Journal* were devoted to the Three Points of Common Grace and the events surrounding their adoption in 1924. John Bolt and Raymond Blacketer, in a total of three articles, revisited the events of 1924 in articles that were unusually sympathetic to Hoeksema and his cause.

There are only two other articles that center on Hoeksema, outside Protestant Reformed circles that is, of which I am aware. The first, by L. Vogelaar, is entitled 'Hoeksema was verbaasd over Schilder.' This can be found in *De Hoeksteen*, Volume 25 (December 1996), afl, 5-6. Pg. 210-213. The second is by P. Rouwendal, entitled 'Herman Hoeksema. Leven en opvattingen van een controversieel theoloog,' and it can be found in the *Tijdschrift voor Nederlandse Kerkgeschiedenis* IV. 3 (September 2001), pages 70-82.

There have been three academic theses that deal with Hoeksema to a greater or lesser degree; his name is in the title of each work. The first one of these was a thesis written by A. C. de Jong for the Free University of Amsterdam in 1954 entitled *The Well-Meant Gospel Offer: The Views of H. Hoeksema and K. Schilder.* This work shows little sympathy for Hoeksema's theological distinctives. I analyze this work in some detail in chapter 7. In 1985 a dissertation by H. David Schuringa was submitted for the degree of Master of Theology in the department of Practical Theology at Calvin Theological Seminary. Entitled 'The Preaching of the Word as a Means of Grace: The Views of Herman Hoeksema and R. B. Kuiper.' This dissertation concentrates almost exclusively on R. B. Kuiper, with Hoeksema and his 'rationalism' little more than a subtheme. The final thesis was written by David B. McWilliams and submitted for the degree of Doctor of Philosophy at the University of Wales, Lampeter in January 2000. It is titled, 'Herman Hoeksema's Theological Method.' McWilliams brings together a huge amount of material in the course of his discussion. It seems, however, that all his sources are, in one way or another, used simply to castigate Hoeksema. McWilliams subscribes to the school of Reformed thought centered on Westminster Theological Seminary in Philadelphia, Pennsylvania. Because of this McWilliams show a preference for paradox and mystery that was not shared by Hoeksema. Hoeksema was logical to a fault, and his enemies criticized him endlessly for it. McWilliams does the same. Hence, there is little in Hoeksema's method that McWilliams finds attractive. I will deal with much of this in chapters 3, 6 and 7.

There is one other thesis that, while not being strictly about Hoeksema, devotes some space to his thought. Entitled 'Grace without Christ? The Doctrine of Common Grace in Dutch-American Neo-Calvinism,' this work was submitted by Walter Campbell Campbell-Jack in 1992 to the University of Edinburgh, Scotland in fulfillment of the degree of Doctor of Philosophy. In what seems to me to be a relatively balanced work, the author investigates the common grace of Abraham Kuyper, Herman Hoeksema and Klaas Schilder. Out of 325 pages the author devotes less than 20 to Hoeksema, which seems to be a deficiency, but, while Campbell-Jack is more sympathetic to common grace than its denial, which Hoeksema does, he is fair in his presentation of Hoeksema's views.

In 2000 Richard J. Mouw, President of Fuller Seminary in California, was invited to deliver the Stob Lectures at Calvin Theological Seminary. This he did with distinction under the title *He Shines in All That's Fair: Culture and Common Grace*. Much is said in these lectures of Hoeksema and much is sympathetic. David Engelsma of the Protestant Reformed Seminary in Grand Rapids, Michigan wrote a response to some of Mouw's conclusions entitled *Common Grace Revisited: A Response to Richard J. Mouw's He Shines in All That's Fair*—see the bibliography at the end of the thesis for further information on both books. Both books are very informative and they complement each other well.

This book, with slight modifications, was originally submitted to the Vrije Universiteit in Amsterdam, the Netherlands under the sponsorship of Professor A. van de Beek of the Vrije Universiteit and Professor R. J. Mouw of Fuller Seminary, Pasadena, California, in fulfillment of the degree of Doctor of Theology.

Part One

Herman Hoeksema: A Spiritual/Intellectual Biography

Chapter 1

The Early Years in Holland

Herman Hoeksema was founder and, for nearly forty years, the unflinching leader of the Protestant Reformed Churches in America. Over the course of his long and often tumultuous career he has been labeled a rationalist (Hoeksema 1969:230-231, Wielenga 2000, McWilliams 2000:6 also p. 54); he has been called unkind (Veldman 2000); and he is consistently remembered as someone who had to be right, irrespective of the consequences (Hoeks 2000, Hoeksema 2001). G. C. Berkouwer of the Free University of Amsterdam, one of Hoeksema's strongest critics and, as such, not intending to be complementary, wrote that 'I have seldom met a theologian who reasoned through so consistently from his original standpoint; he never wavered from his starting point' (Berkouwer 1977:98). Herman Hoeksema was a man who, throughout his life and in all his endeavors, embodied unusually bold distinctives.

In this first chapter my aim is to investigate certain lines of influence that contributed to the shaping of Hoeksema's distinctive thought. First of all, the details of his family history and his early years in the Netherlands, prior to his immigration to the United States, will be discussed in order to determine what influence this period had on his later thought. In conjunction with this history, brief mention will also be made of the events that shaped the Reformed Churches in the Netherlands at the time. Secondly, I will scrutinize those events and people that helped to mold Herman Hoeksema, both personally and theologically, prior to his arrival in the United States in 1904.

1.1 The Provenance of Herman Hoeksema

According to the population records of the Gemeente Hoogezand-Sappemeer, Herman Hoeksema, registered under the name 'Harm,' was born on 13 March 1886 in the *dorp* (town) of Hoogezand in the province of Groningen (Mulder 2001). However, according to his daughter-in-law Gertrude, he was actually born on 12 March, but 'his father neglected to register Harm's birth with the town clerk, and when, at his wife's insistence, he finally got around to it, he registered the date as March 13, which date Harm always afterward celebrated as his birthday' (Hoeksema 1969:17).

Herman's mother, Johanna Bakema, daughter of Jan Lulofs Bakema and Aaltje Kempinga, was born in Kropswolde on 5 July 1856. His father, Tiele Hoeksema, son of Harm Hoeksema and Everdina Steenhuis, was born in Muntendam on 26 January 1856. Johanna Bakema and Tiele Hoeksema were married in Hoogezand on 27 May 1881. Herman's sister, Everdina Aaltina, was the first to be born on the 27 November 1882; Johan followed on 21 July 1884, but passed away the following year on the 12 May 1885. The family relocated to the city of Groningen in 1888 when the young Herman was two years old. After Herman, two more sons, Albert and John, were to be born to Tiele and Johanna before the union ended in divorce on 22 June 1897 (Mulder 2001).

The divorce of Tiele and Johanna seems to have been the result of years of hardship and neglect. Daughter-in-law and biographer Gertrude Hoeksema questions whether 'during their traditional Dutch courtship, had she [Johanna] forgotten to look beneath his dark, even features and his charming dashing manner? Or did he truly seem to be a serious, sincere young man, only to change later?' (Hoeksema 1969:17). 'Before the youngest was born,' Gertrude informs us, 'the father had stopped supporting his wife and children and left the church, had drunk too much and become a full-fledged philanderer. Then he enlisted in the foreign military service of the Netherlands' (Hoeksema 1969:17). According to granddaughter Nell Phillips, Tiele Hoeksema 'deserted grandma time and time again, and he even had a mistress' (Phillips 2001). In the words of another granddaughter, Lois Kregel, daughter of Herman Hoeksema, 'everybody feared Tiele Hoeksema, grandma even sought court protection from him because he was a mean and nasty drunk' (Kregel 2000). Herman Hoeksema Jr. confirms the fact that Tiele Hoeksema had an affinity for the bottle, adding that he also liked to play the horses (Hoeksema 2001). Herman was four when his parents finally separated in 1890. This was, according to Herman Hoeksema Jr., to have a profound effect on Herman's life (Hoeksema 2001). It must also be kept in mind that divorce at this time, especially in church circles, was very rare. And that those involved in a divorce were ever after 'marked' people (see Schilling 1991:58-60).

Herman Hoeksema's mother was, by all accounts, a godly woman imbued with a deep personal piety. The only real remembrance of her, though, are the recollections of Nell Phillips, a daughter of Herman's sister Everdina, and Gertrude Hoeksema, Herman's daughter-in-law—she was married to Herman Hoeksema's youngest son Homer, until his death on 17 July 1989. In the wake of her separation from Tiele in 1890, Johanna took to sewing in order to make a living (Phillips 2001). Alone in the city of Groningen with four small children, writes Gertrude Hoeksema with obvious admiration, Johanna 'spread the word that she was an excellent seamstress. Every day she went out to sew for her wealthy clients, and each evening she came back with the day's wages, equivalent to one American dollar' (Hoeksema 1969:17-18). Even for her ingenuity, money and food were scarce. Bread lines were common, but Johanna detested the experience all the while 'desperately needing the nourishment of the piece of bread that was thrown to them' (Hoeksema 1969:18). Gertrude Hoeksema relates the effect this had on Herman and the resulting lifelong social concern:

> After the humiliation of being treated like animals they were compelled to eat the bread while still standing in line; but the belittling climax came when they were searched to see that they took no bread home in their

> pockets. Is it any wonder that young Harm's whole being rebelled at this inhumane treatment, and that in later life he spoke with an earnestness approaching vehemence on the evils of the rich oppressing the poor? (Hoeksema 1969:18-19.)

Because of these personal experiences, years later, even after having lived in the United States for some time, Herman would still 'hold up to contempt the idealistic loyalty of immigrants who could sing the praises of their fatherland and the House of Orange. His jovial "*Oranje boven, en niets te eten* (Orange above all, and nothing to eat)," said enough' (Hoeksema 1969:44).

Gertrude Hoeksema goes to some length to assure readers of her biography that Hoeksema's mother Johanna was devout but not legalistic in her religious outlook. She recounts a story illustrative of Johanna's ardent devotion. Apparently, one Sunday morning, after a particularly strenuous week, Hoeksema's mother

> discovered that she had forgotten to sew the fresh white collar to her simple black dress. Quickly force of habit took over, and she threaded her needle and sewed it on. Then her conscience stung her. She had done unnecessary work on the Lord's Day. Reproaching herself, she carefully loosened the stitches she had just taken, removed the collar and wore the black dress, unadorned, to church that day. (Hoeksema 1969:21.)

Gertrude Hoeksema is quick to point out that while 'to a casual observer her [Johanna's] brand of piety might have been legalism… her family knew it welled from the depths of her being' (Hoeksema 1969:21). Johanna's actions, according to Gertrude, could best be described as just piously Reformed. It is interesting to note, however, in conjunction with this disclaimer of legalism, that Herman Hoeksema was himself very sensitive to being tarred with this same brush. According to his granddaughter, Eunice, whenever the family was on vacation, Herman was not remiss to swimming on Sundays. If the charge of not properly observing the Sabbath ever surfaced, Herman would curtly reply '*Ik ben geen Jood*' (I am no Jew) (Kuiper 2000).

'She [Johanna] taught them the fear of the Lord,' Gertrude Hoeksema remembers, 'she took them to church, and sent them to the local Christian school. This loving care by his God-fearing mother was the other side of Harm's life' (Hoeksema 1969:22).

1.2 Stories of Youth

Most of what is known of Herman Hoeksema prior to his immigration to the United States is in the form of family stories. These are stories that Herman himself must have told at one time or another. I come to this conclusion because very little is said of other family members in all of Hoeksema's writings. In fact, Herman had two younger brothers who immigrated to the United States with their mother Johanna in 1906, yet there seems to be no distinct recollection of these two men anywhere in the current family. When Johanna died in 1929, one of these two younger brothers, Albert Hoeksema, was the one to provide the details on Johanna's background to the Cook County (Chicago, IL) Coroner. Based on the information given, Albert lacked any substantive details of his own mother's life. He knew her father's name, but that was the extent of his knowledge. Most of the lines on the death certificate are filled with the word 'unknown.' Those that are not, contain incorrect information, such as the ones requesting the birthplace (city or town) of Johanna's father and mother that simply say 'Groningen.' From this I think it reasonable to believe that Johanna, having left her former husband in the Netherlands along with her many hardships, simply chose not to remember her life before immigrating to Chicago any more, much less discuss it. The children, Everdina, Herman, Albert, and John, had their own memories and that was the extent of it. Hence, all information concerning Herman Hoeksema's early years in the Netherlands are his own recollections, transmitted over the years to his children and to their children in the form of stories. In this regard, that portion of Gertrude Hoeksema's biography of Herman Hoeksema, which deals with his early years before immigrating to America in 1904, is just a compilation of these family stories.

Taken together these family stories paint a rather dark picture of the young Hoeksema, depicting him as anything but a polished young man. The first chapter of Gertrude's biography recounts many instances of a young Harm (Herman) swimming illegally in the canals of Groningen, fighting, playing unwanted practical jokes on innocent victims, and thumbing his nose at police (Hoeksema 1969:15-33). After attending grammar school, Hoeksema won a scholarship of sorts to the Ambacht School (a technical school) where he learned the blacksmith trade. Afterwards, he apprenticed in both a country setting and in his hometown of Groningen, both of which, while learning experiences, did not provide fond memories. Gertrude Hoeksema tells us that amidst all the hardship,

> He [Herman] grew up to be a young man who could form opinions for himself. His thinking may have had a philosophic or imaginative bent; but it had objective standards, those of the Scriptures and the Reformed Creeds, with their definitiveness of right and wrong, of sin and grace, of God's sovereignty and man's responsibility. ... [Hence-PB] he was not satisfied with life in the Netherlands, the economic, the cultural, the religious. Convinced that the Reformed truth was the purest interpretation of the Scriptures, he was not wholly satisfied with the conditions of the Reformed church in his country. (Hoeksema 1969: 30-31.)

In Groningen, the Hoeksema family attended the *Afscheiding* or Secession church; more commonly known as the 'A' congregations in contradistinction from the churches of the *Doleantie* or 'B' congregations. In order to understand more fully Hoeksema's religious development, it will be of benefit if we look at the origins of the *Afscheiding* and *Doleantie* churches in some detail.

1.3 The Origins of the Afscheiding

The *Afscheiding*, also referred to as the Reformation of 1834, was a loosely organized secession from the *Hervormde Kerk*. The

Hervormde Kerk was not, however, an official 'state church,' though the influence of the king was very strong after 1815. Eventually, in 1848, a constitution with provision for the separation of church and state was adopted. The *Afscheiding*, or Secession of 1834 was not something that occurred in response to a specific event, nor was it something that took place on the spur-of-the-moment. It was, instead, a considered response to a perceived series of abuses on the part of those with ecclesiastical power. Further, it was a response to what was perceived as an abandoning of the principles of the Reformed faith on the part of the leadership of the *Hervormde Kerk*. The *Afscheiding*, writes K. H. Miskotte of the *Hervormde Kerk*, 'as a struggle for the exclusive right of God's word was a movement of profound and holy import' (quoted by Rasker 1981:55). He concludes by saying that this reformation was a warning from God concerning a 'ruined church' (quoted by Rasker 1981:55). Many things, however, contributed to the 'ruin' of this church. It did not happen in isolation. In many ways the problems were as much political as they were theological.

The Netherlands, since the days of the national Synod of Dort in 1618-1619, had long been a stronghold of the Reformed faith (see Reitsma 1933, Knappert 1911). 'By 1650,' writes Walter Lagerwey, 'approximately one-half of the populace had membership in the Netherlands Reformed Church' (Lagerwey 1964:86). For almost a century these churches held tenaciously to the distinctly Reformed 'Three Forms of Unity' (The Heidelberg Catechism, The Belgic Confession, and the Cannons of Dort) as their theological foundation (Wintle 1987:5). Yet, by the end of the century, Walter Lagerwey informs us, 'there began a gradual decline in the fortunes of both church and state' (Lagerwey 1964:87). 'Among the factors which contributed to the decline of Dutch Calvinism' Lagerwey continues,

> one of the most important was doubtless the close relationship of church and state. The church was subject to the control of the state at crucial points. No national synods could be called without state concurrence, and that was not forthcoming. The fact that the Hervormde Kerk was a national church made membership in it desirable and respectable, but the church could exercise little control over its members. Consequently, the church was

plagued increasingly with the problem of nominal membership. (Lagerwey 1964:87.)

Both Lagerwey and Wintle also attribute this decline in confessional Calvinism to the rise and assimilation of humanistic ideas into the Dutch Reformed Church. Quoting J. A. Bornewasser with approval, Wintle opines further that: 'The churches engaged in a defensive struggle against rationalist criticism, anthropocentrism, human autonomy and individualism, without wanting to distance themselves entirely' (Wintle 1987:8). For Lagerwey, this assimilation of ideas took an entirely different form. Instead of a battle with abstract ideas, as Wintle believes, Lagerwey writes that 'the outbreak of the French Revolution was hailed by Dutch liberals as ushering in a new period of political enlightenment, tolerance, and democracy' (Lagerwey 1964:89). The result for the Netherlands and the Dutch Reformed Church was, writes Lagerwey,

> [that] a large segment of the Dutch populace became hostile to the House of Orange and welcomed the invasion of the Netherlands by French forces in 1795. As a result of this invasion the Dutch Stadtholder was compelled to go into exile. A new state, the Batavian republic, was established on the ideals of the French Revolution: fraternity, equality, liberty, and the sovereignty of the people. The establishment of the Batavian Republic at once rendered the position of the Netherlands Reformed Church problematic. The idea of an established Calvinistic church was in radical conflict with the equalitarian ideals of the revolution. (Lagerwey 1964:89.)

For a Calvinistic church so dependent upon state funding, as was the Netherlands Reformed Church, these developments were disastrous. 'Theology was now under attack,' Wintle writes, 'from philosophers influenced by the new rationalism and humanism' (Wintle 1987:9). New ideas, including 'freedom of religion' which was declared in 1795, only added to the woes of this financially troubled church (Wintle 1987:10).

French dominance of the Netherlands was mainly the result of Napoleon's successes. Conversely, when his success was replaced with defeat in 1813, French dominance collapsed and the Netherlands, literally by default, regained political independence.

'On 16 March 1815,' writes E. H. Kossmann, 'William, who until then had been provisionally called Sovereign Prince, took the title of King of the Netherlands' (Kossmann 1978:111). This burgeoning 'constitutional republic' had previously agreed upon and drafted significant constitutional modifications in the form of eight articles. Kossmann relates that these modifications were discussed at length in April of that year by a joint Dutch-Belgian commission (Kossmann 1978:111). Kossmann further argues that:

> The draft agreed by the commission was intended to establish a moderate form of monarchy which would be a mean between the British system and that of the Central European restoration regimes. It was a synthesis of traditional but contradictory tendencies rather than a compromise between old and new. Neither the conservatives nor the liberals at first seemed dissatisfied with the result. (Kossmann 1978:112.)

One would have thought that the end of French rule also meant the end of French influence. This, however, was not to be. As Walter Lagerwey writes, 'in the new government French reforms, penal codes, political ideology persisted' (Lagerwey 1964:90). In the resulting state of affairs, the church was deemed to be, for all intents and purposes, a branch of the government—actually, even in the time of the Republic the local church had no autonomy. Extreme centralization had deprived her of her autonomy. Walter Lagerwey summarizes the situation as such:

> The status and organization of the Netherlands Reformed Church was now determined by the *state*, and a new church order was formulated by the Ministry of Internal Affairs. This order abolished the presbyterian pattern of church government (destroying the local autonomy of the congregation) and introduced a centralized, administrative, synodical system. The democratic character of the church was changed to one that was autocratic, control of the church from congregational level to synod being vested in administrative bodies which were responsible to the government (king). (Lagerwey 1964:90-91.)

The Reformed Church in its new, government imposed, context was seen by the majority of the orthodox Reformed populace as, in the words of the medievalist Steven Runciman's description of the Orthodox Church in the hands of the Seljuk Turks, 'The Great Church in Captivity' (Runciman 1968).

State control over the church also led to an emphasis on tolerance, the meaning of which was inherited from the French and their concept of *liberté*. This, combined with a growing diversity of theological views in the state church, prompted the government to intervene even further to ensure ecclesiastical peace. As P. Y. de Jong says:

> It sought to stem the disaffections by urging toleration in doctrinal formulations, hoping to promote peace in the churches. When occasionally classes or provincial synods imposed discipline on unfaithful ministers, the state refused to approve. Thus toleration, originally intended ... to provide some greater liberties for those who were not Reformed, opened the door to departures from the confessions within the church itself. (De Jong 1984a:10.)

This trend continued throughout the nineteenth-century; its express purpose being to purge the church of narrowness. D. H. Kromminga has described this trend as such:

> Toleration could be understood and applied in quite diverse meanings and ways; its meaning and application widened gradually, and the government stood by to see to it that the churches learned to practice tolerance. The silencing of theological disputes involving university professors had occurred earlier and is intelligible since those institutions were not of an ecclesiastical but of a civil character, supported and controlled by the government. But the government came to apply the same policy with increasing frequency also to disputes not involving professors, and it showed a growing tendency to exercise control also over the calling of ministers in vacancies. This whole development of government control in ecclesiastical matters was the more possible, since part of the ecclesiastics supported it. In other words, this

> development went hand in hand with the growth of a party within the Church that stood for and preached tolerance, whether in their own interest or from love of peace or failure to appreciate the issues of the controversy. These ecclesiastics naturally approved of the governmental policy, and the combination in the course of time forced toleration on the Church. (Kromminga 1943:68.)

This 'overemphasis' on toleration and the 'maintenance of the organization', Kromminga continues, 'forced the adherents of the Reformed tradition into conflict with the church Boards and led to the expulsion of their leaders' (Kromminga 1943:79). The more aristocratic of the Reformed churches, however, were not amenable to secession (Kromminga 1943:81). While many of these were not happy with the growing doctrinal laxity of the church, they viewed secession as a betrayal of their commitment to the Church of Christ. One member of this more aristocratic coterie was Guillaume Groen van Prinsterer (1801-1876); a lawyer, accomplished writer, historian, and the holder of two doctorates. 'Groen did not approve of the separation from the National Church,' writes James McGoldrick, 'but he affirmed the rights of the *Afscheiding* and decried the persecution of its adherents' (McGoldrick 2000: 27).

Next to tolerance, the influence of contemporary philosophy was also very strong. Leading persons, especially the professors who trained the students of theology, followed mainly philosophical trends. A good example of this was the influential professor J. H. Scholten (1811-1885) of the University of Leiden who exhibited a strong inclination towards Hegel (McGoldrick 2000:32). As a result, the church at this time was, in both organization and in thought, not so very much a resident alien in the world.

1.4 Hendrik de Cock

In the year 1834, all things seemed relatively sedate. No one was expecting a break within the church. In fact, no one was either preparing or agitating for such a break (De Jong 1984b:21). Neither, muses P. Y. De Jong, 'could anyone have expected it to begin in the north far from influences such as the Swiss Reveil, the teaching of

Bilderdijk and "the club of Scholte"' (De Jong 1984b:21). But, begin in the north it did. The initial break from the *Hervormde Kerk* began in the small agricultural town of Ulrum in the province of Groningen, and the man who spearheaded the break was Hendrik de Cock. 'Within a few years,' De Jong relates with obvious pride, 'what began in Ulrum flashed across the land like an uncontrollable prairie fire' (De Jong 1984b:21). Is it any wonder that Hendrik Algra calls this event and the years of 'reform' that followed '*Het Wonder van de Negentiende Eeuw*' (The Miracle of the Nineteenth-Century) (Algra 1966)?

Hendrik de Cock, educated for the Gospel ministry in the Dutch Reformed Church at the University of Groningen, found his life turned upside down, soon after his installation in Ulrum, by a lowly day laborer and conscientious catechetical student named Klaas Pieters Kuypenga (De Jong 1984b:22). This catechetical instruction inadvertently led the newly installed minister to reflect upon his own life and work. Shortly thereafter, De Cock 'began to seek something richer and fuller for his own soul' (De Jong 1984b:22). To this end, he began to investigate seriously the confessions of his own church, apparently for the first time, as well as works by Baron Van Zuylen van Nyevelt and John Calvin. As a result of these investigations De Cock underwent a change. He also began to attract attention. As Kromminga says:

> His changed preaching drew hearers from neighboring villages, and enlargement of the church building became necessary. ...While the renovation was going on de Cock filled neighboring pulpits, thus spreading his influence and arousing hostility among his colleagues. ...At a fraternal classical meeting it came to a clash between him and these opponents in which they challenged him to publish an attack on them. (Kromminga 1943:82.)

Things eventually came to a head for De Cock, as disciplinary measures were instituted against him by Rev. A. P. A. du Cloux; an orthodox minister who chose to remain in the Hervormde Kerk and not join the Secession (Grosheide & Itterzon (eds.) 1957:227-228; Rasker 1981:60). However, 'the first secession from the state church,' writes Walter Lagerwey, 'was the result of direct violations of the state-imposed church order' (Lagerwey 1964:95). In 1834 De Cock violated this church order by baptizing infants whose parents were not members of his congregation in Ulrum. For this he was censured and deposed from the office of minister of the Gospel. Afterwards, 'De Cock appealed with his consistory to the Synodical Board and the king;' all of which, according to De Jong, was to no avail, as he was even forced to pay for the ecclesiastical procedures against him (De Jong 1984:25). After much time and wrangling, the secession from the Dutch Reformed Church became a fact; if not with great fanfare, then simply by default.

1.5 Various Assessments

While most writers who explore the history of the *Afscheiding* seem agreed that it was a reformation of sorts, not all are agreed as to its significance for the Reformed Church in the Netherlands. The Faculty of Mid-America Seminary, who collaborated on a series of essays on the *Afscheiding* in commemoration of its one hundred and fifty-year anniversary, view the Secession of 1834 as a continuation of the Reformation of the Sixteenth-Century. They believe it to be utterly 'Reformed' in every way. Walter Lagerwey, while acknowledging the actions of De Cock and his supporters, does not seem as enthusiastic as the professors at Mid-America Seminary regarding the singularly Reformed character of this secession. Conversely, Gertrude Hoeksema, writing from the perspective of the *Doleantie* churches, is inclined rather to disparage the *Afscheiding* movement altogether. In her comparison of the *Afscheiding* with the later secession from the Dutch Reformed Church, the *Doleantie*, under Abraham Kuyper, Gertrude writes:

> The first, the *Afscheiding*, or Secession of 1834, was a movement of the "*kleine lui* (little folk)," or common people. Among its weaknesses was a lack of strong leadership among a people with mystical tendencies, stemming from a pietistic background. Their conception of the doctrine of God's counsel and of the doctrine of regeneration was weaker and not so well defined as that of the later reform movement, the *Doleantie*, the reformation

of "the grieving ones." Through the influence of their capable leader, Dr. Abraham Kuyper, their doctrinal positions were better defined and followed the sound principles of the early Calvinistic reformers. (Hoeksema 1969:31.)

A. J. Rasker, in his widely read *De Nederlandse Hervormde Kerk vanaf 1795*, is somewhat more pointed in his assessment of things. Concentrating specifically on the pietism associated with *Afscheiding* assemblies, he writes:

> In these meetings, or conventicles, lived the spirit of the 'Nadere Reformatie' [the second reformation-PB] which always accompanied the orthodoxy of the 17th and 18th centuries, and which was fed from the springs of both Pietism and Methodism. ...After the Synod of Dort, sympathy for such assemblies can certainly be understood as an expression of the want of Pietistic practice and as a reaction against the scholasticization of theology and the intellectualization of the preaching in which the common man could find no spiritual nourishment. (Rasker 1981:55-56.)

Rasker sees the *Afscheiding* primarily as a pietistic backlash against a church that could provide neither the spiritual nourishment nor the spiritual experience demanded by the common people.

The church historian, W. van 't Spijker, agrees with Rasker that the origins of the *Afscheiding* lie in the *Nadere Reformatie* (Van 't Spijker 1984:147-148), but his position is significantly more nuanced. According to Van 't Spijker, De Cock did not see an inherent tension between doctrine and life (piety); for him, they simply belonged together. In fact, they could not be divorced, or separated, in any way; because life, or fruit, flowed inexorably from doctrine, be it good or bad (Van 't Spijker 1984:151). The fertile ground in which spirituality had to be rooted (*geworteld*) in order to produce good fruit was a combination of God's Word, an encounter (*ontmoeting*) with God, and a commitment to His service (Van 't Spijker 1984:148). As I understand Van 't Spijker, his use of the term encounter (*ontmoeting*) designates a life lived before God's face (*voor het aangezicht Gods*) and a continuous relationship and life with God by prayer, reading, and meditation on the Scriptures that would permeate the whole of one's life. Hence, for Van 't Spijker, an encounter with God is not an event but a way of life. Additionally, as Van 't Spijker points out, for De Cock, these truths were nothing other than those expressed in God's Word and witnessed to in the time of the Reformation (Van 't Spijker 1984:148).

To summarize: I think it would be correct to say that, for De Cock specifically and for the *Afscheiding* in general, a proper relationship with God is the central tenet of the Christian Faith. And, it is from this relationship that a true spirituality, or piety, necessarily flows. While this relationship is grounded firmly in the truths of God's Word and the Confessions of the church, it nevertheless contains another element. This element is, for all intents and purposes, what makes *Afscheiding* theology more than just believing true sentences about God. It is what gives *Afscheiding* theology life. Van 't Spijker terms this element 'an encounter with God' (Van 't Spijker 1984:148). While I agree with Van 't Spijker's categorical architecture, I cannot help but think that it is here, especially, that we are confronted with that mystical element that both Rasker and Van 't Spijker see as an essential part of the *Afscheiding's* inheritance from the *Nadere Reformatie*. Although he never spoke of an encounter with God *per se*, this element of 'relationship' is not absent from Hoeksema's theology either. This is simply part of his *Afscheiding* heritage. This heritage is most evident in his writings on the covenant, which he defines as a bond of friendship between God and man (Hoeksema 1966: 321-322). More will be said of this *Afscheiding* influence later when we examine the influence of both Foppe ten Hoor and Herman Bavinck on Hoeksema's theology.

Despite its several and varied shortcomings, the *Afscheiding* was a spontaneous movement to correct perceived deficiencies in the Dutch Reformed Church by means of disassociation, and it was not the only such movement. Fifty-two years later, in 1886, there was another secession from the Nederlandse Hervormde Kerk, which is commonly referred to as the *Doleantie*. This time, while the complaints were similar, the theological issues were thought out to a much greater degree and the leadership was much more organized. This was all due essentially to one man, Abraham Kuyper.

1.6 Abraham Kuyper and the Doleantie

Abraham Kuyper was one of the Netherlands' most influential theologians; as well as a newspaper editor, member of parliament, Prime Minister of the Netherlands, founder of the Anti-Revolutionary Party and Free University, and the author of many books. While the sheer scope of his activity was breathtaking, his output was equally astonishing. It is understandable, therefore, that his biographer James McGoldrick subtitles his biography 'God's Renaissance Man' (McGoldrick 2000).

Leading up to the second secession from the Dutch Reformed Church in 1886 was a further fragmentation of the Reformed faith. McGoldrick outlines three competing schools of thought, the 'Groningers,' the 'Ethicals,' and the 'Moderns' (McGoldrick 2000:29-34). The Groningers, according to the description afforded us by McGoldrick, were essentially Unitarian in their view of God (McGoldrick 2000:30). As the century passed the halfway point, they became increasingly anti-supernatural, eventually abandoning their previous 'reservations about radical criticism of the Bible and joined the Moderns (modernists) in opposition to a resurgent orthodoxy within the Dutch Reformed Church' (McGoldrick 2000:31).

By contrast, the Ethicals were genuinely interested in theology, especially in its everyday practical considerations. Since the name 'ethical' gives little insight into the beliefs of the group under consideration, it would be well to clarify what is meant. Professor J. Veenhof, in his massive study of Herman Bavinck, offers some significant insights in this regard. In speaking of 'Ethicals' founder Daniël Chantepie de la Saussaye, Veenhof explains that,

> The idea 'ethical' with its complex historical background has essentially the sense of the present 'existential'. This is amplified by a further analysis of his

idea of conscience, which is dependent on Vinet and the German theologians. In positing the 'ethical' character of truth, he wishes to break through the intellectualism of supernaturalism with its separation of doctrine and life and its primacy of the intellect, and the rationalism of modernism. The sources of life, in his opinion, lie in the heart, not in the intellect. The 'ethical' character of truth implies that the truth, supernatural in origin, is not superhuman but truly human. The ethical principle is at the same time Christological and anthropological. This vision of the truth is also decisive for his view of dogma and confession (aversion for confessionalism, emphasis upon significance of 'the faith of the church'). (Veenhof 1968:670.)

While I would consider the Ethicals to be in a direct line of both ideological and spiritual development from the *Réveil* and the *Afscheiding*, McGoldrick seems to consider them proto-Barthians, of a sort, in their view of revelation, saying that 'they argued that Scripture becomes the Word of God for an individual when it speaks to his or her conscience' (McGoldrick 2000:31). Further, he claims that 'the Ethicals tolerated a broad diversity of beliefs because they held dogma to be of little importance. ... [And] they became highly intolerant of Kuyper when he rose to defend the historic Christian faith' (McGoldrick 2000:247). If McGoldrick bases his case for the Ethicals' 'aversion' to doctrine on their intolerance of Kuyper's strict confessionalism, as he seems to, then I do not find his view substantiated. Just because the Ethicals opposed Kuyper's robust confessionalism is no reason to assume, out of hand, that 'they held dogma to be of little importance' (McGoldrick 2000:247). McGoldrick does, however, use the contrast with the Ethicals to point out the vigorous nature of Kuyper's confessionalism, which, as we will discuss later, is also seen in Hoeksema.

The final school of thought present in the Dutch Reformed Church at the time was the Moderns. According to McGoldrick, 'the Moderns comprised the third and most radical opposition to the Reformed faith in the Netherlands' (McGoldrick 2000:32). 'As their name suggests,' writes historian Louis Praamsma 'the moderns wanted to be men of the present, not of the past' (Praamsma 1985:35). McGoldrick adds that

> The University of Leiden was the centre of this teaching, where Professor J. N. (sic) Scholten (1811-1885) was its most vigorous spokesman. Moderns regarded themselves as agents of enlightenment, as they espoused Darwin's hypothesis of evolution and critical theories about the Bible. They believed they were progressives leading church and society forward so as to make the Christian faith compatible with a naturalistic world-view. (McGoldrick 2000:32.)

It was another student of Leiden, Abraham Kuyper, which, as Praamsma points out, 'was to be most energetic in fighting against this spirit' (Praamsma 1985:35).

Abraham Kuyper fought the spirit of the Moderns in print, in government, and especially in the church. 'After rejecting it [Modernism-PB] in favor of orthodox Protestantism,' writes British historian Peter Heslam, 'he spent the rest of his career in fierce opposition to its effects and in open conflict with its representatives' (Heslam 1998:267). This fierce war of words continued unabated until 1886, at which time Abraham Kuyper 'led 100,000 orthodox Calvinists from the *Hervormde Kerk* in the *Doleantie* (from the Latin *dolere*-to mourn) to form the *Gereformeerde Doleerende Kerk*' (Campbell-Jack 1992:6). In 1892, after much official and unofficial discussion and after much hope and many setbacks (see Bouma 1995 for details), the major elements of both the *Afscheiding* (the 'A' Churches) and the *Doleerende* Churches (the 'B' Churches) united to form the *Gereformeerde Kerken*, which Walter Campbell-Jack refers to as 'the second largest Protestant denomination in the Netherlands' (Campbell-Jack 1992:7).

1.7 Dissent

Not all of the *Afscheiding* people, however, were happy with this union. Under the unofficial leadership of Reverends Henstra and Drayer, who were not themselves *Afgescheiden*, those who refused to become part of the *Gereformeerde Kerken* 'continued their church life under the traditional name—the Christian Reformed Church' (Plantinga 1995:213), only changing it to the plural 'Churches' in 1947 (Plantinga 1995:221). The objections of 'the dissenters of 1892' were essentially doctrinal. Aside from a dislike for the way Kuyper seemed to disparage the Secession of 1834 (Plantinga 1995:215), these dissenters firmly believed that the *Doleantie*, with Kuyper at the helm, had a basic misunderstanding as to the very nature of the church. This misunderstanding manifested itself, according to Rev. Henstra, in questions of justification, election, and faith, all of which are subsumed under the rubric of the covenant. More particularly, Plantinga writes:

> In the churches dominated by the thinking of Kuyper, the doctrine of election is central and becomes the basis of a system of thinking which Rev. Henstra characterizes as the "covenant system." The justification of the sinner takes place in eternity, for Kuyper, and it has nothing to do with man or his faith. ...Kuyper's order was: justification, regeneration, calling, conversion, faith, sanctification. The dissenters of 1892 claim that the order, according to Scripture, is: calling regeneration, conversion, faith, justification, sanctification.... Kuyper subordinates the covenant of grace to the doctrine of election and therefore maintains that the covenant includes only the elect. ...Rev. Henstra writes that because Kuyper thinks of the covenant of grace as having been established with the elect, virtually all who are born within the covenant circle are elect. "This election takes place in Christ, which means that the elect stood before God eternally as recipients of grace and as justified. Therefore we may assume, when they come into the world, that regeneration has taken place at the time of their birth or before it. This regeneration, according to Kuyper, does not as a rule take place by means of the Word, which is also why he speaks of an 'immediate regeneration'".... According to Rev. Henstra, the Christian Reformed Churches of the Netherlands maintain that the covenant "...is established *in time*, and not in eternity; it is established with Abraham and his seed, and later, in the New Testament terms, with believers and their seed. Thus it does not include the elect

alone but believers and their *natural* seed. Ishmael, Esau, and others were also included in the covenant".... Such a covenant demands a human response, in the form of faith and conversion. The response that is needed represents a fulfillment of the covenant. That the covenant has indeed been fulfilled in the life of a particular believer is also a matter of experience (*believing*). Rev. Henstra writes: "The covenant thus asks for *experience*, and this is primarily the characteristic difference between the Reformed and Christian Reformed views of the covenant ... we on our side believe that God gives His promise as a *basis for our plea*; it is on this basis that we beseech Him for what He has promised, namely, salvation and blessing (*heil en zaligheid*)." The difficulty with the Reformed (as opposed to Christian Reformed) view of his matter is that "...we *have* and *possess* all of this; we already *are* justified before God, and therefore also regenerated. Faith is only a becoming aware that one is justified".... Rev. Henstra writes that disagreements regarding this area of doctrine were also the cause (*oorzaak*) of the liberation of 1944...indeed the events of 1944 are to be regarded as "a justification of our ecclesiastical standpoint" .... (Plantinga 1995:218-219.)

Contrary to the objections voiced by the Christian Reformed Churches, I believe Kuyper takes a more logical approach to matters of the covenant and its outworking in the everyday life of the believer. For Kuyper, it is God who decides from eternity past about our status with Him. This status is set, clear, and not dependent on the ambiguities of life. For the Christian Reformed Churches, in line with the *Afscheiding* before them, God goes a way with His people through life so that ambiguities of life are part and parcel of our relation with Him, not so much from His side as from ours.

The reason for bringing these issues to the fore at this time is to underscore them, because we will be returning to these themes again and again, and to demonstrate, even amidst significant differences, Kuyper's influence on Hoeksema's thought. Although Hoeksema took issue with Kuyper's concept of 'presumptive regeneration,' the idea of which is that regeneration could remain in a dormant state for an indefinite period of time and hence one must assume the regeneration of a person once baptized until evidence proves otherwise, it appears that, while allowing for a different doctrinal perspective, the practical outworking of Hoeksema's view was still essentially the same as that of Kuyper. Furthermore, Hoeksema can be viewed as allied with Kuyper in all the other charges of the dissenters of 1892. In fact, many of these objections go right to the heart of Hoeksema's more mature theology. Like Kuyper, Hoeksema also held that the covenant was established with the elect alone, albeit in Christ. This was part and parcel of his stand on sovereign, particular grace (see Hoeksema 1939, ET 1939). He therefore could be said to subordinate 'the covenant of grace to the doctrine of election' (Plantinga 1995:218), as Rev. Henstra charges. Unlike Kuyper, however, who used the concept of 'presumptive regeneration' to broaden his definition of 'the elect,' Hoeksema maintained that election cut right through the covenant, citing the story of Jacob and Esau in Romans 9 as proof (see Hoeksema 1979:1-28). Jacob and Esau were both born into a covenant family, a patriarchal one; both, by Kuyper's definition, were members of the covenant by virtue of circumcision (the forerunner of baptism); yet, as God declared, 'For the children being not yet born, neither having done any good or evil, that the purpose of God according to election might stand, not of works, but of him that calleth.... As it is written, Jacob have I loved, but Esau have I hated' (Bible, AV 1983:1177). Referring specifically to this passage Hoeksema would later hold, contra Kuyper, that Jacob and Esau were in reality not members of the covenant, but, prior to any evidence of either election or reprobation, both were rather in the 'sphere of the covenant' (Hoeksema 1971:134-137, Hanko 2000:375). This same ambiguity in the covenant concept, as illustrated in the difference between Kuyper and Hoeksema, is shared by the Christian Reformed Churches in the Netherlands. However, for them, entrance into the covenant with God is determined by the life of human beings in their relation to God and not some prior determinism.

Beginning with his concept of the covenant as a relationship and not a promise (Hoeksema 1971:139-140), Hoeksema underscored his view that this relationship was initiated and maintained by God alone (election) and not dependant upon humanity in any way. Still, by his use of various phrases to say the same thing, Hoeksema injects a measure of uncertainty into his argument, causing one to question exactly what he means. He alternately speaks of the ungodly seed being 'in the covenant,' 'under the covenant,' and 'in the sphere of the covenant' (Hoeksema 1971:136, 141). His use of these terms in an apparently synonymous way is evidenced by his definition which only encompasses those operations which can be observed in the institutional local church, such as: baptism, the Lord's Supper, and the instruction and preaching (Hoeksema 1971:141). Hence, according to Hoeksema, the ungodly in the church are only 'in the covenant' to the extent that they come into contact with the ministrations of the local church institute. Here Hoeksema differs substantially from Kuyper in his formulation of this matter, but, since the elect and the ungodly are clearly indistinguishable within the confines of the local church, one is not to define, or view, the local manifestation of the body of Christ as anything but the body of Christ, and not as a 'mixed multitude' (Hoeksema 1971:110)—on this point Hoeksema also differs significantly with the Christian Reformed Churches in the Netherlands. This mixed multitude, however, is eventually rendered into its constituent parts by the ministrations of the church, especially the preaching of the Word (Hoeksema 1971:143). So, for Hoeksema as well as Kuyper, those in the church are supposed regenerate until, under the visible ministry of the church, they prove themselves otherwise. For Hoeksema, this happens sometime in one's youth, while for Kuyper no specific determination is mentioned. Hence, both presume regeneration, with the difference being that one seems to be willing to presume a little longer than the other is. Even with these differences of opinion, I believe that Kuyper's early influence in clearly distinguishable in Hoeksema's doctrinal formulation.

1.8 *The Influence of Abraham Kuyper*

The major doctrinal differences between the Secession churches (1834) and the churches of the *Doleantie* (1886) are outlined succinctly by Herman Hanko. He writes:

Although there were many minor issues, the main issues were four in number. The Churches of the Secession were chiefly infralapsarian, maintained strongly justification in time, mediate regeneration and the promise of the covenant as the basis for the baptism of infants. The Churches that were organized from the State Church under the leadership of Dr. Kuyper rather were committed to supralapsarianism, eternal justification, immediate regeneration, and presupposed regeneration as the basis for infant baptism. (Hanko 1976:61.)

Just listing these doctrinal differences does not seem do them justice; given their importance, further clarification is definitely in order. And, since there are a myriad of opinions as to the exact meaning of these doctrinal formulas, I think it helpful to enlist Herman Hanko, emeritus professor at the Protestant Reformed Seminary and former student of Herman Hoeksema, to explain just what these formulas would mean from Hoeksema's perspective. With typical Protestant Reformed verve, Hanko writes:

> The question of supra and infra lapsarianism is basically a question of the order of the decrees of the counsel of God. Infralapsarian maintains that the decree of salvation in Christ follows upon the decree of the fall. Supralapsarianism maintains that the decree of the salvation of the elect in Christ precedes the decree of the fall. It is interesting to note that our confessions are infralapsarian. This is especially true of the Canons of Dort, although the supra position was argued on the Synod and was not condemned. …Our Protestant Reformed Churches have no definite stand on either supra or infralapsarianism other than the position of our Confessions. Nevertheless, Rev. Hoeksema has always maintained his preference for supralapsarianism in that it is more Scripturally correct. Cf. Col. 1:15-19 and Prov. 8: 22-31. With this I agree. …The question of justification was also a question that involved the decrees of God. The emphasis of Kuyper and his followers was on the fact that God eternally justifies His people in Christ so that in His counsel the elect stand before God as an eternally righteous people. This question is closely connected with

the question of supra and infralapsarianism. Undoubtedly, eternal justification is taught in Scripture. The question of mediate or immediate regeneration is a question of whether God affects the work of regeneration in the hearts of His elect people through the means of the preaching of the Word (mediate regeneration) or without the means of the preaching of the Word, e.g., directly through the operation of the Spirit (immediate regeneration). Although this is an interesting and important question, it is sufficient for us to point out that the very first seed of the new life takes place directly and without the mediacy of the preaching of the gospel. The ability to hear the gospel and appropriate its truth presupposes the life of Christ already present. The growth of the new man of regeneration, dependent upon the food of the gospel, presupposes that the new man is already created. The question of the basis for baptism of infants is something else. …The view of Kuyper, that the baptism of infants rests upon the basis of presupposed regeneration is wrong. His idea was that we must presuppose that all children born of believing parents are regenerated, and that therefore, on this presupposition we must baptize them. But this rests the truth of infant baptism upon a figment of the imagination which is obviously contrary to Scripture. The Churches of the Secession rather maintained that the basis for the baptism of infants is the promise of the covenant, namely that God will establish His covenant in the lines of continued generations. This is surely correct. Our Churches maintained this in the fury and strife of the controversy of 1953 and preceding years. Yet we must remember that these same Churches of the Secession later on came to the position that this promise of the covenant was for all that were baptized and was therefore also conditional. (Hanko 1976:61-63.)

While Hoeksema, during his early years in Groningen, attended an 'A' congregation, he seemed to have more affinity with the *Doleerenden* churches, especially with their emphasis on sovereign, particular grace—a doctrine that was to become the hallmark of Hoeksema's later theology. On this Gertrude Hoeksema writes:

> In the years of Harm's childhood there were several "A" and several "B" congregations in the city of Groningen. Harm's mother belonged to the "A" church, and Harm went to catechism there. One of his best friends belonged to the "B" church, and Harm's mother gave him permission to attend the "B" church with his friend occasionally. When the boys were old enough to go to a young men's society, Harm joined the society in the "B" congregation of his friend. The ties of friendship were not the only reasons for Harm's leanings toward the "B" church. Possibly they were not his strongest reasons. For Harm was attracted towards Dr. Abraham Kuyper and his interpretation of Reformed theology, particularly Dr. Kuyper's emphasis that grace is always particular. (Hoeksema 1969:32.)

David Engelsma, current professor of dogmatics at the Protestant Reformed Seminary also speaks of Kuyper's influence on Hoeksema (Engelsma 1998:29). He says categorically that 'although Hoeksema corrected, developed, and put his own stamp on the theology of Kuyper, the theology of Hoeksema is essentially that of Kuyper' (Engelsma 1998:29). Elsewhere, Engelsma, in order to give some distance to Kuyper's influence on Hoeksema because of the former's common grace formulations, seeks to distinguish between Kuyper's theological and philosophical works. Engelsma believes that Kuyper's theology is contained in *Dat de genade particulier is* (his treatise on particular grace), *E voto dordraceno* (his commentary on the Heidelberg Catechism), *De leer der verbonden* (the teaching of the covenants) and his famous theological lectures at the Free University: *Dictaten dogmatiek* (Engelsma 1998:29). By contrast, Kuyper's philosophical, and thus more 'speculative' work, is contained primarily in his *Lectures on Calvinism* and in his three volume work on common grace, entitled, *De gemeene gratie* (Engelsma 1998:28).

1.9 A Different Paradigm

In contrast to Engelsma's paradigm for understanding Kuyper's influence on Hoeksema, I would like to suggest an alternative. Rather than trying to distinguish Kuyper's theological works from his philosophical ones, an effort of dubious benefit for our purposes, I think it better to concentrate on Kuyper's influence as a whole and seek to understand Hoeksema's reaction to Kuyper's different themes. Hence, I think it helpful to divide Kuyper's influence on Hoeksema into both a positive and a negative category. In what I would call the positive and constructive, or influential, category, I would classify works such as Kuyper's treatise on particular grace, or his work on the covenant. In a second category, which I would designate as negative, or reactionary, I would classify works such as Kuyper's *Lectures on Calvinism* and *De gemeene gratie*. The positive category would contain those works that shaped Hoeksema's theology in a positive and constructive way. The negative category would contain works that Hoeksema developed his theology in opposition to. This is why I maintain that Kuyper had both a positive and a negative effect on Hoeksema's theology. Additionally, I think it is also true that Hoeksema's background in the 'A' churches helped dictate which of Kuyper's works influenced him in a positive way and which he wrote in reaction to. His 'A' background would have caused him to eschew the more philosophical or speculative of Kuyper's works altogether. Since the 'A' spirituality was of a less certain nature, more overtly spiritual, even mystical, and certainly less optimistic, its theology required a conscious, and visible, biblical grounding. The 'B' mindset, being of a more rational, optimistic bent and more certain of its eternal standing (election), would undoubtedly explain to a large degree Hoeksema's attraction to those works of Kuyper in which the latter's Calvinism was more clearly reasoned and closely defined. Yet, I believe it is impossible to understand Hoeksema properly without taking both the positive and the negative into account, regardless of how these Kuyperian themes receive their final formulations in Hoeksema's thought.

1.10 A Positive Influence

In the positive category, Kuyper's exposition of particular grace, which had such a profound affect on Hoeksema, was published in the *Uit het Woord* series, second series, part one, and titled, *Dat de genade particulier is*. The book is divided into four sections, the first of which is designated: '*Geen Christus pro omnibus*' (no Christ for all). Kuyper grounds this statement on the historic Reformed concept that there is no election on the basis of a foreseen faith in the individual, but that faith follows from God's sovereign election (Kuyper [s.a.]:15). In the first forty pages of the book Kuyper deals with the three main biblical texts that he believes are used in support of the idea of 'Christ for all' i.e. I John 2:2, I Timothy 2:4, and II Peter 3:9 (Kuyper [s.a.]:17-38). His conclusion is that these verses do not teach what those who want a 'Christ for all' claim (Kamps 1998:39). 'The false doctrine of a Christ for all, general grace, or universalism for Kuyper was a God dishonoring doctrine which robbed the church of the essence of her calling, that is, to *worship*,' writes Marvin Kamps, a former Protestant Reformed minister. 'How can the believer worship, when the preaching presents a God who cannot accomplish His will, whose Son is made a beggar, and whose grace is made in most instances insufficient to save, or when sinners are made to believe that their salvation is dependent on their own efforts?' (Kamps 1998:39).

In the course of his analysis of particular grace, Kuyper made it a point to stress its individual application. 'The entire work of redemption is personal, and on the individual person applied,' wrote Kuyper. 'The tie, or bond, of this mystic union with Jesus must be personal, also on this ground, that by this tie [the mystic union with Jesus-PB] enters into the [very] depths of our life, of our character, and our existence' (Kuyper [s.a.]:64). The grace of redemption that Kuyper elucidates here is entirely personal, entirely particular, and as such, entirely sovereign. This is the concept of grace expounded by Kuyper that so captivated Hoeksema. In his book, *God's Goodness Always Particular*, Hoeksema, following Kuyper's lead, goes on to say that

> the doctrine of general grace is in deep conflict with what Scripture teaches us concerning the deep corruption of man and his total incapability to accept the proffered redemption; is contrary to what Holy Writ teaches us concerning the unity and veracity of our God; cannot be

harmonized with the doctrine concerning the person of our Redeemer, who was ordained from eternity as head of his own, nor with his work of redemption which was a payment for the guilt of sin and, on the basis of it, liberation from the power of sin, and therefore necessarily particular, for if it is not particular it could be no atonement for sin. (Hoeksema 1939:67-68.)

1.11 A Negative Influence

From a negative, or reactionary, perspective, Kuyper's influence on Hoeksema was embodied in his doctrine of common grace. This theme was expounded by Kuyper in great detail first in a series of articles in a newspaper under his editorship, *De Heraut*, and later collected into three volumes under the title *De gemeene gratie*, published between 1902 and 1904. Reverend Bernard Woudenberg, minister emeritus in the Protestant Reformed Churches, told me several times that Hoeksema's commentary on these volumes was not of a favorable nature. Hoeksema often said that the three volumes of *De gemeene gratie* could be reduced to sixteen typed pages; single spaced, and not lose anything (Woudenberg 2000). Cornelius Hanko, also minister emeritus in the Protestant Reformed Churches and for many years an associate pastor under Hoeksema at First Protestant Reformed Church in Grand Rapids, said categorically that Kuyper's articles on common grace were an attempt to justify his political associations (Hanko 2000, Terpstra 1998:41). Hanko was referring to the cooperation of Kuyper's Anti-Revolutionary Party with Catholics (later the *Rooms-Katholieke Staatspartij*) in the political sphere in the Netherlands. Hoeksema, however, was a bit more diplomatic in his assessment of Kuyper's motives in this regard. Hoeksema believed that while Kuyper

> was undoubtedly a man of keen intellect and mighty vision…. [I]n his attempt to apply the principles of the Reformed faith to every sphere of life, he did not keep in view that the struggle of the people of God is a purely spiritual one. For the Reformed element in the Netherlands he desired and sought a place of power in the World, and in this pursuit of power the principles of the

Word of God were not always maintained and applied. And it is in this light that we also must view the attempt to develop the theory of common grace alongside of the truth that the grace of God is particular. The theory served to create a synthesis between the church and the world. (Hoeksema 1947:309.)

Charles Terpstra, Protestant Reformed Minister in Holland, Michigan, elaborates on what he sees as additional aspects of Kuyper's motivation in developing his theory of common grace. He concludes that,

> Kuyper's motivation ... was not solely theological; it was also very practical. For one thing, he sought to answer the growing effects of modernism in the church-world. He noted that modernism had a broad vision of the world and for the world, but that this vision was grounded in humanistic rationalism. He wanted the Reformed faith to have the same broad vision, but to be grounded in the sovereign work of God. Common grace gave him the answer, he thought. ...Still more ...Kuyper had developed a growing aversion for what he believed was an "Anabaptist" spirit in the churches of the Netherlands. There were Reformed Christians who believed that being true to the Reformed faith meant living a godly life of separation from the world. That meant no cooperation with the world in any realm, whether it be labor, religion, or politics. Kuyper's common grace sought to reprove this narrow view of the Christian's life in the world and create a full-orbed world and life view. (Terpstra 1998:41.)

At this point it would be helpful to gain some idea as to just what Hoeksema understood by Kuyper's theory of common grace. I do not wish to enter into a prolonged discussion of common grace at this point, as an extended discussion will be more appropriate later in our analysis. However, Hoeksema was able to distill Kuyper's theory down to three points, which I believe are both succinct and judicious. Under the heading of the 'chief elements of the Kuyperian conception of common grace,' Hoeksema summarized as follows:

1. That God, though with a view to eternity and the eternal blessedness of the Kingdom He is gracious only to the elect, with a view to things earthly and temporal He is gracious to all men.

2. That there is a restraining influence, ever since the fall of man, of the common grace of God upon the physical and ethical corruption of the world and of the heart of man, so that the principle of total depravity cannot work through.

3. That there is a positive influence of God's common grace upon the mind and will of man, whereby he is so improved that he can still live a positively good world-life. (Hoeksema 1947:313.)

Hoeksema was thoroughly convinced that Kuyper's doctrine of common grace led to a blatant denial of the Reformed truth of the 'antithesis.' This is the concept whereby God after the fall put enmity between the seed of the serpent and the seed of the woman as recorded in Genesis 3:15. The enmity, or antithesis, spoken of in this verse, popularly known as the '*moederbelofte*' or mother promise, details the beginnings of a division between the 'church' and the 'world' that would presumably continue until the return of Christ. This division is both spiritual and ethical. Furthermore, it is ethical and all pervasive in the life of the child of God precisely because it is spiritual. It is believed that God has put a profound separation between the 'elect,' those whom He has chosen for eternal life and the 'reprobate,' those whom He has not. This separation, or antithesis, becomes visible in individual morality. Unlike people in general, Christians are to be the salt of the earth. They are to be in the world but not of the world (Zwaanstra 1973:90-91). Hence, the Reformed concept of the antithesis precludes any cooperation between the church and the world in any area of life (see Zwaanstra 1973:117 for a fuller discussion of this theme), a concept put in immanent danger expressly because of Kuyper's theory of common grace (Terpstra 1998:42-43).

1.12 *Kuyper's Further Influence*

Kuyper's three volume *De gemeene gratie* was enormously popular, and influential, in the Netherlands. The success of *De gemeene gratie* was followed with two more multi-volume works, *Pro rege* (3 volumes) and *Antirevolutionaire staatkunde* (2 volumes), in which Kuyper worked out the principles of common grace in a much broader scope. All three works, never having been translated into English, were to have a limited affect in America. However, in 1898 Kuyper was invited to deliver the Stone Lectures at Princeton Theological Seminary in New Jersey. This he did with distinction. The result was a renewed interest in Calvinism (see Heslam 1998 on this history) in both Reformed and Presbyterian circles. The published version of these lectures, known simply as *Lectures on Calvinism*, was to become a classic, and it was by means of these lectures that Kuyper's influence preceded Hoeksema to America.

According to Gertrude Hoeksema, the ecclesiastical picture in the Netherlands continued to be fraught with controversy. Even after the Union of 1892, the 'A' churches and the 'B' churches, for all intents and purposes, continued their separate existence and only gradually merged. She writes that:

> As the unrest between the two groups escalated, at times into theological battles, the leaders called representatives of both factions to Utrecht in 1905. At this session they drew up the Conclusions of Utrecht, an attempted compromise to bring peace to the GKN. The result was that the true peace they had anticipated was not achieved. The best they could do was establish an uneasy truce between the two Reformed groups. For about three decades the GKN lived with this truce, until the period near the end of World War II, when problems again began to surface. After the war the A and B wings parted ways. (Hoeksema 1992:7.)

Hoeksema, however, was not around to witness the events following the Synod of Utrecht in 1905, as he already left for America in 1904.

1.13 Conclusion

During the course of this chapter I have outlined Herman Hoeksema's origins and early years in the Netherlands. In the course of this outline, I have sought to sketch, at times in some detail, those influences which helped to shape Herman Hoeksema both personally and theologically.

His personal life was a difficult one; one fraught with deprivation. In a sense, as a result of this state of affairs, his early years were wild and unsupervised. In many ways, he was anything but a polished young man.

In conjunction with this general lack of training went an interest in things theological. The most significant influences in this area were his mother, his upbringing in the *Afscheiding* churches, and Abraham Kuyper. Hoeksema's mother was a devout woman who cared very deeply for the spiritual welfare of her son. Her efforts, the results of which were not always visible, were eventually to bear abundant fruit. Hoeksema's upbringing in the 'A' churches gave him an appreciation of God's relationship to His people. This 'relationship' eventually would become the basis of his all-important doctrine of the covenant. The great catalyst, at least in Hoeksema's early years, was Abraham Kuyper. I have also sought to demonstrate that Kuyper's influence was in many ways a double-edged sword, so to speak. Hoeksema's theology was influenced in a positive way by Kuyper's insistence that God's grace is both sovereign and particular. He reacted strongly, however, to Kuyper's formulations of a common grace of God. Much of Hoeksema's later theology was developed, albeit by default, in response to theory of common grace. While holding to God's sovereign particular grace, Hoeksema, thoroughly repudiated any notion of a common grace of God. These themes, already visible in Hoeksema's early years, were only to develop further after his arrival in the United States in 1904.

Chapter 2

The Seminarian and the Dutch Reformed Church

Herman Hoeksema immigrated to the United States in 1904. He was eighteen years old at the time and spoke no English. In the course of this chapter I propose to outline Hoeksema's exploits in his new country. More specifically, I will chronicle, in some detail, his theological odyssey from his arrival in Chicago to his beginnings in the pastorate, concluding with some more personal observations.

Before entering into a discussion of Hoeksema's early years in America, I think it proper to sketch the ecclesiastical terrain. America has had a long and rich Reformed history, and, as in the Netherlands, it has been fraught with controversy. In fact, many of the same controversial themes that characterized the church struggles in the Netherlands were also evident in their American counterparts. It is within this theological environment that Hoeksema's distinctive Reformed theological tenets would develop and come to fruition. It is to this history that I would now like to turn.

2.1 A New Home

In the nineteenth-century America became home to many from the Netherlands who espoused the Reformed faith. Because of persecution, a significant number that left the *Hervormde Kerk* in the Secession of 1834 came to America to start a new life. Many others came because of severe economic conditions in their homeland. Herman Hoeksema fits into the latter category; he came primarily to find a better life.

As early as 1890 the Christian Reformed Church (CRC), based in Grand Rapids, Michigan, had a mission to arriving immigrants, especially those from the Netherlands. In fact, 'restricting the evangelistic outreach of the church to Holland immigrants and other people of Holland ancestry was defended on the grounds that a church is most obligated to those who share with it a common origin, language and history' (Zwaanstra 1973:29). This mission was geared specifically to advance the cause, and increase the numbers, of the Christian Reformed Church. This is not to say that immigrants were looked upon solely as objects for proselytization, but it does appear that the Christian Reformed Church was of mixed motives. 'At Ellis Island,' Zwaanstra writes, 'new arrivals were introduced to the Christian Reformed Church, given spiritual counsel, and assisted with settlement problems. Later the church appointed a commission to prevent the scattering of Holland people in America' (Zwaanstra 1973:29).

Despite the services provided by Christian Reformed Church, Herman Hoeksema passed through New York City, his point of entry, alone. Gertrude Hoeksema captures well this sense of being totally alone. She writes:

> Alone and bewildered in a strange land! With his meager baggage, Harm had passed through customs, docilely allowing himself to be pushed through the routine inspections, not understanding the reasons for all the formalities. Now he stood blinking at the New York of 1904, its streetcars, trains, and other conveyances, and wondered what was in store for him next. (Hoeksema 1969:35.)

Hoeksema's stay in New York, however, was a short one. Almost upon arrival, he boarded a train for far away Chicago, and his sister. Hoeksema's sister, Everdina, had immigrated two years earlier to Chicago's West Side, where she lived with her husband, Jacobus Veldman (Hoeksema 1969:36). Hoeksema's fondest recollection of his arrival in America was not, however, of the Statue of Liberty, or of New York City, or even of the cross-country train ride to the 'Windy City.' What he remembered most was his first taste of apple pie, the beginning of a life-long love affair (Hoeksema 1969:36).

Hoeksema's arrival in Chicago was uneventful. Chicago was just emerging from the financial panic precipitated by the assassination of President McKinley some three years earlier. 'For one who could not communicate,' relates Gertrude Hoeksema, 'finding work presented a double difficulty' (Hoeksema 1969:36).

Because of his training in the Netherlands, it was natural that Hoeksema would seek out work as a blacksmith. He had no trouble securing a job despite the language barrier—Everdina's husband was instrumental in this regard.

This first job, however, was also to be Hoeksema's first encounter with another aspect of the American workplace, the labor union. One evening he was brought to a meeting, the particulars of which were kept secret until the last minute. At this meeting, he was asked to swear an oath for reasons he did not fully comprehend. His stubborn Dutch nature, however, would not allow him to do such a thing. He did not run. Instead, he bellowed out 'no' to the questioner in the most adamant voice that he could muster (Hoeksema 1969:37). Herman Hoeksema Jr. related that the next firm he worked for was about to go on strike, and he was to be used as a strikebreaker. When two union 'enforcers' arrived to prevent him from working, Hoeksema responded with the whip that was usually reserved for the horses. He quit the job shortly thereafter for one that was non-union, but not before, as Herman Hoeksema Jr. says, 'cussing out the owners' (Hoeksema 2001). His next job was to haul the ashes 'from the basements of downtown buildings and industrial plants' (Hoeksema 1969:39) and dump them on Chicago's lakeshore, the current home of Chicago's famous Museum of Science and Industry. It was grueling work, which caused Hoeksema to decide that there must be something better out there for him. The final, and probably the best job he had in Chicago, was at the Aermotors Corporation. It was here that Hoeksema's trade school background, including his ability to draw-up blueprints, was an asset. He finally left this job in order to study for the ministry.

From this diverse and rather sordid assortment of job experiences, two things emerged in Hoeksema's makeup that remained with him for the rest of his life. First, he came to the firm conclusion that labor unions were, plainly and simply, wrong. They were, he reasoned, rebellion against the lawful owners or managers of a business. To this day, one cannot be a union member and simultaneously a member of the Protestant Reformed Churches. Secondly, while he repudiated union membership as a hedge against a capricious boss, Hoeksema reserved his vehemence and vitriol for the employers, whom he viewed as perpetrators of the greater evil (Hoeksema 2001). Or, as Hoeksema himself says in a sermon on

Lord's Day 2 of the Heidelberg Catechism, circa 1930: 'The man that has piled up money and then gives away a little of that money which he has first sucked out of the poor, may say, "I am a pretty good man." And the biggest thieves put the little thieves in jail. That is our corrupt nature' (Hoeksema 1930).

Jacobus Veldman's brother, Richard, was a minister in the Christian Reformed Churches in the Chicago area (Grotenhuis 2000). Maybe for this reason Herman Hoeksema's church affiliation since arriving in Chicago was the Christian Reformed Church 'known as Chicago I, on the corner of 14th and Loomis' (Hoeksema 1969:41). His son tells me that during his stint as blacksmith in Chicago, Herman also taught Sunday school at a local Baptist Church (Hoeksema 2001). Still, it was in the Chicago I Christian Reformed Church that Herman Hoeksema would meet his future wife, Nellie Kuiper. Also at this time, around 1906, he obtained the money needed to pay for passage for his mother and his two younger brothers to come to America. Upon arrival, they also settled in with Everdina and Jacobus Veldman.

In order to understand the Christian Reformed Church as it existed in America at the time Herman Hoeksema began his ministry, it would be helpful to look at some of that church's history. The Christian Reformed Church had its beginnings as the Classis Holland of the Reformed Churches in America, the denomination from which it subsequently split in 1857. Hence, a bit of this earlier history is in order.

2.2 The Reformed Church in America

The Reformed Church has been in America for over three hundred years. The celebrated Collegiate School in Upper Manhattan can be dated from the arrival of the Reverend Jonas Michaelius, 'the first Minister of the Dutch Reformed Church in New Amsterdam from 1628-1632' (Frost 1985:2). That is only a decade after the famous Synod of Dort. Gerald de Jong writes that, 'although growth was slow during the Church's first quarter century in America, a solid foundation was laid for future development' (De Jong 1978:28).

The church that emerged out of the next two centuries of development on American soil was the Reformed Church in America (RCA). While over the course of this time there were a steady stream of immigrants that attached themselves to the Reformed Church in America, in the wake of the Secession of 1834 immigration seemed a more important, and pressing, matter. Two of the most prominent names associated with the exodus from the *Hervormde Kerk*, and the Netherlands, after the Secession of 1834 were Reverends Albertus C. van Raalte and Hendrik P. Scholte. Van Raalte was initially not of a mind to emigrate, but many lay people, even members of his own congregation, began to view the Netherlands as a hindrance to the truths they held dear, especially after seeing the treatment Hendrik de Cock received at the hands of the state (De Jong 1984:25-28). Van Raalte viewed these events with concern both for the people who were leaving and their plight (Bruins 1996:20). 'Perhaps,' concludes Elton Bruins, 'Van Raalte was also influenced (to emigrate-PB) by the visit to the Netherlands of Thomas De Witt, a minister in the Dutch Reformed Church in New York, who met with his Afgescheiden colleague Hendrik P. Scholte in the spring of 1846' (Bruins 1996:20).

Van Raalte arrived in America in November 1846 (Bruins 1996:22), and immediately set about looking for a suitable place for 'his' colony. 'After the decision was made to establish the Holland colony in the western part of the State of Michigan,' writes Elton Bruins, 'Van Raalte and the first party arrived on February 9, 1847' (Bruins 1996:23). To one viewing Van Raalte's settlement in its early stages, its future was by no means certain. Harsh winters, lack of money, and scarcity of food all contributed to what Elton Bruins calls 'the grim reality of life on the Michigan frontier' (Bruins 1996:23).

Van Raalte's colleague in the Netherlands, Hendrik Scholte, also immigrated to America. In 1847, he led a 700 to 800 member group west of the Mississippi to the town of Pella in Iowa (Vander Hart 1984:68). After arriving in Pella, Scholte chose to have very little contact with Van Raalte, as, 'he felt more comfortable on his own' (Vander Hart 1984:68). Scholte's contribution is, no doubt, of great significance for the history of the Reformed faith in the United States, but he chose to remain independent and, subsequently, had little influence on either the Reformed Church in America or, after 1857, the Christian Reformed Church.

Over the course of the next decade, Van Raalte's settlement became a viable, even thriving, community, known today as Holland, Michigan. Although there were many issues to settle in the community, Elton Bruins argues that 'the most momentous decision was the decision to join the Dutch Reformed Church in the East then known officially as the Reformed Protestant Dutch Church of North America [known today as the Reformed Church in America-PB]' (Bruins 1996:25). The Dutch Reformed Church in the East was the only Dutch Reformed Church present in the United States at the time of Van Raalte's arrival. Hence, similarities in religious observance were coupled with feelings of commonality in both language and culture. Moreover, 'from the start,' relates Elton Bruins, 'Van Raalte had a positive feeling for the Dutch Reformed Church. Many Members of the Dutch Reformed Church in America surrounded him and his people with arms of love when they arrived in New York.... In this denomination, Van Raalte felt he had found a branch of the old church in which he had been raised in the Netherlands and of which his father had been a pastor' (Bruins 1996:26).

Because of Van Raalte's efforts motivated by his innate love for the Dutch Reformed Church in America, a daughter of the Nederlandse Hervormde Kerk, the settlement founded by Van Raalte in Western Michigan became the Classis of Holland in the Dutch Reformed Church in America in 1850. There was, however, much hesitancy among the rank and file in Van Raalte's community over the proposed union with the Dutch Reformed Church in America. There were questions whether Van Raalte himself was aware of the nature of the church he was proposing everyone to join (Kromminga 1943:106). The whole affair seemed to have a hidden, even sinister, side (Kromminga 1943:102-106). Herman Hanko questions 'whether the immigrants in fact authorized the union with the RCA. Van Raalte was present at the synod where the immigrants were accepted into the fellowship of the RCA, and Van Raalte himself expressed the willingness of the settlers to enter this union. But whether he was given official sanction by the colonists to commit them to union with the RCA is not at all clear from the records' (Hanko 2000:27).

The next seven years of union with the Dutch Reformed Church in America were not tranquil ones for the settlers in Michigan. Doubts among the settlers concerning the union, it seems, were never fully addressed. Additionally, writes Herman Hanko, there were 'reports from the East that all was not well in the RCA. Some churches there did not administer the sacraments in divine worship services. Lodge membership was not at all uncommon. Hymns were sung in place of the Psalms. A certain spirit of worldliness and willingness to conform to American ways was common' (Hanko 2000:22). Because of these things, many began to feel that 'they had made a serious mistake in joining the RCA' (Hanko 2000:22). In 1857 this dissatisfaction with the Dutch Reformed Church in America led directly to the founding of the Christian Reformed Church. While it is undoubtedly true that all the reasons mentioned had a hand in the eventual split of many of Van Raalte's followers from the Dutch Reformed Church in America, and the founding of the new denomination, the central reason had its origin in the Netherlands. The Dutch Reformed Church in America was a daughter church of the *Hervormde Kerk* in the Netherlands, the church from which Van Raalte and his followers had just seceded and that had persecuted them so severely (Hanko 2000:22-27). Hence, by joining with the Dutch Reformed Church in America they were, in effect, repudiating the very reasons for which they immigrated in the first place. This fact was brought out clearly, writes Elton Bruins, 'when the church of Graafschap (Graafschap is a suburb of Holland, Michigan-PB) sent a letter to the classis on 7 April 1857, notifying the classis of its separation from the Reformed Church. The congregation gave as the main reason for its action: "And it grieves our heart most in all this that there are members among you who regard our secession in the Netherlands as not strictly necessary, or [think that] it was untimely"' (Bruins 1996:33).

Van Raalte himself remained a member of the Dutch Reformed Church in America until his death and was deeply grieved by the whole affair. RCA historian William van Eyck, recounting the Minutes of Classis for April 8, 1857, relates that Van Raalte said:

> he is grieved to see such grossly inconsiderate accusations, as for example, that we reject the principles of the secession in the Netherlands. He was not conscious of any estrangement from these brethren, and that it was

nonsense to call the emigration from Holland and union with Reformed Church a separation from the brethren there in an ecclesiastical sense, since they in Holland had never seceded from the Reformed church, but only from the illegal and heretical church government (kerkbestuur) which was imposed in 1816.... (Van Eyck 1950:111.)

The Classis of April 8th, however, set in motion the split. The Reformed Church in America, for all its protests, was not able to undo what was happening. Professor H. Bouwman of the Theological School in Kampen commented that:

> it was a matter of duty before God and men to be 'by themselves' as they had begun to do, in the fear of the Lord. As an independent group, leaning on God's might, standing at the side of other Calvinistic manifestations of the body of Christ, they were to coöperate in the great work of the kingdom of God, and the development of a typical Reformed-American Church as the final result. (quoted by Beets 1946:63.)

The split of 1857 had many ramifications for the fledgling group as well as for the burgeoning frontier of Western Michigan; the most immediate of which was that of families divided in the split and the matter of affiliation. Although these problems pale in light of many contemporary concerns, Albert Hyma, in his biography of Van Raalte, puts the matter in perspective. He writes that:

> As long as there had been no formal secession, the Separatists coming from the Netherlands were not confronted by the question as to which denomination they should join. They automatically were enrolled in a congregation belonging to the Classis of Michigan or the Classis of Holland. But the moment the Secession of 1857 became a well-known fact, people had to make a choice. Particularly after 1880 the newly founded denomination, having the same name as that to which the Separatists all belonged originally, grew by leaps and bounds. The great majority of the *Gereformeerden*, whose numbers in the Netherlands swelled to a million members, felt that their church must be that of the old Separatists. The latter represented the purified, the orthodox churches, while the

Reformed Church in America was often looked upon as being nearly or entirely identified with the *Hervormde Kerk* in the Netherlands. In short, the Secession of 1857 has become one of the great developments in the history of Michigan.... (Hyma 1947:215.)

While immigration provided a steady stream of growth for the new denomination, the growing influence of the denominational publication, *De Wachter*, also contributed significantly (Beets 1946:74). Yet, for a time, Rev. K. Vanden Bosch was the only ordained man among the entire group (Beets 1946:75). In the years that followed, ministerial needs were provided either through the immigration process or local training, which at the time was still a product of the manse. Finally, the year 1876 marked the beginning of a denominational theological school, Calvin College and Preparatory School, formally charged with the training of future ministers for the denomination. With Rev G. E. Boer installed as regular *Docent* in February 1876, the school grew at a gradual and steady pace (De Jong 1926:24). Between the installation of Rev. Boer in 1876 and Hoeksema's arrival in 1908 several prominent 'American Secession Theologians' (Faber 1996) had already become affiliated with Calvin College and Seminary. In addition to Rev Boer, there was L. J. Hulst (1825-1922), G. K. Hemkes (1838-1920), Gerhardus Vos (1865-1949), William Wijnand Heyns (1856-1933), Hendericus Beuker (1834-1900), and Foppe Martin ten Hoor (1855-1934) (Faber 1996:17).

2.3 The Seminarian

After residing for four years in Chicago, Herman Hoeksema decided to pursue a career in the ministry in the Christian Reformed Church. It was 1908 and he had already met his future wife, Nellie Kuiper, at the Chicago I Christian Reformed Church. He was, however, not to marry her until 1914 (Hoeksema 1969:60), at the start of his senior year. A seminarian getting married prior to his graduation was a rather unusual thing in the Christian Reformed Church of 1914, but Hoeksema was able to do so because of the money he made tutoring, teaching and preaching. As Hoeksema himself would say: 'I was tired of having my feet under someone else's table' (Woudenberg 2001). By this time, he had also mastered the English language sufficiently enough for it to be his medium of instruction at school (Hoeksema 1969:44).

Herman Hoeksema entered the 'Theological School and Calvin College' (Stob 1955:175) in the fall of 1908 in order to begin his preparations for the ministry (Hoeksema 1969:45). From all accounts, Hoeksema was an exceptionally good student. According to Gertrude Hoeksema, 'to supplement his classical support money, Herman began tutoring fellow students in Dutch and Latin, and teaching an English class under Professor J. Vanden Bosch' (Hoeksema 1969:54).

During the course of Hoeksema's ministerial training, it was Professors William Heyns and Foppe M. ten Hoor who left the deepest and most lasting impressions.

2.4 William Wijnand Heyns

William Heyns, having begun his theological training at Kampen in 1877 (Faber 1997:301), immigrated to the United States in 1881 and arrived in Paterson, New Jersey—he was 25. He went on to complete his theological education at the Theological School of the Christian Reformed Church in Grand Rapids, Michigan, subsequently becoming Professor of Diaconiology there from 1902 until 1926 (Faber 1996:23-25). Unfortunately, although William Heyns played a significant role in the history of Calvin Theological Seminary, there is very little biographical information available on him.

The teaching of Professor Heyns during his tenure at Calvin Seminary hinged in large measure on the doctrine of the covenant. His first publication, following closely the lectures upon which it was based, was entitled *Verhandelingen over het genade-verbond* (Essays on the Covenant of Grace) (Faber1997:301). When compared with the teachings of Herman Bavinck, however, Heyns's writings demonstrate that there was a distinct lack of unanimity within the Secession churches on this cardinal doctrine. It is in the midst of this tension that Hoeksema's own doctrine of the covenant began to take shape.

In regard to the nature of God's covenant, Heyns taught that its essence is: 'the promise of salvation in the form of a covenant' (Heyns 1926:125) or elsewhere: 'every Covenant of God with man is actually a promise given in the stronger, more binding form of a covenant' (Heyns 1926:126). Moreover, Heyns declared that the covenant of grace is 'unconditional.' So conscious was Heyns of being labeled an Arminian, writes Jelle Faber, that he eschewed the word 'condition' in his remarks on the covenant preferring instead to speak of 'obligations'(Faber 1997:303). He wrote:

> When, therefore, we are accustomed to speak of conditions of the Covenant and mention as such faith and obedience, this must not be misunderstood. Faith and obedience must not be regarded as conditions for becoming participants in the Covenant, for we are participants in it from the time of our birth. Even in the Covenant of Works the condition of obedience was not a condition for being taken into the Covenant, but for keeping the Covenant and for gaining its reward. In the same way faith and obedience are conditions for keeping the Covenant of Grace and for inheriting the promise, Heb. 6:5, whereas unbelief and disobedience make the Covenant member a Covenant breaker, who shall not enter in: Heb. 3:18-19. Hence the earnest admonitions of the Lord Jesus to abide in Him, John 15:4-6. It might be preferable to call faith and obedience not conditions but obligations of the Covenant. (Heyns 1926:131.)

Furthermore, for Heyns, election had no bearing on the scope of the covenant. As Faber points out, since the concept of Christ as Head of the covenant of grace was abandoned, Heyns excluded 'any identification of covenant and eternal election or any confusion of God's covenant and His eternal counsel of peace' (Faber 1996:37).

The great Secession theologian Herman Bavinck viewed these matters in a decidedly different light. Bavinck began his treatment of the covenant of grace with humanity's need for redemption (Bavinck 1956:262); the whole of which 'begins and ends in Him' (Bavinck 1956:265). Additionally, Bavinck did not posit part of the responsibility for the covenant with God and part with man, as did Heyns. Instead, Bavinck saw the covenant as a function of God's eternal election, bestowed upon humanity as a sovereign gift of grace. He writes:

> After all, when the covenant of grace is separated from election, it ceases to be a covenant of grace and becomes again a covenant of works. Election implies that God grants man freely and out of grace the salvation which man has forfeited and which he can never again achieve in his own strength. But if salvation is not the sheer gift of grace but in some way depends upon the conduct of men, then the covenant of grace is converted into a covenant of works. Man must then satisfy some condition in order to inherit eternal life. In this, grace and works stand at opposite poles from each other and are mutually exclusive. If salvation is by grace it is no longer by works, or otherwise grace is no longer grace. And if it is by works, it is not by grace, or otherwise works are not works (Rom. 11:6). (Bavinck 1956:272.)

Hoeksema's covenant view is not entirely coincident with Bavinck's, however. Elsewhere, writing in his *Gereformeerde Dogmatiek*, Bavinck conceives of the covenant of grace as harboring both the elect and also those who are not to be considered sincere believers. He calls these insincere believers 'evil tendrils on the vine,' 'chaff among the grain,' and 'earthen vessels' in the covenant, which he further distinguishes from the elect or 'golden vessels' (Bavinck 1929:213). But, he says, 'they are to be treated as allies,' and that 'while they are here on earth, they are bound up with the elect in all sorts of ways' (Bavinck 1929:213). Hoeksema never denied that the chaff and the wheat grow together within the confines of the church institute, this idea is thoroughly Reformed. Hoeksema did, however, deny them a place in the covenant. For him, as with the children of believers which we discussed earlier, those whom Bavinck classifies as 'not sincere believers' (Bavinck 1929:213) would be consigned to the sphere of the covenant or the jurisdiction of the covenant, i.e. the local church, and not to the covenant itself. Hence, in the local church they could be said to be in the sphere of influence of the covenant, nothing more.

Grace also seems to have had a different meaning for Heyns than for Bavinck. From the above quote, Bavinck can be said to view grace as God's favor, objectively considered. For Heyns, covenant grace is subjective, with the express purpose of rendering its object without excuse. As Faber writes: 'It is not a grace which as such renders the covenant member capable of faith and repentance. It is a grace which takes from him or her all excuse for not bringing forth the desired fruit of the covenant' (Faber 1997:309). Additionally, while Heyns may say that the covenant is bestowed unconditionally, its maintenance is most certainly conditional. In fact, maintaining the covenant seems to be solely the work of humanity, with God's grace simply a vehicle for rendering any who fail inexcusable.

Hoeksema wanted nothing to do with the concept of God's covenant that was espoused by Professor Heyns. Rather, following what he liked of Bavinck, Hoeksema chose to identify the covenant closely with election. That is to say, for Hoeksema, the number of the elect is the exact number of persons included in the covenant. Thus, the covenant is for the elect alone, i.e. those whom God has chosen to save and make partakers of the covenant in Christ. Moreover, the covenant is both established and maintained by God alone, without any help from fallen humanity (Hoeksema 1966:323-325). Since God establishes and maintains His covenant, there is no room for 'conditions,' or as in the case of Professor Heyns 'obligations,' within the covenant; either for the express purpose of gaining entrance into the covenant or, ultimately, for maintaining one's position within it. Another prominent member of the Calvin faculty, F. M. ten Hoor, also saw the covenant as 'the bond between the offended God and the offending but elect sinner. It is a bond, [a] communion of life,' Ten Hoor insisted, 'and not a mere offer' and, as such, 'the covenant is a deed of God only, and is in its origin monopleuristic' (Ten Hoor [s.a.]:121-122). Following the lead of Bavinck and Ten Hoor, Hoeksema began to see the covenant as more of a relationship (Hoeksema 1966:321-324), rather than simply a promise, as was taught by Professor Heyns. As Hoeksema himself puts the matter:

> The essence of the covenant ... is not to be sought in a promise, and that, too a promise in the sense of a certain general offer to the children of believers, as Prof. Heyns would have it. ...But the essence of the covenant is to be sought in this living relationship of friendship whereby God the Lord is the sovereign friend of His people, and

they are the Lord's friend-servants, partaking of His fellowship, by grace possessing and manifesting His life and fighting the battle of His cause in the midst of the world. (Hoeksema 1971:65.)

Professor Heyns did have his influence, however, as Hoeksema would later write:

> Prof. Heyns's [covenant-PB] presentation has for years been imbibed by many who now serve as ministers in the Christian Reformed denomination. If we keep this in mind, it is no longer surprising that the general offer of grace on God's part in the preaching of the gospel to all who hear that gospel not only could find reception but also could be so readily officially adopted by the Synod of 1924 as the only pure Reformed presentation. (Hoeksema 1971:20.)

In addition to its being in some ways circumscribed by election, Bavinck, and Hoeksema after him, believed the essence of the covenant to be 'organic' in nature. In fact, an important characteristic that allied Hoeksema's covenant view with that of both Bavinck and Ten Hoor was, according to Reverend Woudenberg, its quality of 'organic development' (Woudenberg 2001). All of which tends to underscore the fact that, for this particular branch of Secession theology, as represented by Bavinck and Ten Hoor, and eventually Hoeksema as well, 'relationship' was considered a defining characteristic in the nature of the covenant. On this theme, Bavinck wrote:

> The second peculiarity or remarkable characteristic of the covenant of grace is that in all of its dispensations it has an organic character. ...The elect, accordingly, do not stand loosely alongside each other, but are one in Christ. ...It is one communion or fellowship, endeavoring to keep the unity of the Spirit in the bond of peace. ...Thus election cannot have been an arbitrary or accidental deed. If it was governed by the purpose of constituting Christ as Head of the church His body, then it has an organic

character and already includes the idea of the covenant. (Bavinck 1956:276.)

Similarly, Ten Hoor contended that 'in the covenant of grace the relationship, the organic comes to the foreground.... The covenant in its progress does not jump from individual to individual, but proceeds organically and historically, joins itself to the genealogical line, and takes up into itself parents with their children and all that is theirs' (Ten Hoor [s.a.]:134).

Unlike Heyns who wanted to make the covenant something that God established with each and every believer, writes Reverend Woudenberg, Hoeksema, again following Ten Hoor, saw the covenant relationship as something that broadens out into the line of human generations, i.e., organically (Woudenberg 2000:99). It is not surprising that Herman Bavinck also subscribed to this view (Van Genderen 1995:58). Reverend Woudenberg concludes:

> This perhaps more basically than anything separates his [Hoeksema's-PB] views from that of Schilder, who, like Abraham Kuyper before him "had a preference for judicial categories and for terms like statute, obligation and legal status, defined by the *speaking God*, the God of the *Word*, both for those who will respond positively, and for those whose response will be negative." Meanwhile, however, the Rev's H. Danhof and H. Hoeksema had followed Bavinck's suggestion and focused on the organic relationship of friendship as the heart of their covenantal thought. To them the idea of the covenant as a living relationship was far more Biblical and far richer in thought than that of a legal right to something that might not even be realized in the end. (Woudenberg 2000:99.)

While much of what Ten Hoor wrote regarding the covenant of grace mirrors that of his well-known contemporary and life-long friend, Herman Bavinck, there is equally much that does not. Ten Hoor begins his discussion of the covenant by first laying down its parameters. Ironically, even after stating unequivocally that 'the leading thought is that only the elect are in the covenant, [and that] those who are not elect, are not in the covenant, [and that] for them there is no promise, and even when they are baptized, their baptism is not real' (Ten Hoor [s.a.]:149), two pages later he vacillates almost to the point of agreeing with his colleague at the seminary, William Heyns. To add to the confusion, elsewhere Ten Hoor writes that: 'No matter how unbelieving a member of the covenant may be' and then concludes with a paragraph that is as unintelligible as it is long (Ten Hoor [s.a.]:153-154). Yet, there seems to be no mistake when later he writes:

> Also those who have no saving faith stand in a spiritually organic relation to Christ ... and they enjoy spiritual gifts of grace.... They are not standing as detached individuals in the covenant, not with respect to God, nor with respect to the true believers. They do not form a separate circle either, but they are within the organism of the covenant as it exists as God's institution of salvation. They are even responsible for the promise of the covenant to its full extent. (Ten Hoor [s.a.]:155.)

Both students and professors alike were struggling with these weighty matters all during Hoeksema's time in seminary. Hoeksema lived through it. Still, he was going to bring about a solution one day, in *The Banner*.

2.5 *The Origin of Professor Heyns's View of the Covenant*

Where did Professor Heyns's view of the covenant, which Hoeksema later referred to as 'Arminianism injected into the covenant' (Hoeksema 1971:20), and which differed so much from that of his Secession colleague Herman Bavinck, come from? Klaas Schilder, whose theological roots go deep into the Secession of 1834, said that his church had not 'adopted any official conception of the covenant' (Schilder 1996:104). This statement by Schilder would seem to indicate that there was more than one view on the covenant in vogue in the Secessionist Churches at the time.

Herman Hanko and Herman Hoeksema's son, Homer, attempted to trace the provenance of these divergent covenant views in their *History of Dogma* (1982). In the course of evaluating the various views of the covenant held among the Secession Churches in the Netherlands, they write that 'it is not at all surprising that with these views of the covenant there were also those among the churches of the Secession who maintained a general offer of the gospel. Already very early in the history of the churches of the Secession the leaders were split over this question of the general offer. These doctrinal emphases continued' (Hoeksema & Hanko 1982:93).

Hendrik de Cock is acknowledged by all as the father of the Secession Churches, and Herman Hanko sees in De Cock's view of the covenant the beginnings of the well-meant gospel offer, or conditions within the covenant. 'DeCock,' argues Hanko, 'maintained that those born within the church and baptized by the church were a part of the church visible and were only externally part of the covenant community. They could be said to be outwardly in the covenant, but they were not actually in the covenant until they came to the assurance of faith' (Hanko 2000:12). The change, according to Hanko, began in earnest with Hendrik De Cock's son, Helenius. While professor of theology at the *Afscheiding* seminary at Kampen, Helenius de Cock would, over time, change his views markedly. And Professor Heyns did study in Kampen. On this change Hanko writes:

> While first Helenius agreed with his father, he gradually changed his position and adopted a radically different view of the covenant. While he did not abandon his views on election, he pushed election aside and said that the truth of predestination was irrelevant to the administration of the covenant in time. And pushing election aside in the administration of the covenant, Helenius DeCock took the position that the promise of baptism was a promise to all the children baptized, so that all are in the covenant, though outwardly, and are participants of the covenant. Their unbelief cannot invalidate God's covenant, although it deprives them of the blessing of the covenant. Thus, all the promises of the covenant (as outlined in the first part of the Baptism Form) are given to all the children, though only objectively. And the baptized children are "sanctified in Christ" only objectively, that is, they are only separated from other unbaptized children by the mark of baptism. Because Helenius DeCock took the position which he did

> on the question of baptism, it was not strange that he also adopted the view of the well-meant offer of the gospel, which teaches that the gospel is offered to all who hear it as an expression of God's intention or desire to save all. ...If the promise made in baptism is to all the children baptized, that promise, because it is of God, expresses God's desire to save all these children. Even though many go lost. So also the gospel offer expresses to all who hear the preaching God's earnest desire to save them, even though they may go lost. (Hanko 2000:13-14.)

Thus, Hanko sees the free offer of the gospel developing logically and naturally from a certain Secessionist view of the covenant. Moreover, primarily via immigration, this tenet of common grace became a staple in the Christian Reformed Church. Hanko illustrates the prolonged saturation of the Christian Reformed Church with these ideas by pointing to a series of sermons published around 1900 from Dr. C. Bouma entitled, *Genade Geneest*. In this series, Bouma states categorically that 'Christ does not want any one to go lost' (quoted by Hanko 1989:174). Elsewhere, Hanko quotes Rev. J. Keizer, from around 1910, who concluded a sermon with the words: 'Many walk no longer with us; they have turned their backs to God's covenant and words, even their heel, their neck, "the cold shoulder." Their end is the ways of death; as children of the kingdom, they will perish. Return still, ye who are so averse; the Lord will still accept you; he still waits to be gracious to you' (quoted by Hanko 1989:174).

More recently, however, with the impending publication of the first English translation of Herman Hoeksema and Henry Danhof's 1923 monograph *Van Zonde En Genade* (Of Sin and Grace), Herman Hanko, by way of introduction to the views of the fathers of the Secession, writes:

> In proving the fact that the Reformed churches since the time of the sixteenth century Reformation held firmly to sovereign and particular grace, the authors [Hoeksema and Danhof] give a ringing endorsement of the Secession of 1834. This is heart-warming, because even in Reformed circles the Secession is openly criticized. This endorsement is found, to cite but one example, in the following quote

> [from *Van Zonde En Genade*] in which the Secession is referred to. ...They refer to the strong emphasis on sovereign and particular grace found among most of the leaders of the Secession (Hanko 2002:104-105.)

This more recent offering from Herman Hanko seems to put a decidedly different twist on his earlier opinions of the Secession of 1834 and the views of its leaders.

While much of what Herman Hanko has to say regarding the origin of the differing covenant views in the Secessionist Churches in the Netherlands is interesting, especially for pinpointing the origin of professor Heyns's view of the covenant, Anthony Hoekema's 1953 doctoral thesis for Princeton Theological Seminary provides, at least to my mind, a more convincing scenario. Although, at the same time, it is altogether possible that different lines of influence are in evidence here. Nothing ever seems to come from one identifiable source, and this is undoubtedly the case with Professor Heyns's view of the covenant. Hoekema, however, contends that the fathers of the Secession, Hendrick de Cock, H. P. Scholte, A. Brummelkamp, and S. van Velzen, were all faithful to the Three Forms of Unity in their view of the covenant and baptism. Their successors, however, did not maintain the prevailing view, and 'a view of the covenant and baptism quite different ...uttered itself in a publication by K. J. Pieters and J. R. Kreulen published in 1861 under the title, *De Kinderdoop volgens de Beginselen der Gereformeerde Kerk* (Infant Baptism in the Light of the Principles of the Reformed Church)' (Hoekema 1953:50). 'These authors,' Hoekema maintains,

> in setting forth their doctrine of the covenant, do not take their point of departure in God's decrees. They do not wish to identify election with the covenant of grace. They say that, when we consider baptism, we must let eternal election rest, and leave it aside. These men stress the two-sidedness of the covenant, and make much of the demands of the covenant, and of the conditional form in which God's promises appear. The covenant promise, that God will take us to be His children and heirs, must not be interpreted as being equivalent to salvation, but must be understood in a covenantal way (verbondsgewijze): that is,

objectively. The conclusion is inescapable ...that the covenant promise is here simply thought of as an offer of salvation.... Baptism, so say Pieters and Kreulen, is not a seal of internal grace, but only a sign and seal of the promise of the covenant. (Hoekema 1953:51-52.)

There was much opposition to these views (Hoekema 1953:53), and they appear to have generated a good deal of confusion as well. The result was that the Synods of Franeker (1863) and Amsterdam (1866) 'issued compromise formulations which, while they did not condemn Pieters and Kreulen, refused to hail their conceptions as the most exact expression of the convictions of the Reformed' (Hoekema 1953:53).

The origin of Professor Heyns's views on the covenant and baptism can be clearly discerned in the earlier writings of Pieters and Kreulen. It is difficult, however, to make the connection definite. In his manual of theology, *Gereformeerde geloofsleer* (1916), Heyns quotes primarily from Scripture with little other citations. In his *Handboek voor de catechetiek* (1907: 144-145), Heyns deals at length with subjective grace versus objective grace, but nowhere does he mention Pieters or Kreulen by name or cite any of their works. Neither in his earliest work specifically on the covenant, *Verhandelingen over het Genade-Verbond* (Essays Concerning the Covenant of Grace), does Heyns specifically refer to Pieters and Kreulen, but it is interesting that he classifies the differences in theological viewpoint within the Reformed camp on the covenant as differences between supra- and infralapsarianism (Heyns 1914:32). Commenting further, Heyns characterizes the difference between '*supra en infra*' as the difference between two poles (*twee polen*) following the principle of God's sovereignty (*Souvereiniteit Gods*) and man's responsibility (*de verantwoordelijkheid des menschen*) (Heyns 1914:32). Again, those on the faculty of the Seminary, as well as the student body, were struggling with weighty and seemingly insoluble matters; matters for which Hoeksema would one day propose a decidedly different solution, in the pages of *The Banner*.

Professor Jelle Faber of the Canadian Reformed Church, in his work on the 'American Secessionist Theologians,' points out a possible connection between Heyns and Pieters and Kreulen when he mentions that several of the Secession theologians who eventually taught at Calvin Seminary sat at the feet of Reverends Pieters and Kreulen as part of their theological training (Faber 1996:26-29). Ultimately, however the transfer of ideas took place, the influence of Pieters and Kreulen on Heyns's view of the covenant and baptism is unmistakable.

2.6 A Chance Encounter

A chance encounter on a train, as recorded by Gertrude Hoeksema, illustrates Hoeksema's lasting impression of Professor Heyns.

> One day during his pastorate in Holland, he [Hoeksema] met his former professor, William Heyns, in the inter-urban. Prof. Heyn's (sic) book, *Gereformeerde Geloofsleer* (*Reformed Faith* or *Reformed Doctrine*) had just come out and the professor asked his former student what he thought of it. In his student days, Herman Hoeksema would not have expressed his opinions candidly, for this professor was vindictive against those who did not agree with him. Now he was free to discuss the contents and viewpoint of his former professor's book, which he had already read. The discussion centered on Heyn's (sic) belief in the conditional promise, the promise of salvation for all those in the sphere of the covenant, on the condition that they believe. Hoeksema stared out of the window of the inter-urban for a few moments and then told Prof. Heyns, "With your thought, professor, you do not save one reprobate, and you do not build up the elect. Under my preaching the elect are instructed and built up and the reprobate are not deceived that they have an imaginary heaven." These were the words which Rev. Hoeksema had been longing to voice, and Prof. Heyns was angry as they parted. (Hoeksema 1969:109-110.)

Long after leaving his professor's tutelage, the debate over a conditional covenant versus an unconditional covenant remained a subject of intense interest for Hoeksema. From a positive perspective, because it spurred him on to develop his own conception of the covenant beginning in 1918 in his rubric 'Our Doctrine' in *The Banner*. Negatively, because any view of the covenant that contained even a hint of conditionality made its author immediately suspect in Hoeksema's mind and worthy to be branded a 'Heynsian.' Years later Hoeksema would equate the covenant views of the famous Dutch theologian Klaas Schilder with those of his former professor. As Jelle Faber relates, within the Protestant Reformed Churches of the 1950s 'Schilderianism was being equated with Heynsianism and Heynsianism with Arminianism' (Faber 1996:47).

On a more personal level, Gertrude Hoeksema tells of Hoeksema's shock at hearing of Klaas Schilder's deposition by the Synod of Sneek-Utrecht in 1944. Later, Hoeksema's 'astonishment knew no bounds when he read in the first church papers after the war that Dr. Schilder and his followers adopted the Heynsian view of the covenant, the view that Hoeksema could not accept when he met it in his student days, the view that he had battled ever since' (Hoeksema 1969:275-276). Less than a decade later, Gertrude Hoeksema reminisces, Hoeksema would see these same views beginning to crop-up in his own Protestant Reformed Churches (Hoeksema 1969:313).

2.7 *Foppe Martin ten Hoor*

The man who eventually became Hoeksema's mentor at Calvin Seminary, F. M. ten Hoor, received his diploma from Kampen in 1880, the same day as his more famous friend and contemporary Herman Bavinck, but he did not arrive in the United States until 1896. Ten Hoor was later called, in 1900, to serve as Professor of Dogmatics at the Theological School, a position that he discharged faithfully until his emeritation in 1924 (Faber 1996:23-25).

Writing in direct response to Jelle Faber's essay on the 'American Secession Theologians' and their influence, Bernard Woudenberg scrutinizes the influence of both Heyns and Ten Hoor on Hoeksema. He argues that:

> Faber deals with the last two of these men, William Heyns and Foppe M. Ten Hoor, as though they were of one theological cut, while I recall distinctly how Herman Hoeksema, who studied under both of them, took strong exception to the teachings of Heyns, while he was quite fond of Ten Hoor and in a certain way looked upon him as his own theological mentor. (Woudenberg 2000:97.)

Elsewhere, while trying to situate Ten Hoor within the larger Reformed continuum, Woudenberg compares and contrasts him to his more illustrious contemporary and friend, Herman Bavinck. Woudenberg writes:

> Foppe Ten Hoor and Herman Bavinck...shared basically the same theological positions, but with a difference. Bavinck...in time became a close friend of Dr. Abraham Kuyper, working with him to bring together the *Afscheiding* (Secessionists) and the *Doleantie* (Aggrieved) into the new Reformed (*Gereformeerde*) denomination. Their theological backgrounds and outlooks were different, but Bavinck was convinced that they could work together for the good of the Reformed faith, and to the glory of God. This conviction, however, was not shared by Ten Hoor. Already in the Netherlands, and even more after he moved to the United States to teach and write as a professor at Calvin Seminary, he was deeply disturbed by what Kuyper was bringing into the churches. It was not so much what Kuyper taught as the way in which he approached it. Rather than extracting his views from the confessions and Scripture, Kuyper—by every measure an academician—sought to take the learning of worldly scholars, including their speculative philosophies, and using it to develop the Reformed faith. This Ten Hoor rejected—as in principle did also Bavinck—and constantly spoke out against it, warning that this could only end in molding the church after the image of the sinful world.... It was under this influence that Herman Hoeksema received his theological education, and Ten Hoor's warning he believed to be true. It was only that, with his clear and analytic mind, he came to focus on what he considered to be the underlying fault in it all, Kuyper's

theory of Common Grace by which he was excusing this bringing the thinking of the world into the church of God. (Woudenberg 2000:101.)

Reverend Woudenberg also recounts the story, often told by Hoeksema, of Ten Hoor's view of common grace as given on the floor of synod during the height of the controversy in 1924. 'Ten Hoor remarked, "I have studied Common Grace for forty years and, although I believe there is such as thing, I still do not know what it could be." Just what he meant with this it is hard to say, but it would seem to imply that he had a great deal more sympathy for Hoeksema's position than he dared say at the time' (Woudenberg 2000:101).

Ten Hoor was especially well-known for his strong opposition to what he saw as Abraham Kuyper's 'agenda,' something that he fought vociferously on both sides of the Atlantic. According to Cornelius Pronk of the Free Reformed Church:

> Long before union took place (1892), questions had been raised in connection with some of the teachings of Dr. Kuyper. His views on science, theological education, common grace, culture, the church, the covenant and baptism, the order of salvation as well as many other subjects, left many of the Seceders wondering whether this great man was truly Reformed in every respect. But Kuyper was very popular and few dared to openly oppose him for fear of being ridiculed by him or by his supporters. Yet there were some who had the courage of their convictions to speak out against what they believed to be serious departures from the old Reformed truth. (Pronk 1987:3.)

Ten Hoor was one who had convictions as well as courage, and speak out he did. He began by scrutinizing what he saw as Kuyper's 'philosophical' presuppositions.

Ten Hoor began his investigation by looking into the historical origin of the ideas that motivated the Doleantie. After carefully weighing his options, Ten Hoor concluded:

> these new ideas are the result of modern philosophy rather than the old Reformed theology. The leaders of the

> Doleantie ...have been influenced by the philosophy of Kant and Hegel, which has given birth to a whole new concept of science. According to Kant, science is concerned only with objects that can be known and scrutinized by reason. This implies that theology is not a true science, since its object, God, being outside of the cosmos, cannot be subjected to scientific investigation. (Pronk 1987:74-75.)

Ten Hoor firmly believed that this new understanding of science would eventually undermine theology. If theology could not find its object within the created order and study it by means of observation and experimentation, how could it claim to be a science? Kuyper's solution, as demonstrated in his monumental *Encyclopedie der Heilige Godgeleerdheid*, was to show that 'God, in addition to being truly beyond the cosmos as the object of faith, is also in some way part of the cosmos' (Pronk 1987:75). For Ten Hoor, this view had serious implications for the training of ministers, as well as other concerns. If theology is just one branch of the larger tree of the 'sciences,' should not all the sciences be taught together in 'Christian university' so their interrelationships can be studied together (Pronk 1987:76)? Kuyper certainly believed this to be the case and it became one of his primary motivations in the founding of the Free University in 1880. It was also on this basis that Ten Hoor objected strenuously, although to no avail, to the appointment of Ralph Janssen as professor in the Theological School in 1904 (Stob 1955:276-277). Janssen was considered a 'university man;' one who 'subscribed to the Kuyperian idea of the sovereignty and freedom of theological science,' which according to Ten Hoor, 'constituted a wide-open door for the intrusion of a non-confessional teaching into the Theological School of the Christian Reformed Church' (Stob 1955:283).

In contrast to Kuyper, Ten Hoor further distinguished between the 'concept' and the 'idea' of theology. While the concept of theological sciences may be taken from this world, the idea of theology, which he equated with revelation, is derived from God alone. 'Kuyper constructs his system not out of the divine idea,' Pronk insists, 'but out of the human concept of theology, not out of God, but out of man, not out of the object, but out of the subject'

(Pronk 1987:77). Theology is not just one of the many branches of science. Ten Hoor believed:

> We put all the emphasis on the concept theology, not on the formal, human thought processes. We do not by our reflection make theology a science. Theology is science in God, and is revealed as science by God. We do not proceed from the subject, but from the object. We do not just derive the idea but also the concept of theology as science from God and not from man. We must indeed systematize our knowledge of God, but we do not create this knowledge. It is there. It is given. It lies in the revelation of God. (quoted by Pronk 1987:77.)

Kuyper, however, chose to maintain his distinction between 'theology as a science and the knowledge of God as the church possesses it' (Pronk 1987:80), simply ignoring Ten Hoor's criticisms in the process. In his 1883 address in Kampen, Bavinck seems to agree more with Ten Hoor than with Kuyper. Paraphrased, Bavinck says:

> Is everything that is invisible for that reason unknowable? No! Faith proves the scientific character of theology, for faith investigates things spiritual. Faith perceives the Object of theology. One cannot blame theology for the fact that unbelievers are not able to perceive what is clearly seen by believers and for that reason dispute its right to the name science. Because of its non-cosmic object, theology is Regina Scientiarum and transcends all other sciences. Theology is, however, related to the other sciences since all their objects have their origin in God. As universal science theology resembles philosophy, because both disciplines cover the entire spectrum of life. But the big difference is that philosophy is anthropocentric while theology is theocentric. (Bavinck 1883:32-35.)

In the same address (Bavinck 1883:24), Bavinck argues convincingly that the attempt of modern universities to assign theology a place among other sciences implies that God will no longer be viewed as the object of theology but as religion, as a historical phenomenon. He writes: 'When Christendom is put on the level with other religions, theology becomes anthropology and loses its unique principle and object' (Bavinck 1883:25). This is exactly what Ten Hoor also feared was going to happen under Kuyper's idea of theology as one of the many cosmological sciences (Pronk 2005). Ten Hoor, as Bavinck, also regarded theology as the Regina Scientiarum.

As a true son of the Succession, Bavinck firmly believed, along with Ten Hoor, that God in Himself is the true object of theology, not just the Word of God as Kuyper preferred to have it. Bavinck concluded that 'God is the only object [of theology] and everything else is to be related to Him and arranged and subsumed under Him' (Bavinck 1883:30). In fact, according to Reverend Pronk, they each saw Kuyper as teaching that God is not accessible except through His word (Pronk 2005).

I am convinced that it is in these early quotes from Bavinck, as mediated through Ten Hoor, that we also begin to see the origins of Hoeksema's own thought on this particular subject. It was in a direct line from the positions of both Bavinck and Ten Hoor that Hoeksema would later launch his attack on Professor Janssen, which was to have such unforeseen consequences. Additionally, Hoeksema clearly shows Bavinck and Ten Hoor to be the origin of his own thoughts on theology, when, at the beginning of his *Reformed Dogmatics*, he carefully distinguishes between theology as the knowledge of God and theology as just one of many branches of science. He writes: '1) That the science designated is intended to be theology, knowledge of God, (and) 2) That the purpose was to set forth the loci, the principia ...of this knowledge of God' (Hoeksema 1966:3).

In addition to the above, Ten Hoor also took issue with Kuyper over what could be termed his 'cultural mandate,' which, according to Ten Hoor, exhibited a divided concern on the part of God. John Bolt of Calvin Seminary sums up Kuyper's idea of the 'cultural mandate' as such:

> Because Kuyper did not wish to see Christian socio-cultural activity, including political activity, under the protective arm of the church, and because he also valued the cultural activity of non-Christians, he insisted that cultural activity is a fruit of "common grace," a given of

creation, rather than a product of special regenerating grace. (Bolt 1984:142.)

This perception of God having parallel concerns arises from Kuyper's idea of the 'dual role of mediator,' which he sees as inherent in the work of Christ. For Kuyper, 'Christ is not only the Mediator of redemption, but also, and that first of all, Mediator of creation' (Pronk 1987:125). Especially in his work on common grace, Kuyper puts a stronger emphasis on cultural activity than his Reformed predecessors, even 'assigning to each of Christ's mediatorial functions its own distinct terrain, namely common and particular grace' (Pronk 1987:128). Moreover, according to Pronk, what upset Ten Hoor so much was

> Kuyper's statement to the effect that the soteriological element in divine revelation must be regarded as accidental, bearing an intervenient character and remaining dependent on the fundamental conception of revelation given in the creation itself. For Ten Hoor divine revelation is both theological and soteriological at the same time. It is theological with respect to God and soteriological with respect to man. All theology, therefore, is soteriological, because knowledge of God is eternal life. He saw in Kuyper's system a real danger, namely that preoccupation with natural revelation and culture would eventually result in a serious decline in vital, spiritual religion. (Pronk 1987:128.)

Kuyper used his concept of common grace to assist his theory of the dual role of Christ as mediator. This in order to show that Christ's redemptive work had benefits for the elect as well as the creation at large; particular, saving grace for the redemption of the elect, common grace in the bestowal of temporal blessings on the creation as a whole. By means of this common grace God's curse on humanity from the fall is mitigated and, thus, human culture is possible. Common grace is therefore a necessity because 'God has decreed not only that His elect will be saved, but also that the entire creation be redeemed. When God saves us, it is not as individuals that we are saved, in isolation from the rest of the cosmos. The Christian has a task in this world. He is to carry out his cultural mandate and fully develop the creation's potential' (Pronk

1987:132). According to Pronk, Ten Hoor would have none of Kuyper's formulation. Rather, he would agree with J. Douma that 'all grace is directed at salvation and the knowledge of God' (quoted by Pronk 1987:138). It seems that in spite of Kuyper's reputation as a potent supralapsarian, and perhaps his personal claim as well, the view, as stated above reflects more an infralapsarian way of thinking, namely, that election is not the first decree, but rather one of two decrees. Infralapsarianism, in distinction from supralapsarianism, would see the creation exclusively as the first decree of God. That is to say, that when expounding his concept of the 'cultural mandate' or developing his views on common grace and the creation, Kuyper very readily made use of infralapsarian constructs to explain and even bolster his position; he simply used whatever theory was suitable to the discussion at hand.

Infralapsarianism, however, was the view most widely held by Hoeksema's teachers, but this is one area where Hoeksema did not follow his mentor F. M. ten Hoor. Most of the 'American Secession Theologians' were infralapsarian in their view on the order of God's decrees (Faber1996:15-54). Faber also believes that 'Herman Hoeksema as a supralapsarian theologian was influenced by Abraham Kuyper and his follower Geerhardus Vos,' and that, 'although he [Hoeksema] rejected Kuyper's ideas of common grace, of baptismal grace, and of presupposed regeneration, he accepted his organism idea, his concept of the antithesis, and his definition of the essence of the covenant' (Faber 1996:43).

2.8 *The Lines of Influence*

Earlier, I sought to demonstrate that there are lines of influence in Hoeksema's theology from Kuyper as well as a select group of Secession theologians. I have also shown, by references to Herman Bavinck and F. M. ten Hoor, the origin of Hoeksema's concept of 'organic.' It is true that Hoeksema's understanding of the essence of the covenant primarily as a 'relationship' has much in it attributable to both Bavinck and Ten Hoor, while his idea of the antithesis is rather a common theme among many of the Reformed fathers. It must also be acknowledged that Hoeksema found Kuyper's supralapsarian position attractive (Hoeksema 1969:96 also

p. 105). But even here Hoeksema did not adopt Kuyper in a slavish manner and he would later propose an alternative. Hoeksema himself once voiced the criticism that a very wooden conception of the decrees of God from a supralapsarian perspective was in danger of injecting a 'temporal order in the decrees of God' (Hoeksema 1966:164). In other words, Hoeksema wished to be careful and not inject any element of temporality into that which is eternal. Hoeksema considered both infralapsarianism and supralapsarianism simply as paradigms for understanding, as both of these paradigms use a temporal construct for the decrees of God to aid in that understanding. It is true that Herman Hoeksema preferred the trappings of a supralapsarian paradigm, with its distinctive chronological temporal construct, to distinguish the priority of the eternal decrees of God. Yet, he was only too aware that the act of distinguishing this priority in itself superimposed a temporal chronology on that which is eternal. Hence, he viewed infralapsarianism and supralapsarianism as aids to our human understanding, nothing more, and if these temporal constructs were pressed too far, their usefulness was negated. In this Hoeksema was following an old Reformed tradition, as laid out by Herman Bavinck:

> with Calvin the supralapsarian and infralapsarian representation alternates. This is also true of most of the later theologians who embraced supralapsarianism. They regard the supralapsarian view to be admissible but they do not think of condemning infralapsarianism or of demanding that their view be embodied in the official confession of the church as the only standard of truth. They do not ask that their own be *substituted* for the infralapsarian representation but they plead for *actual recognition* of both views. (Bavinck 1977:363.)

All through seminary it would appear that, even while surrounded with views from every side: Heyns (conditional Arminianism), Janssen (the Neo-Calvinist) and Ten Hoor (the adamant anti-Kuyperian), Hoeksema was seeking to balance them off and come to his own conclusions. Furthermore, he firmly believed that historical Reformed theology could be demonstrated as having arisen directly from the Scriptures by way of the Reformed confessions.

2.9 The Student and His Predilections

From Herman Hoeksema's student days there are only two known, extant writings. The first is a senior college paper, written at the close of his senior year in the preparatory division of Calvin, prior to his entrance to the seminary division, entitled *Rousseau and Education*, and dated 1912. By modern standards, it is a rather poor specimen. The paper is poorly constructed; it is handwritten and contains no footnotes. Yet, in another sense, it is a tour-de-force. *Rousseau and Education* is based almost exclusively on Hoeksema's reading, in the original French, of Rousseau's *Émile, ou de l' Éducation* (1762). Throughout his analysis of Rousseau and his educational concepts, Hoeksema searches desperately for something positive to say. And, although he struggles continuously with the positive, he ends up saying something negative every time. As he says in the introduction concerning his reading of Émile:

> If we should begin by reading the Emile, the book in which Rousseau expounds his educational theories we would perhaps like Kant forget to take our usual afternoon's stroll and read it at one sitting, we would very likely be strangely impressed by it and exclaim after we had finished it: all of this is passionate, much of it is wonderful, a good deal of it is bad and some of it is good! But we would not grasp it in its full significance. (Hoeksema 1912:1.)

And, adds a youthful Hoeksema:

> Although we must not be blind for the good characteristics of Rousseau's educational system and admit that in some respect his influence upon the world of his and of our own day has been salutary, yet when we consider his system in broad outlines and estimate its principles, its aim, its method and its character from a biblical point of view, we cannot but condemn it in its entirety. (Hoeksema 1912:3.)

At this point, the struggle to find anything positive in Rousseau ends abruptly. Summing up, Hoeksema writes that, 'in its aim

Rousseau's system of education is positively immoral' (Hoeksema 1912:5). Although this summary judgment occurs before the halfway point in his paper, what follows tells us as much, if not more, about Hoeksema as it does about Rousseau. Hoeksema brands Rousseau a 'fantastic theorizer' (Hoeksema 1912:6); one who, 'because he never saw the practical consequences of his theories in real education, …came to tell us the most wonderfully impracticable and strangely impossible things' (Hoeksema 1912: 6). This sweeping assessment is based largely upon Hoeksema's incessant dislike for Rousseau's aristocratic bent. But, it is at this juncture that Hoeksema pulls back the curtain a bit and reveals some of his own sentiments, sentiments which, as we shall see, go beyond just educational theory. Concerning the character of Rousseau's system, he writes:

> In its character, Rousseau's educational system is to be condemned because it is exclusive, aristocratic. Like Montaigne and Locke, Rousseau wrote for the higher class of people only. His pupil, Emil, is rich and his education is based upon the supposition that his wealth is sufficiently large to provide for him during his entire life. For the education of the masses and for the education of women Rousseau had no use. With all his pretended sympathy with the common people Rousseau did not understand that education fulfills but a small fraction of its task as long as the masses are neglected. (Hoeksema 1912:7-8.)

Hoeksema's criticisms here seem to be motivated more by his dislike of all things 'aristocratic;' a dislike no doubt nurtured by the breadlines of his childhood in Groningen. He always distrusted the aristocracy, or upper class, and Rousseau's playing up to the upper class and the intelligentsia of his day was simply a sham. Moreover, while Hoeksema believed that Rousseau did not know what he was talking about, because he pitched his ideas to high society, more specifically the intelligentsia, he still became very influential, more so than his ideas alone would warrant. By contrast, Hoeksema saw pandering to any group as all politics, anti-Scriptural and, hence, dead wrong. He believed the upper class, or political class was, plainly and simply, not worth it.

The only other early extant writing from Hoeksema's student years, again prior to his entrance into the seminary division, was a play entitled *Dominee Kouwenaar of Zedelijk Dualisme* (Reverend Kouwenaar or Ethical Dualism), which, according to its author, 'the drama has in view to present the idea of sin, hidden to the eyes of men behind a mask of sham holiness and never confessed before God, brings forth sin, and finally death' (quoted by Hoeksema 1969:53). A melodramatic work worthy of Thomas Hardy, it was purchased by Eerdmans Publishing Company for publication in 1910, but it was not until 1919 that it was finally available for purchase. By 1919, however, Herman Hoeksema was in his first pastorate, and this youthful work became the occasion of no little embarrassment (Hoeksema 1969:54). The major theme of the play, though, remained an underlying theme for Hoeksema throughout his life. His sermons constantly warned against a reliance on works, and emphasized that it is the spiritual nature of the heart that is of concern before God. All else is simply not genuine. In this regard, many of the concepts he emphasized in his paper on Rousseau are developed further in his play. As Hoeksema himself said in an early sermon on Lord's Day 2 of the Heidelberg Catechism:

> If we look at the outward precepts, we find a good many little deeds in ourselves. But, if we look at that law as the sphere, as the boundary of the love of God, and that His consuming wrath follows all that is not in harmony with the boundary of that love of God, do we find any good within us then? To be within the bounds of the love of God means that we never do anything, never will anything, never desire anything that is not within the bounds of that love of God, so that we love God with all our will, with our heart, with our mind, with our all. I say, if we look at the law of God in that light, and that His consuming wrath follows all that is outside of it, then let us speak again. (Hoeksema 1930.)

These sentiments may also account for Hoeksema's opposition to Common Grace, and his insistence that God cannot be pleased with those who do not love him regardless of how admirable their works might seem to others.

Sometime later, though, Hoeksema's own over-confidence seems to have gotten the best of him. Becoming a bit too sure of himself, he was censured by the faculty at the seminary for his 'extreme statements.' As former Calvin College professor Harry Boonstra writes:

> In the period which the author knows best, such men as Herman Hoeksema and Henry Van Wesep delved into religion and philosophy to the extent of causing real faculty concern over their beliefs. This concern finally led to discipline and ...in the case of Hoeksema to apology and retraction of his extreme statements. (Boonstra 2000:40.)

Although it is not mentioned what these 'extreme statements' were, Hoeksema's sister, Everdina, sternly rebuked both the statements, and the attitude that produced them. Hoeksema's son Herman Jr. relates that in his days in seminary Hoeksema was called a 'rebel,' probably for becoming a 'highbrow' in both his attitude and behavior, something that would, nevertheless, have been detestable for the everyday *afscheiding* family. As a result, according to surviving family members, his sister Everdina 'read him the riot act' (Hoeksema 2001, Kuiper 2001) sometime before his formal entrance into the ministry. It appears that this experience had a profound effect on the young Hoeksema. He went from a 'highbrow,' of sorts, to a more serious and spiritually minded student. This encounter with his sister also goes a long way towards explaining Hoeksema's distrust, even dislike, of the upper, or political, class within the church, as is evidenced both in his play and in his paper on Rousseau.

2.10 The Young Minister

Louis Berkhof, Professor of Theology and eventually President of Calvin Theological Seminary, married Herman Hoeksema to Nellie Kuiper on the 7th of June 1914. The following year, 1915, according to Gertrude Hoeksema, held two more 'very important events in [Herman Hoeksema's] life—his graduation and the birth of his first child. Both came in June. Johanna Dorothy arrived on June 15, a short while before he became eligible for his first call to serve a congregation' (Hoeksema 1969:61).

Hoeksema's first ministerial call came from the Fourteenth Street Christian Reformed Church of Holland, Michigan. According to Gertrude Hoeksema, Herman did not want the call, but rather than decline it outright, he decided to 'put out a fleece' (Hoeksema 1969:66-67). Consistent with his decision to 'put out a fleece,' he asked the consistory of the calling church if he might meet the congregation. Before the meeting a minister from a neighboring congregation sought to give the candidate some friendly advice on pastoring a large congregation. This friendly advice was rebuffed with the old Dutch expression: '*Ik kan mijn eigen varken wel wassen*' (I can wash my own hogs) (Hoeksema 1969:67). 'At the meeting,' writes Gertrude Hoeksema,

> he found the whole congregation present to listen to him. He told them about his firm stand in the Reformed truth and his intention to preach forthright, exegetical, Scriptural sermons. And he told them about themselves. He scolded them about their wrong views of Christian education. He told them that they were not Reformed in doctrine and practice. He told them that they almost killed their former minister. He promised them that they would hear the Christian school issue from the pulpit; furthermore, the congregation might never dictate to him what he should preach. "Now," he concluded, "if you still want me to come, shake hands with me after the meeting." (Hoeksema 1969:67.)

Despite this diatribe, in September of 1915 Herman Hoeksema was ordained as minister of the Gospel at the Fourteenth Street Christian Reformed Church in Holland, Michigan.

2.11 *The Man and the Minister*

Thus far I have concentrated almost exclusively on Herman Hoeksema's intellectual and spiritual development, interspersed with some pertinent history both personal and ecclesiastical. Now I would like to delve into the man in a more intimate way. To this end, the portrait of Hoeksema that follows is a synthesis distilled from questions I had and answers provided by surviving family members and colleagues, as well as a more personal literature.

While there is indeed truth to the contention that he loved what he considered the truth so much that he would go to any lengths to protect it, Herman Hoeksema could, at times, have an unusually brusque way about him. We might venture to say that Hoeksema loved his God and his Church so much that at times he seemed overzealous. His writings betray a love for theology and a mind that was concerned for its clear exposition and development. And while this is certainly to be commended, there was also a dark side that I would be remiss not to mention.

Most of those who currently attend the Protestant Reformed Churches would never say a word against their esteemed founder. This would be akin to defaming an icon. However, family members who are not currently members of the Protestant Reformed Churches felt a bit more at ease airing their views.

Ella Veldman, wife of the late Reverend Richard Veldman, Hoeksema's nephew and former Protestant Reformed minister—he rejoined the Christian Reformed Church in 1960—told me that 'Herman Hoeksema was a very unforgiving man; a man who had to be right, no matter what' (Veldman 2000). Ella's nephew, Henry Hoeks, emeritus professor at Calvin College, echoed Ella Veldman's sentiments, adding that Hoeksema could brook no opposition (Hoeks 2000).

Cornelius Hanko, emeritus minister in the Protestant Reformed Churches, who for years was co-pastor with Herman Hoeksema at First Protestant Reformed Church in Grand Rapids, Michigan, was very helpful at this point. He admitted that, while he probably knew Herman Hoeksema better than anyone, he did not know him all that well. 'Hoeksema was aloof,' he said, 'and while I was as intimate with him as any, he remained distant' (Hanko 2000). Hoeksema's son, Herman Hoeksema Jr., came close to agreeing with Ella Veldman in her assessment of his father. He said that his father had this overwhelming sense that he was always right. He just could not be wrong! This coupled with the feeling that 'if you disagree with me, you don't love me' (Hoeksema 2001). One can easily see how this emotional mix could cause problems. Add to this Hoeksema's insistence that that he was just 'hating' the enemies of the Lord, and you have a combustible mix to be sure. One wonders, though, whether Hoeksema was always just hating the enemies of the Lord. Still, it seems that Hoeksema's motives had more than a little resemblance to the Genevan Reformer. As Jean-Daniel Benoît writes of Calvin:

> On his death-bed he begged the pardon of the City Council for his "over-vehement expressions, which he regretted." It is interesting however that Calvin should allow himself a defense for his vehemence and his violent words, and a justification for his attitude against much more bitter and relentless opponents. He felt constrained in spite of himself to use cutting words, "I feel I deserve some indulgence," he claims, "if in defense of the true religion I am forced to attack (*tractus invehor*) such obstinate men as would, I am sure, have received no gentler treatment at the hands of apostles or prophets." "You prefer gentleness," he writes to Zurkinden, "and indeed I am no enemy to it. If I appear too severe, believe me, I am driven to it out of necessity. On the other hand, does it never strike you how much your 'gentleness' actually harms the Church, this 'gentleness' which allows the wicked to go on with impunity, which confuses good and evil, and which does not differentiate between black and white.... As for me, I would rather be transported with rage than never be angry at all." (Benoît 1966:74.)

I asked Herman Hoeksema Jr. what single factor he believed influenced his father's development the most. Expecting a profound theological answer, I was shocked when he told me that he thought it 'was the complete lack of parental supervision growing up' (Hoeksema 2001).

It should also be acknowledged, however, that Herman Hoeksema was not altogether oblivious to his own faults, as when he noted in a sermon, circa 1935, on Romans 2:17-21a, 'Behold, thou art called a Jew, and restest in the law, and makest thy boast of God ... which hast the form of knowledge and of the truth in the law. Thou therefore which teachest another, teachest thou not thyself,' he added the comment:

> Now I must be careful in speaking about these words of the apostle—and you in listening—lest we become filled with indignation at the self-righteous Jews. What if we do? We are more self-righteous than the Jew, for this self-righteous Jew is a picture of what we are by nature. You and I are just what the apostle says here of the Jew. I am the worst Jew, next are the elders, then the deacons, then the teachers and leaders, and then the common members; but I'm the worst Jew. I'm not joking. I mean it. It is the mystery of the ministry of the word that God chooses such a Jew as I am, one who preaches and does not do what he preaches. Don't you see that we can read the text this way, "Behold thou art called a Christian, and thou restest in the Reformed Doctrine, and makest they boast of God, and knowest his will, and approvest the things that are more excellent, being instructed in Reformed doctrine, and trustest that thou hast the purest form of the truth, and that thou art an instructor of the foolish, a teacher of babes, a guide of the blind, and a light to them that are in darkness. And thou hast not only the form of the truth but the truth itself. Thou therefore which teaches another, teachest thou not thyself? Thou that teachest that we must glorify God above all, gloriest thou not God thyself? Thou that teachest that we must not seek the things below but the things above, seekest thou the things below? Your religion, your piety, your baptism, your doctrine, your faith, your hope, is taken away as a basis of your righteousness in the day when God shall judge the secrets of men." That is the text. (Hoeksema 1935.)

Like every true Christian Hoeksema was not oblivious to his own faults, but like so many of us it was not an easy thing for him to show what he knew to be true in his heart.

> No doubt those who like Herman Hoeksema will ascribe his single-mindedness and his abrasiveness, as well as his charisma, to his singular love for the truth. Those who do not like Hoeksema will

undoubtedly ascribe these personality traits to his overarching need to be right. To varying degrees, both are true, and I would not be inclined to disparage one in favor of the other. Equally, I would not be inclined to speculate on the mix, I do not think anyone could, because for many Hoeksema simply loomed larger than life in the conflicts that befell him.

In a sense, Hoeksema's psyche can be exemplified in his retort: 'I can wash my own hogs.' That is to say, Herman Hoeksema, as he grew up, developed the attitude that it was for him to take care of himself; he could not and would not rely on anyone else. He had this mindset even as a child on the streets of Groningen. He was able and willing to work hard. He had a quick mind that could grasp a situation and take care of it. He also had a charismatic personality that drew people to him. What he resented were situations, like the bread lines of his childhood, in which he was dependent on other people (the rich, the upper class) who clearly looked down on him as someone who could not be trusted—as came out in the preceding paragraph of the Lord's Day 2 sermon from the Heidelberg Catechism quoted above:

> As long as we say, I may not do this, and I may not do that, we may think that we are pretty good. The man that has piled up money and then gives away a little of that money which he has first sucked out of the poor, may say, "I am a pretty good man." And the biggest thieves put the little thieves in jail. That is our corrupt nature. (Hoeksema 1930.)

Additionally, he developed the determination to be straightforward and open with all, being thoroughly convinced that it would become evident in the end just how right he was (*The Banner* 1921:101-102).

All of this was reinforced in his school years. He worked hard at his studies, especially at mastering the English language which set him apart from nearly all of the other students who had grown up in thoroughly Dutch communities in which little but Dutch was spoken. In fact, he left them feeling very uncomfortable with both their own English and their heavy Dutch accents. Hoeksema fought diligently to learn English, taking every difficult pronunciation and repeating it over and over again until it sounded the way it should, to the point that he was one of the few students that could handle comfortably the English church services that were just beginning to be introduced into the more progressive congregations of the Christian Reformed Church. The result of his diligence was that from the start there was a strong demand for his services, and he was sent several summers to serve a vacant church in New York State which had a large proportion of members who were unfamiliar with Dutch and which he welcomed because it gave him an opportunity to improve his English even more.

The demand for his services was accentuated by his pulpit abilities. He quickly developed an attractive pulpit style, writing out his sermons completely beforehand and memorizing them word for word to the point where he could preach very naturally without notes. This he did with the kind of authoritative confidence and conviction that people loved to hear, and particularly so because he did so in defense of the historical traditions of the Secessions churches, from which he and nearly all of them had come.

All of this came across with a charisma that never left him. When he entered a room, his very appearance and composure—to say nothing of his deep, piercing eyes and strong resonant voice—made him the center of attention without his ever saying a word. When he spoke, whether in private or from the pulpit, what he said came across with a natural simplicity that made people feel that this was exactly what they thought and believed as well, which in the end perhaps became one of his greatest faults. He and they for the moment took it for granted that they were agreed, only to have many of these followers leave him and take up positions quite contrary to what he had taught, often leaving him and them with a sense that each had been betrayed. They had been drawn by his presentation, but never came to terms with what he taught.

In the end, perhaps it was his very strength and self-sufficiency that proved to be his Achilles heel. Had he listened to the kind offer of the elderly pastor to advise him on what he would encounter in the ministry, he might have gained a friend, while his curt retort—I can wash my own hogs—may well have alienated him completely in the end. And so, throughout, his sense of not needing anyone would seem to have left him separated from those he really needed to accomplish his desired end—this pattern is repeated over and over throughout his career.

Throughout, it appeared to be Hoeksema's conviction and desire that doctrinal differences should be talked about forthrightly and openly, possibly with the presumption that, if that were done, it would become evident to all that he was right, particularly because he had the advantages mentioned above. However, never having established that sense of mutual respect required for such a discussion, few would ever take him on under those terms; and, if they did, it was a battle in which each was committed beforehand to a conclusion from which he was not about to waver. The point was that, while Hoeksema had many admirers, by essentially his own refusal, as Reverend Cornelius Hanko's remarks bring out; he had few, if any, true friends. Maybe that is why he cried out for what he personally had missed. He simply would not, and possibly could not, let them in—and how ironic for one who made 'friendship' the cornerstone in his theological thought.

2.12 Conclusion

In this chapter we have looked at a variety of subjects: Hoeksema's arrival in the United States, his ecclesiastical affiliation and some of the history of that church, and some insights into the man and what motivated him. I have tried to paint a picture of the man and his theological landscape. We will see this landscape take on further dimensions in the following chapter as the conflicts begin. But for now, I have tried to scope out the man; the parameters of what defined 'Herman Hoeksema.' He was a man of singular interest. He was focused in ways most are not. Maybe his focus was too inward. Many would say it was, and that this was the source of his inability to handle those with whom he disagreed. Maybe it was his unswerving love for what he saw as the 'truth.' I think that a combination of the two give us a more complete picture of the man. It is my contention that this is the picture of Herman Hoeksema that emerges in the course of his theological odyssey from the docks of New York City to the beginning of his life in the ministry. I would now like to turn to this man in his theological context, his beginnings in the ministry and, especially, his writings in *The Banner*.

Chapter 3

The Origin and Development of Hoeksema's Theology

In September of 1915, Herman Hoeksema entered the ministry of the Christian Reformed Church armed with of a zeal for the truth of the Reformed faith as he saw it and a self-confidence unabated by anything that had gone before. He would prove his mettle in a controversy over a flag in his first pastorate. This may seem a relatively minor matter from our perspective, but the tensions of those days were so intense that Hoeksema bought a gun to defend himself.

It is not my intention in this chapter to outline a whole theological taxonomy for Hoeksema. I merely wish to investigate those events, including his development of a distinct theological methodology, which occupied Hoeksema's energies at this point in his career. These themes are, to my mind, essential to a proper understanding of the mature Hoeksema to come. In this regard I have drawn heavily on the writing he did for *The Banner*, the denominational organ of the Christian Reformed Church, as it is here that we get a first hand glimpse of Hoeksema as he comes into his own.

3.1 The First Pastorate

Herman Hoeksema's first pastoral charge at the Fourteenth Street Christian Reformed Church in Holland, Michigan—the largest Christian Reformed Church in Holland, Michigan—began in a downright stormy manner, but, as I said in a previous chapter, he insisted he was 'going to wash his own hogs' (Hoeksema 1969:67). The congregation, it appears, was of a divided mind and therefore not as 'Reformed' as the young pastor would have liked. Hence, Hoeksema's constant references to 'predestination' and 'election and reprobation' in his sermons, Sunday after Sunday, grated on some of his hearers (Hoeksema 1969:69). What Gertrude Hoeksema refers to as the 'liberal element' (Hoeksema 1969:73) began to agitate against the proclivities of their new pastor; going so far as to seek affiliation with a local Presbyterian church. As unrest began to seize the church, a frightened parishioner came to Hoeksema after having 'heard that the liberal element were actively conniving with the Presbyterian Church and were working to leave the denomination and to take the property with them' (Hoeksema 1969:73). Nonplussed, Hoeksema responded to his worried charge, saying: 'you are like the doctor who gives his patient a dose of castor oil and then gets scared when it begins to work. Now a *good* doctor will give him one more dose. That's what the congregation will get next Sunday morning' (Hoeksema 1969:73). The next Sunday, with a preparatory sermon scheduled, Hoeksema chose Galatians 5:7-10 as his text:

> Ye did run well; who did hinder you that ye should not obey the truth? This persuasion *cometh* not of him that calleth you. A little leaven leaveneth the whole lump. I have confidence in you through the Lord, that ye will be none otherwise minded: but he that troubleth you shall bear his judgment, whosoever he be. (Bible 1983:1214.)

Believing full well that the trouble was doctrinal and that another dose of spiritual 'caster oil' was needed, Hoeksema ended his preparatory sermon with a stinging three-point conclusion:

> Three things I have to say, and I hope to be so plain that misunderstanding is impossible. In the first place, to the troublers, and by them I mean those that oppose the official truth of their own church, and those that have gone to the length of working for another congregation, while still belonging to the church, I have this word. This week you stand before two alternatives: Repent and submit and come to the Supper of the Lord. That is your duty. Even now I maintain that the Supper must remain

the standard in the congregation. Or, if this is impossible, there is but one thing left: Leave the church, for your own sake, and for the sake of the congregation, as soon as possible, for the truth of the church stands or falls not with number, but with the truth of the Word of God. In the second place, to the congregation as a whole, this warning: Be not led astray by troublers, whoever they be. The Lord shall judge them. And finally, let the coming Supper be the means to remove all the envy and the hatred from your hearts, so that again we may manifest our unity in Christ Jesus to His glory on the basis of the truth. That truth shall stand; that truth shall conquer. And all else, all personal pride and vain glory the Lord shall judge. Standing on that truth you may be of good cheer, for the everlasting Lord of His church has promised us the victory. Amen. (Hoeksema 1969:77.)

Upon hearing this, the 'liberal element' had had enough. Several of them went so far as to voice their intention to leave the church. In the end, it appears the number exiting was comparatively small. This sermon, and its effects, writes Gertrude Hoeksema, were 'the turning point of Pastor Hoeksema's ministry in Holland. After that the congregation flourished' (Hoeksema 1969:77). Hoeksema consistently and steadfastly preached the Reformed faith, as he saw it. He set the parameters of this faith for his sheep very carefully, and any who did not agree with his staunch confessionalism were simply 'un-Reformed.' Of this, Hoeksema was sure.

3.2 Reformed and Nationalistic

During Herman Hoeksema's pastorate at the Fourteenth Street Church, World War I broke out in Europe. 'Suddenly,' writes Gertrude Hoeksema, 'World War I and its propaganda and patriotism was upon them' (Hoeksema 1969:81). Everyone, with a renewed sense of love of country, was waving the American Flag. It was also on display in most of the churches at the time, but not in Fourteenth Street Christian Reformed Church. On the morning of 10 February 1918, however, 'a flag appeared there before the service' (Hoeksema 1969:81). Seeing the flag, Hoeksema asked the elders to see that it was removed before the evening service, and it was. For Hoeksema, this rather innocuous act proved to be the opening of a proverbial 'can of worms.' Three days later, on a Wednesday, the Holland *Daily Sentinel* carried this rather minor occurrence on the front page. The article said in part:

> Rev. H. Hoeksema, pastor of the 14th Street Christian Reformed Church, believes that the American flag has no place in a church and that the national anthem should not be sung there. He told a committee so yesterday afternoon when they called on him to discuss statements he was rumored to have made in a sermon preached last Sunday.... He gave the following statement for publication to one of the members of the committee, explaining his reasons for saying what he did in his sermon: "The church as an institution as the manifestation of Christ's body on earth is universal in character; hence that church as an institution cannot raise the national flag nor sing the national hymns. As Christian citizens the members of the church, however, are in duty bound to be loyal to their country, to go when their country calls, in obedience to the government. But the flags should be raised from the home, on the streets, and on all public and Christian school buildings. Anyone who is pro-German in our time has no right to the name of Calvinist and is a rebel and a traitor to his government." (Hoeksema 1969:81-82.)

A certain Reverend Cheff responded to Hoeksema's contentions on the first page of the *Sentinel*. 'I do not care to argue the theological contentions advanced (i.e., Hoeksema's interpretation-PB),' he wrote, 'I fail to see the slightest connection' (Hoeksema 1969:82). Also responding in the *Sentinel*, G. J. Diekema, the President of Hope College, said that 'if at this crisis we spend our time in theological hair-splitting instead of patriotic devotion we are near to treason' (Hoeksema 1969:83). Unlike Hoeksema, Diekema 'cast the war in sacred, apocalyptic terms.' He believed that 'in this final conflict between freedom and tyranny, God was using the United States to "give birth to the universal brotherhood of man and ... usher in the promised reign of the Prince of Peace."' Additionally, Diekema contended that '"the flag stands for all that is pure and noble and good" [and] that the cause of Christ and country were the same' (Bratt 1984:88). According to James Bratt, 'Hoeksema, the resident champion of Antithetical Calvinism, responded by turning to Calvinism, the Constitution, and personal insult. Since Cheff and Diekema appeared to be incapable of sound thinking, he declared, a constructive discussion was impossible; he would have to content himself with showing that "it is very well possible to be fully as loyal and truly patriotic as those that make it their business to advertise their patriotism at every opportunity"' (Bratt 1984:88).

While Bratt has much that is good to say on the subject, my own opinion is that Hoeksema, as evidenced in the front page article in Holland *Daily Sentinel*, put forward a more thorough theologically based interpretation of the events surrounding the removal of the flag from his church than that of his detractors. For Hoeksema, a Reformed believer may be, and even must be both a good nationalist and a good Calvinist, but that nationalism must not be confused with the eternal Kingdom of God, especially where it concerns the church. These two must stand separately, therefore, if they are to stand at all. For Diekema, this reasoning would be considered mere 'theological hair-splitting,' because, for him, both the temporal duties associated with nationalism and the eternal obligations of a Reformed believer seem to run together. Methodologically, while Diekema just proposed a convenient label for those who disagreed with what he considered the proper behavioral response to the 'crisis' at hand, Hoeksema sought to discover any theological principles that might apply in the situation and thus dictate a proper behavioral approach. Hoeksema, throughout his career, always seemed to use this same method regardless of the circumstances. In his response to Diekema, Hoeksema stressed that, 'the church is not a building but the church is the people of God as a whole, united in Christ as their head as members of His body. And when the people as such do not meet in the church building, there is no church there. ... [Hence] the church as such never raises a flag' (Hoeksema 1969:86-87).

It would seem that Hoeksema also derived some of his ideas on the relationship of the church to the state from his mentor in seminary, Professor F. M. ten Hoor. In the course of refuting the idea that Ten Hoor saw the church and state as antagonists, Cornelius Pronk states:

> Ten Hoor ... believed that the church should be completely free from state control or influence, for only then could it be a true New Testament church and be part of an international, spiritual community of believers, governed solely by its King and Head, Jesus Christ. Against those who accused him of dualism, Ten Hoor was careful to point out that this charge was false because he did not say that church and state are antagonists, but rather that they stand independently alongside one another and that each had their own, distinctive terrain which should never be mixed. (Pronk 1987:123-124.)

The way this concept worked out practically, according to Ten Hoor, was that the methods of the world, 'political methods and tactics,' have no place in the Church of Christ (Pronk 1987:122). Conversely, 'the church should never seek to impose its will upon the state in an effort to turn it into a Christian state or society' (Pronk 1987:122). These same themes will be encountered again when Hoeksema begins to write for *The Banner*, but there it will be Kuyper's 'cultural mandate' that will bear the brunt of his scrutiny.

The *Daily Sentinel* continued to satirize and slander Hoeksema over the flag incident (Hoeksema 1969:88). However, during the greater part of this time of satirization and slander Hoeksema was on a trip to Iowa, where he preached for a missionary conference. While there, a minister in a nearby town refused to display the flag during worship for much the same reason as Hoeksema. His church became the object of clandestine extremism; it was burned to the ground (Hoeksema 1969:89). With the increased emotionalism and extremism of the time, duly illustrated by the burning of the nearby church, Hoeksema thought his life might be in jeopardy. According to James Bratt, 'Hoeksema reacted with an interesting display of his own Americanization. He took to carrying a pistol and, walking home one dark night in Holland, actually threatened to use it upon some would-be assailants' (Bratt 1984:88-89). Although Hoeksema never actually had cause to fire on anyone, his son told me that years later he did fire it down a laundry shoot to make noise for a family celebration on the Fourth of July (Hoeksema 2001). The controversy over the flag ended as abruptly as it began. The armistice of 1918 brought the emotionalism and extremism of the war years to an end.

3.3 Growth and Development

During his four and one half years at Fourteenth Street Christian Reformed Church (Hoeksema 1969:107), Hoeksema's fame as a preacher began to grow. So much, in fact, had his reputation as a preacher spread that, in the time that he was eligible for a ministerial call while in Holland, he received nineteen such calls (Hoeksema 1969:77). 'Hoeksema was, throughout his life, a great preacher,' recalled Cornelius Van Til, late Professor of Apologetics at Westminster Theological Seminary in Philadelphia. Van Til remembers when he was young, as

> a Calvin College student [that he] sat spellbound, listening to the young preacher who had just come to Eastern Avenue Christian Reformed Church in Grand Rapids, Michigan. The preacher had the physique of a blacksmith and the mien of a Napoleon. But his name was Herman Hoeksema. With flaming eyes and resonant voice the preacher said: "All flesh is grass, and all the goodness thereof is as the flower of the field ... but the Word of our God shall stand forever" (Isaiah 40:6-8). (Van Til 1968:83.)

In addition to the mechanics and oratory of his preaching, it was during this period that Hoeksema also began to refine its content. As part of this refinement, he began to reconsider theological positions held by the Christian Reformed Church in what he saw as a more critical, and biblical light.

'The Christian Reformed Church after 1890 began seriously to reflect upon its place and future in the American world,' writes Henry Zwaanstra. 'Not only did the church become more conscious of its surroundings, it also became more self-consciously Reformed and more articulate in expressing the implications of its faith in a new environment' (Zwaanstra 1973:25). The implications of its faith came to be called its 'world and life view,' a concept that could be traced to the Netherlands and Abraham Kuyper (Heslam 1998). Actually, it could more accurately be traced to Princeton Theological Seminary and the Stone Lectures for 1898, which Kuyper delivered there with such distinction (Kuyper 1931).

Kuyper's theological concepts, however, were not new to Hoeksema; he grew up with them (Hoeksema 1969:15-33).

Although in many ways insignificant, the 1918 Synod of the Christian Reformed Church appointed Herman Hoeksema to write an editorial column 'Our Doctrine' for the denominational magazine, *The Banner*. In a sense, this was a real coup for one who was only three years out of seminary. In its pages, from 1918-1922, Hoeksema would grapple with a number of subjects both mundane and controversial. More importantly, however, this new found opportunity allowed him to speak to the common people of the denomination; people for whom *The Banner* may very well have been their only source of information, both in and out of the church. These editorials, like the student papers that preceded them, continually disclose as much about the author, as the subject on which he was writing. His method, however, appears to be of special significance, because of both its apparent simplicity and the external motivations it betrays. It is in these pages that we witness first hand the flowering of Herman Hoeksema's theological thought and, based on what has gone before, a flowering in somewhat unexpected directions.

3.4 Our Doctrine

Beginning the editorship of his new rubric on 5 September 1918, Hoeksema announced that his first series of articles would touch on the Kingdom of God. That is to say, he starts with a serious but subtle attack on the Kuyperian *Pro Rege* mentality, beginning as he does with issues relating to the kingdom. Hence, instead of sphere sovereignty, the covenant of friendship becomes the theme, where God is the sole source of strength. Flowing naturally from this covenant of friendship is the principle of the antithesis, a principle primary to his *Afscheiding* background. In this endeavor he is successful. He speaks to the hearts of the people in a way others could not. He naïveté, however, was in his assumption that he could spell things out and people would immediately see the logic of his position and follow him. Although, according to Reverend Woudenberg, Calvin College's long time professor of philosophy William Harry Jellema, stated categorically that by 1924 the denomination as a whole agreed with Hoeksema. Still, in 1918, Hoeksema, in his new position as editor, set out to develop his concept of the kingdom from both a positive and an antithetical point of view, but he could not resist a good fight.

Whether Hoeksema had considered the vastness of his theme at the outset is doubtful. Knowing Hoeksema, he would have told his readers if he had. The first glimpse he gives his readers of his own personality, his own motivations if you will, comes like a blinding flash in the course of a charge, a reprimand even, which he gives to his readers in the opening paragraphs. He writes:

> When I am preaching I like to have an audience. I hate empty pews. And when the church is well-filled I like to see the audience attentive. I dislike to see people sail off to sleep when I am preaching. Perhaps it's my pride, but I confess, that I am very sensitive in this respect. And the same is true in regard to the articles I must write for *The Banner*. I write, of course, because the Synod thought fit, that since I was successor of Rev. P. A. Hoekstra as pastor of my present charge, I should also follow him in being editor of the department, "Our Doctrine" in *The Banner*. So I accepted the appointment, and I am about to assume the responsibilities connected with this new kind of work. I will write. But I want you to read my articles. I will appreciate it very much, indeed, if you do read them. In fact, if you just omit them, I would feel greatly obliged if you would just drop me a card, informing me of your absolute lack of interest. If all of you should feel that same way about my articles, and if you would inform me about your attitude, it would have the same effect upon me as a church running empty while I was preaching. Just as in that case I would stop preaching, so in this case I would immediately discontinue writing. Hence, please, read or let me know that you don't. (*The Banner* 1918:632.)

Typically Hoeksema, in a tone bordering on arrogance but with a genuine concern for his readers and their habits, he proceeds to accept the appointment, all the while alternating between humbly confessing to a certain inability and proclaiming a sense of superior purpose emboldened by a general spiritual malaise which he sees all around him (*The Banner* 1918:632-633). In short, in the first article he seems to say that: I accept this position because only I can do it justice, and as such, I expect you dear reader to read it.

While Hoeksema's motivation is somewhat obvious, his method is decidedly less so. It is, however, as far as understanding Hoeksema is concerned, of no less importance. During his seminary years, the theological concepts that seemed to captivate Hoeksema's sensibilities the most were the covenant and the fine distinctions involved in the perennial debate over infralapsarianism and supralapsarianism. I believe it is these same themes that dominate his methodology in his *Banner* articles, at least until such time as he becomes irrevocably entangled in the Janssen affair.

Hoeksema's covenant view, as discussed earlier, was developed primarily in reaction to the view of the covenant espoused by one of his professors at seminary, William Heyns. Hoeksema, in reaction to Heyns, and even at times to Ten Hoor, conceived of the covenant as a relationship with God, controlled, in turn, entirely by God's sovereign decree of election. Additionally, in contrast to many of his contemporaries, Hoeksema did not see the covenant as a means to an end; rather it was an end in itself. In fact, the covenant, God's relationship of friendship and love with those whom He had chosen from before the foundation of the world, i.e. election, was, for Hoeksema, the highest goal of the Christian faith. It is no wonder then that, from the beginning in 1918, he chose to write his offerings in *The Banner* from the perspective of the covenant. However, in Hoeksema's hands, this covenant perspective was to take on a still more refined approach. And, it is in the furtherance of this more refined approach that infralapsarianism and supralapsarianism are taken from their abstract abode and put to use as a working methodology. In order to understand fully Hoeksema's method in his *Banner* articles, a brief look at the finer points of infralapsarianism and supralapsarianism and how Hoeksema exploited the tension between these two abstract constructs to form a working methodology, is in order.

3.5 Origins of a Methodology

In the Reformed tradition, infralapsarianism and supralapsarianism have been rather technical terms referring specifically to the sequence of the eternal decrees of God, not eternity and history as Hoeksema later worked them out to do. Hence, I think it appropriate to take a look at the traditional understanding before proceeding to how others have 'developed' these concepts. Heinrich Heppe, in his classic *Reformed Dogmatics*, has this to say regarding the differences between infra and supralapsarianism:

> In this sense the *ordo salutis* is expounded by the prevailing Church doctrine in the infralapsarian sense. The contrast between the supralapsarian and the sublapsarian basis is clearly and skillfully set forth by Riissen VI, 20, 23: "Although in the decrees regarding formally and *a parte Dei* no order can properly be expected, because they are *an actus unicus et simplicissimus*, there is nothing to prevent the institution of some order in them, considered objectively and from our side according to our mode of conceiving. —As to what order they are to be arranged in for the purposes of comparison, there is no unanimous finding. Those who ascend *supra lapsum* (above the Fall) or above creation to constitute the decree of predestination are of the opinion that the decrees must be so arranged, that they place the decree of predestination before the decree of creation and of permission to lapse, and God is conceived as having first thought of manifesting His glory in the exercise of mercy and righteousness in the salvation or damnation of men, before He thought of creating man or permitting his fall; so that creation and permission to fall are of the nature of a means for revealing His mercy and righteousness. Thus the first decree about men concerns the manifestation of God's glory in the exercise of mercy and righteousness by the salvation and damnation of men; the second concerns creation; the third, permission to

lapse; the fourth, the sending of Christ for the salvation of those whom He had decreed to save." (Heppe 1950:146-147.)

While the words infralapsarian and supralapsarian may be attributable to the Remonstrants (González 1987:279-282, Bangs 1971:67-68), and while it was the controversy between Arminius and Junius over these two concepts that brought the ideas of infra and supralapsarianism into the mainstream of Reformed thought, the ideas themselves and the tension between them as polar opposites was felt long before the Reformation. As historical theologian Richard Muller writes, 'This problem of the relation of the eternal decree (whether providence or predestination) to its execution in time is, moreover, one of the problems of medieval theology that was profoundly felt by the Reformed theologians of the sixteenth and seventeenth centuries' (Muller 1991:250). Without any reference to medieval theology, Carl Bangs, in his monumental study of Arminius, seeks to demonstrate that the conceptual origin of these two constructs lies in the 'high Calvinism' of Beza, Calvin's successor in Geneva (Bangs 1971:68). For Bangs, it was Beza's 'extreme' views on predestination and providence, and their primacy with regard to the eternal disposition of humanity, that brought the problem to the fore that both supralapsarianism and infralapsarianism have sought to answer (Bangs 1971:68-69). While Bangs makes some important points, I do not think he does justice to the subtleties of Beza's position. The understanding of the order of God's decrees and their outworking in history was never so cut and dry for Beza as his critics would have us believe. In fact, Beza, while believing firmly in the decree of God's predestination, never looses sight of the historical. On his approach to this matter, He writes:

> Likewise, they will discuss this mystery wisely when they use some clear pattern of sound words, as well as the most convenient method for teaching, admonishing, and comforting. In his epistles the Apostle Paul sets down two ways of doing this: the synthetic and the analytic. Here we call "synthetic" the method that is <u>a priori</u>, or that descends from causes to effects, which the Apostle Paul uses in the epistle to the Ephesians. Having explained to us there the ground of the spiritual blessings that we

receive from God through Christ, he treats election and its causes before he comes down to its fruits or effects. These effects are the external calling by the Gospel, internal drawing by the Spirit of adoption, and justification, sanctification, and other similar evidences that confirm our election in us. Furthermore, we call "analytic" the method that is a posteriori, or that ascends from effects to causes, which the same apostle uses in the epistle to the Romans. He discourses at length and extensively on justification by faith, on hope, and its fruits, and then ascends finally to predestination itself, which comprehends in itself the supreme principle of our hope and our justification by faith. From all these things it is apparent that the chief end of the former method (the "synthetic") is knowledge; but the chief end of the latter (the "analytic") is consolation and confirmation in faith, hope, patience, and the rest of the Christian virtues. (Beza 1982:419-420.)

According to Beza, the Scriptures present two viewpoints on the matter and both are found in the 'Apostle Paul' who deals with election and predestination from two completely different perspectives. The Epistle to the Ephesians takes an 'a priori' perspective, starting with election and proceeding to the fall. Conversely, the Epistle to the Romans starts with the fall, only to arrive at election via an 'a posteriori' path in chapter nine. Beza is emphatic that both of these perspectives have value: the 'a priori' approach is good for instruction while the 'a posteriori' approach is better in such areas as pastoral counseling and personal work.

Herman Bavinck follows closely Beza's exposition of infralapsarianism and supralapsarianism, even appropriating much of the language. Beza's distinction between 'a priori' and 'a posteriori,' and his designations of 'analytic' and 'synthetic,' in regard to method, figure largely in Bavinck's account of God's decrees as well. 'Whether predestination is made part of the doctrine of God (the a priori order),' Bavinck concludes after careful consideration, 'or is treated at the beginning or in the middle of the doctrine of salvation (the a posteriori order) does not necessarily imply an essential difference in principle' (Bavinck 1977:358). Again, following Beza's lead, Bavinck proceeds to discuss both the similarities and the tensions involved in the understanding of the analytic method versus the synthetic method and the possibilities and difficulties involved in using either as a working methodology. Bavinck writes:

> the real reason for [the] difference is the fact that for the Reformed the doctrine of predestination has not merely an anthropological and soteriological but especially a theological significance. God's glory, not man's salvation, is considered the chief purpose of predestination. Also the synthetic, a priori order is rooted in a deeply religious motive. Hence, the assertion that this order of treatment presupposes a nominalistic conception of the Deity and that it offers a dry and lifeless dogma lacks every ground. The doctrine of predestination can be treated in a dry and abstract manner in the middle as well as at the beginning of dogmatics. To be sure, a true and saving faith is the prerequisite for the confession of the doctrine of election, but this is also required with respect to all other doctrines, e.g., the doctrine of God, the trinity, man. If this consideration is allowed to decide the issue, every dogma would have to follow the doctrine of salvation. But in dogmatics we do not discuss the truth as it subjectively enters the consciousness of the believer but as God has objectively revealed it in his Word. The synthetic method alone is able to do justice to the glorification of God, as a religious interest. (Bavinck 1977: 358-359.)

Elsewhere, speaking specifically of those who claim to hold the 'synthetic' or supralapsarian position, Bavinck argues that, in reality, both the supra and infra positions are little more than perspectives which alternate depending upon the nature of the inquiry (Bavinck 1977:363). That is to say, for Bavinck, no one holds to either the supralapsarian or the infralapsarian position exclusively. These, in fact, are not positions that any sensitive theologian can hold to be mutually exclusive. For Bavinck, as for Beza before him, these are perspectives, constructs, or models by which to understand God eternal decrees and their outworking in time.

Around the same time as Bavinck, Dr. K. Dijk of the Gereformeerde Kerk in 's-Gravenhage, in the Netherlands, also scrutinized the issues surrounding the infralapsarian and supralapsarian positions, with much the same result. In his analysis, Dijk seems to twist Bavinck around. He is markedly clearer than Bavinck in his analysis, but he also drops the language inherited from the Reformation which makes up so much of Bavinck's case. Writing on the tension inherent in the two positions, and, at the same time, seeing the unity which they seem to demand, Dijk concludes:

> All efforts to reconcile these two opinions have given no single final solution, except to see that there is no principal contradiction between Infra and Supralapsarianism. Also, regardless of one's assumptions, none can eliminate considering the truth of the other; that is, there is no Supralapsarian that does not make use of Infralapsarian terminology, and there is no Infralapsarian who does not retain some of the Supralapsarian presentation. (Dijk 1912:50.)

Even with the more conciliatory approach to these two constructs issuing from the Netherlands, closer to home, F. M. ten Hoor seems rather to have developed his own position in response to the strong supralapsarianism of Abraham Kuyper. In a sense, simply to give Kuyper a supralapsarian label and leave it at that is misleading. Kuyper really must be considered together with his 'cultural mandate,' in which he sought the development of history theoretically. Kuyper wanted to be supralapsarian in his theology, but he also wanted to maintain God's value within the infralapsarian paradigm. In fact, the irony of Kuyper was that he did not want to give up the value system. In contrast to Kuyper and with an obvious preference for legal terminology, Ten Hoor gives a strong defense of supralapsarianism (Ten Hoor [s.a.]: 118-119), only to conclude that although 'man appears in the covenant of grace as elect sinner...with the Reformed (Gereformeerden), the conception of the covenant of grace was infralapsarian' (Ten Hoor [s.a.]: 123). This would appear, on the part of Ten Hoor, to be rather careful anti-Kuyper reasoning, with a tendency towards infralapsarianism, but with a recognition of the place of election more characteristic of supralapsarianism. Giving what appears, on the surface at least, to be a defense of supralapsarianism, but ultimately confirming his preference for the infralapsarian position, Ten Hoor writes:

> As to our willing and actions we cannot take God's secret or hidden counsel or decree as a starting point, likewise we cannot use it as such for our knowing and our thinking either. All knowledge, which in this dispensation is possible for us, God has revealed to us in the Holy Scriptures. We know about God's decree only those things which the Holy Scriptures teach us about it. However, even from this revealed doctrine of election we may not deduce a teaching of the covenant through abstract thinking, and then make the truths, which have been revealed concerning the covenant in the Holy Scriptures, have a cut and dry fit for that teaching. The doctrine of election and the doctrine of the covenant must be understood as they have been revealed to us in the Holy Scriptures, even when the consequences of this is that the relationship between the two cannot be completely understood. (Ten Hoor [s.a.]: 120.)

The significance of all this investigation into these two constructs, infralapsarianism and supralapsarianism, is, to my mind, to preserve two ideas which, if either were held in isolation, would divorce the abstract from the historical. That is to say, infralapsarianism wants to stay close to the historical account as it is laid out in the Bible. Accordingly, it wants to be concerned with the responsibility of mankind, and to deal with God as one who interacts intimately with us. Supralapsarianism, on the other hand, desires to understand the value system of God by understanding the logical order of importance of his decrees. Hoeksema believed that both should be concerned with this order of importance, however, he saw infralapsarianism as not really wanting to get into the decrees of God, but wanting to deal solely with history. The problem with this approach is that once you focus exclusively on the temporal order, the value system becomes very subjective. Hoeksema was determined to find a middle way; to steer between, if you will, the Scylla of supralapsarianism and the Charybdis of infralapsarianism.

In a more recent offering entitled 'Herman Hoeksema's Theological Method,' David McWilliams acknowledges Herman Hoeksema's quest for a middle way and, at the same time, excoriates him for searching for it. Writing with respect to Hoeksema's understanding of the Doctrine of Reprobation, McWilliams comments:

> It is one thing to acknowledge that God's work is an organic whole; it is another to think that we can penetrate it. Does not Hoeksema come dangerously close to this when he admits that the Scripture is infra in its order of events, but insists, nonetheless, that what is ultimately in history is first in God's counsel? Moreover, this highly speculative tendency is clearly discernable in Hoeksema's quest to understand the relationship between God's counsel and reprobation. (McWilliams 2000:99.)

Several pages later, using a rhetorical question, McWilliams warns: 'must we not assume that we can penetrate the divine decree and that, furthermore, we can fully understand what God's ultimate plan is for the universe He has created?' (McWilliams 2000:117). Much of what McWilliams writes concerning Hoeksema's understanding of infralapsarianism and supralapsarianism reflects not so much on Hoeksema's conclusions as such, but that he had the audacity to search for conclusions to these matters at all.

In a section of his conclusion subtitled 'The Place of Mystery,' after quoting a section from Hoeksema's *Reformed Dogmatics* on the darkened understanding of man in his fallen, sinful state (Hoeksema 1966:283), McWilliams frankly admits:

> An analysis of Hoeksema's thought indicates that he would have done well to develop more fully this concept of mystery. As it is he tips his hat to it, recognizes the truth of it, but rarely will his penchant for grasping the organic nature of things permit him to say that there comes a point beyond which we simply cannot conceptualize since the data is not provided for us. This passing reference to mystery never becomes constitutive in his thinking. (McWilliams 2000:116.)

While McWilliams has written a great deal criticizing Hoeksema and the blatant lack of the mysterious in his method, nowhere does McWilliams demonstrate how the successful integration of the idea of mystery into Hoeksema's method could be accomplished nor, for that matter, what benefit it would have.

3.6 Hoeksema's Own Thoughts on the Subject

Hoeksema understood supralapsarianism to hinge on the primacy of God's decree of election, and infralapsarianism to be essentially historical in its perspective (*The Banner* 1920:423-424). It was a synthesis, or the exploitation of the tension these two polar opposites provided, that Hoeksema harnessed as his working method. He expressly wanted to deal with the covenant, or rather covenantally, only within the confines of history. It was this desire to treat the covenant as it unfolded in history that caused him to begin with the topic 'The Fallen King and His Kingdom.' Later, mid-1920 to be exact, he changed to 'The New King and His Kingdom.' Concerning these two topics and their covenantal significance Hoeksema writes by way of summary:

> Historically we found, the matter is thus, that the first king that was ordained, the head and root of the human race arose in rebellion against His rightful sovereign, and that hence he fell. He became the enemy of God, the friend of the devil, and his kingdom became through his fall and rebellion a veritable kingdom of Satan, the kingdom of darkness, the negative line of reprobation, through the history of the world, and we came to the conclusion that along this line we ultimately arrive at the kingdom of anti-Christ, that will exist for a while but will be consumed by the breath of Christ's mouth. And if we would follow this historical line in speaking of a new king and kingdom, we would not have to refer to creation again. All that would be necessary is to discuss the fact that this fallen kingdom is saved again in Christ Jesus. The kingdom is created under Adam as king. The king and the kingdom fall through his rebellion and sin. That same and entire kingdom is saved in Christ Jesus. Such is the

> historical line of development. And here we wish to call your attention to the very obvious fact that history is thoroughly infra. (*The Banner* 1920:423.)

However, Hoeksema does not stop with this. Rather, he is intent on discussing the relationship between supralapsarianism and infralapsarianism in his own thinking and its peculiar covenantal application. He writes that:

> It cannot be denied that Scripture is obviously soteriological in presentation. The redemptive idea, the message of salvation appears emphatically on the foreground. And we do not even hesitate to state, that just because Scripture follows largely the historical line which is soteriological, it is far easier to quote texts that favor the infra-conception than to appeal to separate texts for the supra representation. ...This, however, does not mean that Scripture does not shed the light of God's eternal counsel over this historical development of the plan of salvation. It does not mean that we are obliged to rest in this historical development and that we may not struggle till we have caught a glimpse of the glory of God as He realizes His eternal counsel in the history of the world. It does by no means imply that the supra-view is to be condemned. On the contrary, very often Scripture affords us a glimpse of this higher conception and allows us to see the whole of history in the glorious light of His counsel. ...It is there above all, that the supra-light of God's counsel is abundantly shed upon the infra-historical development of the kingdom of glory! It is in that higher light that we now wish to follow the historical line of development of the New King and His Kingdom. And if we make a study of history in this higher light we will come to the conclusion that it was, indeed, all adapted to the Christ of God and that the stream of history, irresistibly, without turning back to its source for even once, moves onward toward the realization of the Kingdom of our Lord Jesus Christ, according to God's eternal counsel. (*The Banner* 1920:423-424.)

Of major significance, to my mind, is the way in which Hoeksema's insistence that we do not start with election and reprobation per se is worked out in *The Banner* articles. Instead, he insists that we must follow the *Heidelberg Catechism* and speak rather of the 'organism' of the church. Hence, 'the purpose of predestination,' Hoeksema contends, 'is the gathering of the church to live in covenant relation with God. ...He elected there to be a church in order to be to the praise of His glory. And reprobation must serve this election' (Hoeksema 1930b). It is then this 'reprobation serving election' that Hoeksema sees as the unfolding of the covenant in time, which, in turn, is the stuff of which history is made. History is then to be defined as God's way of molding people, the primary purpose of which is the salvation of the elect. While giving an equal ultimacy, of sorts, to both election and reprobation goes back to many of the older writers, Hoeksema wants to distance himself from this conception. God, he believes, does not gain pleasure in simply sending people to hell. Reprobation, therefore, does not have equal ultimacy with election. That is to say, Hoeksema consciously departs from the traditional view of supralapsarianism which simply sees election as a way of showing mercy and reprobation justice. Rather, he sees the goal in God's purpose to bring forth a people, a church, with whom He will dwell eternally in a covenant relationship of love. There is then a very distinct relational purpose in God's mind and a goal which goes well beyond the mere boast of His greatness and goodness. For this reason, Hoeksema's 'modified Supra view,' as he himself calls it in the sermon on Lord's Day 21, begins with the will of God to glorify Himself by creating a creature to share in the covenant of friendship with Him (see Ephesians 1). In this context reprobation takes on more of a temporal connotation, becoming part of the creation along with the fall. That is, in order to realize this covenant relationship, it is God's will that a world would be created in which humanity, including the elect, would fall and need redemption. Part of the means to this end is reprobation. So, reprobation is secondary in nature. And, when speaking of this historical order, infralapsarianism is the language used. In fact, most of the Bible is written from this perspective, but from time to time God reminds man that His purpose is higher (Hoeksema 1930b).

It is just this perspective of the higher purpose, God's covenant of friendship as well as its unfolding in history, which was to become Hoeksema's chosen perspective as well. Whereas Kuyper saw election as the basis of the covenant, Hoeksema bases the covenant on faith. Still, following Kuyper, faith is not the ultimate base for Hoeksema, but election which becomes patent by faith. The purpose of God is with the elect in their lives, and in making all things work together for good. The important thing, however, is faith and it is God who gives it. For Hoeksema, you are not in the covenant unless you believe. Thus, if you come to faith you are elect. The covenant, then, is simply the outworking of the relationship of friendship with God in history, which, in turn, is based on election. This view gives to history an essential reality all its own; it is not just another of Plato's shadows on the wall.

An elemental component of this idea of friendship is communication. In the covenant, then, is the beginning of the possibility of honest communication, which, in turn, is really the very essence of friendship. Christ came as the fulfillment of the covenant and He was the picture of friendliness and kindness and not just to those who were friendly and kind to Him. It is here, however, that the covenant concept broke in Hoeksema's hands. Other than from the pulpit, it is doubtful that Hoeksema ever really understood the idea of communication. He could preach, he could argue, he could debate with the best, but he could not share himself. Maybe this is why, although he wrote much on the covenant as a covenant of friendship, he never expanded to any degree on just what friendship was.

In the course of his pastorate at Fourteenth Street Church, Hoeksema was really intent on picking up where his mentor at seminary, Professor Ten Hoor, had left off, using these concepts to develop a full-blown dogmatics. He was going to show how to answer all the problems Ten Hoor had and, at the same time, avoid Kuyper's idealism. To do this, his intent was to approach the material from a historical point of view, maintaining neither a polemic nor sectarian stance. It was with this mindset that Hoeksema began his writing career on the staff of *The Banner* on 5 September 1918; his first subject being the 'The Kingdom of God.'

3.7 The Banner Articles

For almost four years, from 1918 to 1922, Herman Hoeksema wrote a weekly column under the byline 'Our Doctrine' for *The Banner*. 'Please,' writes Hoeksema at the outset, believing full well that he, as well as all his readers, live in a hopelessly lazy world, characterized by an unhealthy concern for the practical with little room for doctrine or theory, 'don't be frightened by the heading of this department, so that you pass my article by without reading it at all' (*The Banner* 1918:632). 'I am different,' he says, you need to read what I say (*The Banner* 1918:632). Still, maybe because he is a bit older than when he first determined to 'wash his own hogs,' Hoeksema seems at times almost conciliatory. 'We will try to be as constructive as far as possible,' he writes, 'and, therefore, with due respect for the views of others who differ from us in principle or in detail, but at the same time fully convinced of the truth of our own view, we hope to write in a constructive manner conclusively, as much as possible' (*The Banner* 1918:633).

From the beginning, Hoeksema is intent on engaging himself exclusively with the Kingdom, which he sees as the Kingdom of Heaven in terms of the Covenant of Grace (*The Banner* 1918:672-673). That is to say, he aims to show that the whole concept of the Kingdom can be demonstrated from a spiritual point of view. While his intent may have been to lay all this out in a straight line, it is quite obvious that he is feeling his way as he goes. His stated reasons for proceeding from the standpoint of the Kingdom of God are, first, that a fresh approach will generate interest and therefore stimulate readership; second, the Kingdom of God connects with the principle concept of the Reformed Faith, namely, Divine Sovereignty; thirdly, the Kingdom is all-comprehensive which leaves Hoeksema great latitude [fourthly] to combat false views; and lastly, the Kingdom approach connects with the present state of the mind in the times we now experience (*The Banner* 1918:672-673).

The concept of the Kingdom, its essence and its laws, takes on a whole new meaning in Hoeksema's hands; even his unique understanding of both its organic nature and development is expounded upon at some length. On this he writes:

Once more, let us remember, that God created the world a kingdom, and that means, too, that He has sovereignly ordained all His ordinances and laws for every creature. When He created the world, He did not make a chaotic mass of objects, thrown together in a haphazard manner, without any relation between them. He did not make sun, moon and stars, seas and rivers and lakes, trees and flowers, man and beast, as separate objects in order to let them determine their own relation to one another and to their God. No, God also created their relations. God did not make chaos but kosmos, harmony, a kingdom. To every one of His creatures God has assigned its place in relation to all the rest. And that relation of every creature to all the rest, and of the whole to Creator, is the law of the creature. The sun cannot wander through space at random, but must travel a certain path, in relation to the earth, and all the planets are controlled likewise, by what we call the law of gravity. The tree must be planted in the soil, the flower must bathe in the light of the sun, the fish must find its life in the water, the bird must fly in the air. The tree cannot walk over the face of the earth, the fish cannot exist on dry land, the bird cannot swim in the water. There is a definite relation, a definite place assigned to every creature, and that definite place is its law. And together these creatures, standing each in its place as assigned by the Almighty, form one beautiful whole, one grand kosmos, the world, the Kingdom of God. But this is also true for man. God assigned him a place. True, there is a difference between man and the rest of the world, for the simple reason that man is conscious of the law of God, is a rational and moral creature that must keep his place freely, from voluntary obedience. But this does not alter the fact, that also to man God has assigned his place, given His own law. And that place of man was that he should be the king-servant. Have dominion over all things and love the Lord his God with all his heart and with all his mind and with all his soul and with all his strength. That was God's law for man. In the second place we must also understand that the law which God set for every creature was entirely in harmony with the very nature and being of that creature. It is not so, that God made creatures of a certain type and character, and that He assigned to them a place and gave them a law that was in disharmony with their being; but so that in the case of every creature there is harmony between his being and the law of God. The law of the fish, to live in the water, is in harmony with the being of the fish; the law of the tree is in harmony with the essence of the tree. And so it is with all of creation. So it is also with the law of God with respect to man. The law was adapted to man and man to the law. There was harmony. And this implies at the same time, that the creature can be happy only so long as he remains in harmony with the law, only so long as he retains the place and the relation assigned him by God. As soon as he transgresses, trespasses the boundary of the law, he is doomed to destruction. Pull the fish out of the water, and its death is certain. Uproot a tree and it must wither. Imagine that the sun would leave its path, destruction would be the result. The law of God is the happiness of the creature, transgression of the law is his death. And the same truth holds also for man. God has also assigned to him the sphere in which he could live and prosper. That sphere was the love of God. Transgression of the boundary of that sphere must be his death. (*The Banner* 1918:765-766.)

Having laid the foundation for the Kingdom as he envisioned it, Hoeksema proceeds to look at fallen humanity from the perspective of the unfolding of the covenant and the organic development of sin in its historical context. In discussing the latter, Hoeksema makes a sharp distinction between Kuyper's concept of 'common grace' that entered the world to keep it from destruction after the fall and his own burgeoning view of grace, which he refers to simply as 'special grace.' Hoeksema argues that it is because God must be all in all 'that humanity is not destroyed from the start, that it must have a history, that it is allowed to develop. The principle of special grace, however, injected into the human organism from the start and saving it as such, does not save all the branches of the tree. It saves only the elect' (*The Banner* 1918:789). With one stroke of the pen Kuyper's concept of common grace, one that entered the world after the fall to save humanity and thus make room for the preservation of the 'cultural mandate,' is summarily swept away. But, Hoeksema goes further still. Humanity after the fall, he believes, has no God ordained dominion of any kind, whatsoever. The only one who has dominion over the creation is the devil with fallen man under him as king, a situation which, according to Hoeksema, 'will reach its highest manifestation in the dominion of Antichrist' (*The Banner* 1918:789). 'And it is under the influence of this so-called common grace of the Almighty that the world is allowed to exist,' writes Hoeksema by way of summary, 'that sin only slowly develops itself, that the kingdom of darkness receives a chance to manifest its full strength and reveal all the hatred of rebellion against the Most High' (*The Banner* 1918:789). In contrast to Abraham Kuyper, Hoeksema insists:

> Never must we stretch the doctrine of common grace till we speak of two kinds of grace. There is only one kind of grace, and that one kind of grace is special grace, and thru that special grace all the world, with man as king, is to be saved. It saves humanity, but it also saves the world as kingdom. But there are two kinds of people in Adam, separated thru the injection of special grace into the human organism. They are the seed of the woman and the seed of the serpent, the elect and the reprobate, the children of obedience and the children of disobedience. Outwardly, all the children of the serpent share in the blessings of grace. Also they develop, also they have a history, also they develop their kingdom under Satan. But inwardly, even these outward blessings of grace are a curse to them, for they are totally depraved, and there is no receptivity for the grace of God in their hearts. But the seed of the woman is saved in Jesus Christ. He is their Redeemer and their King, and through His grace they become His willing subjects. (*The Banner* 1918:789.)

From this point on, for almost a year and with few digressions, Hoeksema continued to expound on the genealogical lines of both the elect and the reprobate and their growth and development in history. The lines of the elect always represent the outworking of the covenant of God in time. Whereas, the lines of the reprobate are always referred to in close conjunction with the organic development of sin, always with the latter serving the former. That is, the reprobate are in the world, in space and time, for the benefit of the elect. They serve the unfolding of the covenant in time. And while many times this service meant persecution or tribulation for the elect, it is still service because it is accomplishing ends that are predetermined by a sovereign God for His beloved.

3.8 The Bultema Case

Also known as the '"Maranatha Case," from the name of the book in which the condemned views were propagated' (Kromminga 1949:72-73), this seemingly minor disturbance occasioned by the dissemination of premillennial eschatological views more commonly held in Fundamentalist circles (Bratt 1984:96), struck many as really more of a tempest in a teapot, than the full-blown crisis others try to make of it. While the book, written by Reverend Harry Bultema, the relatively obscure pastor of First Church (Christian Reformed) in Muskegon, Michigan, was published in 1917, thus making full eschatological use of the war to end all wars, the ecclesiastical machinery took until the following year to take both the book and its author to task. According to James Bratt:

> The CRC Synod of 1918 found time between its patriotic singing and resolutions to declare his [Bultema's-PB] statements on the two contested points ['the unity of the Church in all dispensations and the Kingship of Christ' (Kromminga 1949:73)] to be in conflict with the Confessions and directed his consistory to admonish him properly. But the Synodical committee acted so tactlessly that Bultema, most of his congregation, and scattered sympathizers left the denomination. (Bratt 1984:97-98.)

It seems that Hoeksema entered the fray purely by coincidence, yet his deliberations on a proper disposition of the matter proved to be decisive. The Synod of 1918, the same one that appointed Herman Hoeksema to his weekly rubric in *The Banner*, also appointed him to a special committee to review the details of the Bultema Case and to make the appropriate recommendations (Hoeksema 1969:93). According to Gertrude Hoeksema:

> During the committee's discussion sessions, some members found it hard to produce Scriptural and Confessional proof that Rev. Bultema was in error. The committee agreed that the confessions did not, in so many words, denounce Rev. Bultema's premillennarian views. But Hoeksema showed the committee that Rev. Bultema was questioning the Kingship of Christ over His whole church. ...After the committee recognized the nature of Bultema's error to be what Hoeksema had said it was, they refuted it with ample Scriptural and Confessional proof, to the satisfaction of the Synod, which adopted the report. (Hoeksema 1969:93-94.)

Since Hoeksema wrote the report on Bultema's views that Synod later adopted (Hoeksema 1969:93), he was, therefore, a major factor in Bultema's departure from the Christian Reformed Church.

Hoeksema's own opinion was that premillennialism was false doctrine. 'Accept the doctrine of the covenant,' he wrote, 'and Premillennialism becomes an impossibility' (*The Banner* 1918:844). While he recognized Fundamentalism in general and especially its premillennial eschatological orientation to be 'one of the most powerful and influential currents in the Christian world of today' (*The Banner* 1918:844), it was just this influence that he saw as so dangerous. Hoeksema contended that:

> Premillennialists have an entirely different view of history than the Reformed people. They cut the thread that runs through all history both of the old and new dispensation. They cannot admit that essentially there is but one people of God, and that one people of God the covenant people, of whom Christ is the Head and King forever. They have no conception of the continuity of the covenant of grace, of the gradual process of its development and revelation, and for that reason they have no eye for the organic unity of Scripture and cannot admit that the New Testament is the fulfillment of the Old. (*The Banner* 1918:844.)

I think Hoeksema's method is particularly well illustrated in his criticism of those who hold premillennial ideas. While God's value system, the supralapsarian viewpoint is represented, Hoeksema's concern is with the outworking of that value, the unfolding of the covenant in time, the infralapsarian perspective. History, therefore, is writ large in his criticism. His concern is not that premillennialists fail to give proper emphasis to election, but that by their hermeneutics they misunderstand history and its natural, organic development. I think this criticism is telling, especially considering Hoeksema's overarching view of the covenant and its historical continuity and development. In this regard, Hoeksema, while continuing his criticism of premillennialism, continued to develop and present his own insights from a distinctly covenantal perspective. On this he wrote:

> Of course, if the truly Reformed covenant idea is grasped at all there is no danger of ever embracing this premillennial view of history. The former stands for the continuity of history, the gradual development of God's plan and the idea of progress in the Revelation of God to man. There is but one covenant essentially, and that one covenant is the covenant of grace established with the people of God in Christ Jesus, but that one covenant passes through various stages of Revelation till at last in the days of the new dispensation it reaches its highest stage of development and manifestation, because then the head of that covenant and the King of His people has become manifest and actually entered into His heritage from Jehovah. From this standpoint there is no essential difference between the old and new dispensation, Israel and the Church are essentially one. True, they represent different dispensations but they are dispensations of the same covenant essentially. They have the same God and the same Christ, are members of the same Body and citizens of the same Kingdom, are saved in the same blood and by the same Spirit through the same faith in the same Gospel. They have the same purpose, namely to exist as God's people in the world and show forth the glories of His Name, let their light shine, and ultimately they are all to be gathered under the same Head into the

Kingdom of Glory that shall embrace all the works of God. But if a true conception of the truth of the covenant ought to guard us against the strong seductive influence of Pre-millennialism it must also prepare us for battle against a still stronger movement that is in the air today, and which after all is nothing but some form of Post-millennialism.... You ask, how in the world the doctrine of the covenant can draw the lines in this respect? You fail to see what this doctrine has to do with the movement pictured above? Well, then, let me tell you that it is my conviction that at the basis of this entire movement in as far as some of our own people are involved in it, lies an altogether erroneous conception of the relation of "common" and special grace, or if you please, a confusion of ideas with regard to the covenant of nature and the covenant of grace. These must neither be separated or altogether confused, but they must be explained in their true and Scriptural relation to each other. Then and then only can we hope to maintain a clear conception of the kingdom of God and its development in this dispensation. Then and then only will we be in a position to distinguish between the world and the kingdom of God. Then and then only will we be able to appreciate truly the value and the purpose of the different institutions God has ordained on earth in this dispensation. (*The Banner* 1918:844-845.)

It was not until a year or so later, in September 1919, that Hoeksema finally spoke of the Bultema Case by name at all, and this only because 'the act of synod 1918 regarding Maranatha has been called mockingly "an heretic trial"; and has been bitterly denounced as a manifestation of religious intolerance and an act of persecution' (*The Banner* 1919:581). Hoeksema vigorously defended his actions with respect to Bultema, whom he regarded as a purveyor of false doctrine. How this particular label differs from 'heretic' is nowhere addressed. However, he was emphatic that,

> one who propagates teachings in disharmony with the Reformed standards is in no wise persecuted or wronged, becomes in no sense of the word a martyr, if he is kindly asked to retract his unreformed teachings or to leave the church. Nor is he in any wise an object of persecution, if

refusing to leave the church on his own account and yet insisting to spread his doctrines he is simply expelled and forced to look for a field of labor elsewhere. (*The Banner* 1919:581.)

The significance of the Bultema Case for Hoeksema was, to my mind, his handling of the affair in print. Both his analysis of the matter for the 1918 Synod and his subsequent writings on premillennialism, including his insightful summary written a year after the fact, scared some people to death. This was a time when, as we have seen, Americanization was beginning to take hold in this once hesitatingly defensive Dutch subculture (Bratt 1984:98). Those who were of a progressive mind could not but bemoan this turn of events. Here was one exhibiting distinctly exclusive tendencies at a time when many, especially those in the vanguard of the Americanization process, were pushing for a more inclusive vision of the church. Hoeksema's handling of Bultema was, to this more inclusive faction, thoroughgoing regression. In addition, while many who were of this more inclusive mind would never have agreed with Bultema's theological orientation, still there had to be room for this orientation as well. Hoeksema, by his thorough and insightful analysis of the matter and his unflinching desire for doctrinal purity, including the expulsion of any who disagreed, became instantly anathema to those who saw progress elsewhere. In turn, Hoeksema considered these 'progressives' to be pseudo-Calvinists, on whom, according to James Bratt, Hoeksema now 'declared war' (Bratt 1984:102).

One aspect of Hoeksema's 'war' on pseudo-Calvinism was his increasingly critical stand on common grace in print. In the above offering he refers to common grace in quotation marks. To my mind, this is meant, as he does elsewhere in other *Banner* articles of this period, to call this concept and its then current usage into question. While over the next several years these questions would multiply exponentially, nevertheless it is at this juncture that he openly begins to question the use of the term itself in a specific context. Clearly, it is with this in mind that, on 6 February 1919, Hoeksema takes time from his discussion of 'Mankind's Relation to the Fallen King' to write:

> One characteristic of Pseudo-Calvinism is, that although is resembles our genuine faith, it would ultimately lead us right into the midst of the world in the evil sense of that word. Evidently, it does not maintain the sharp distinction, so clearly announced in Scripture between "world" and "world", and hence it comes to call Anabaptism what is nothing but the only true Christian attitude and must result in amalgamation with the world in its evil sense. (*The Banner* 1919:6.)

It is my belief that by his insistence on the Reformed truth as he saw it at the expense of unity or inclusivism of any sort, Hoeksema made himself a marked man. This would become more evident with the onslaught of the Janssen Affair. Still, it must be emphasized that while Hoeksema may have insisted on Reformed truth for himself and those in his charge, he was never so one-sided in his view of Christianity in general. Even while excoriating pseudo-Calvinism at length, in the same breath he could say:

> Not all Christians are Calvinists. Mark, I say: "not all Christians are Calvinists." They may be Christians all-right. Sure! Dear children of God, with whom I love to shake hands. I don't believe that there is a Calvinist that denies this. I don't think that there is a Calvinist who maintains that the Calvinists are the only Christians. And those who love to waste paper (and that in this time when paper is so valuable!) by fighting against Calvinists who maintain that they are the only Christians on earth, are fighting a shadow, a product of their own imagination. No, but I claim that a Calvinist is a Christian of a distinct type, with distinct principles and views, in distinction, namely, from other Christians. (*The Banner* 1919:6-7.)

3.9 Eastern Avenue Christian Reformed Church

During his last two years at Fourteenth Street Christian Reformed Church, Herman Hoeksema received many calls to serve other congregations in the denomination (Hoeksema 1969:77). At last, for the congregation, the inevitable happened (Hoeksema 1969:94). After four and a half years at Fourteen Street Church

(Hoeksema 1969:107), Hoeksema accepted the call to Eastern Avenue Christian Reformed Church in Grand Rapids, the largest church in the denomination, in January of 1920 (Hoeksema 1969:114-115). The newly appointed pastor took up his duties in Eastern Avenue in February of 1920. Amidst all the joy of the new charge, Hoeksema could not see the storm clouds that were slowly gathering on the horizon.

3.10 Conclusion

In the course of this chapter, I have tried to give the reader a sense of both Herman Hoeksema the man, and his spiritual/intellectual development. For this reason the chapter has been taken up to a good degree with topical and thematic analysis, in addition to the historical narrative.

I began by outlining Hoeksema's first charge as pastor. It began badly, in part because of a congregation accustomed to one type of minister and partly because of Hoeksema who was definitely not of the expected mold and neither would be. World War I was also beginning at this time with its attendant patriotism and propaganda. It produced many extremes, one of which concerned the display of the American Flag in church. Herman Hoeksema's spiritual/intellectual development influenced and was influenced by all these events. Additionally, beginning in 1918 he began writing in *The Banner*, the denominational magazine of the Christian Reformed Church. It is here that he developed a distinct method. Had things gone differently, maybe he would have completed an entire dogmatics from the perspective of the covenant. As a whole, though, while much of what is written in *The Banner* under the rubric 'Our Doctrine' is of a seminal nature, in the long run Hoeksema becomes too wordy, at times he tends to major on minors, he seems to have trouble getting to the point in many instances, and, as a result, he begins to bore people. It becomes obvious after the first year that he has not thought things through completely and, maybe, he was simply too young to have undertaken such a mature task. Probably, at least in part, because of the Bultema Case, his tone changes noticeably from one of 'gentle' persuasion at the outset to one that is distinctly confrontational. It is also in connection with the premillennialism of the Bultema Case that Hoeksema once again, at least in print, takes issue with the whole idea of common grace. The more polemical Hoeksema, however, began to emerge fully with his critique of Neo-Calvinism in the April and May 1919 issues of *The Banner*.

In all this, Hoeksema's fatal flaw, at least to my mind, was that he allowed himself to get sidetracked, first by the Bultema Case, then finally, and fatally, by the Janssen Affair. His weakness was that he simply could not turn down a good fight. After all, theology developed throughout history through confrontation. Was this not necessary for doctrinal development? All through his childhood on the streets of Groningen, Hoeksema had to fight for everything he got, and he was used to winning. This was just how things were done. He was really a scrapper at heart and he could never resist a good fight. I firmly believe this is what his son meant when he told me that the most telling feature of the mature Hoeksema, in his opinion, was the distinct lack of parental guidance in his earlier years. Anyway, regardless of his motives, this weakness would eventually prove his undoing.

Chapter 4

The Janssen Affair

Herman Hoeksema took up his duties as pastor of the Eastern Avenue Christian Reformed Church in February of 1920. Over the course of the next four years, his world would be turned up side down. In the end, he would no longer be affiliated with the Christian Reformed Church in any way. What happened to bring about this change of fortunes? It is to this question that I would like to direct my efforts in this chapter. The question is, however, not as simple and straightforward as one might imagine. The history of the period is one marked by ecclesiastical conflict, based, in turn, upon detailed doctrinal wrangling, and the things that happened to Hoeksema in 1924 were in many ways the result of these earlier controversies and the part Hoeksema played in them. Paramount among these earlier events was the appointment and subsequent dismissal of Ralph Janssen from his position as Professor of Old Testament at Calvin Seminary in 1922. In this rather sordid affair Hoeksema played a truly pivotal role. Moreover, the issues at stake in the 'Janssen Affair' actually set the stage for the events of 1924.

Since it is really impossible to appreciate the events of 1924 without first understanding the events leading up to and including 1922, in this chapter I intend to investigate the latter. As in previous chapters, I intend to deal with both the historical and the doctrinal, as together they determine the intellectual/spiritual development of Herman Hoeksema, and, in turn, lay the necessary foundation for our later discussion of common grace.

4.1 Professor Janssen

Harry Boer, in an early article written on the Janssen Case, concluded that 'in the entire history of the Christian Reformed Church no significant event has been so silenced by the ecclesiastical structure nor has any event cast so long and oppressive a shadow over its life as the disposition of the Janssen case by the Synod of 1922' (Boer 1973:21). While biographical material on Professor Janssen is 'extremely meager' (Boer 1972:17), George Stob, in his thesis on the history of the Christian Reformed Church, was able to supply some necessary details.

Roelof (Ralph) Janssen was born on a farm between Holland and Zeeland, Michigan in 1874 (Stob 1955:301, Bratt 1984:105). According to Herman Hanko, he studied at Hope College, received his baccalaureate from the University of Chicago in 1898, and went on to study at several major European universities finally receiving his doctorate from Halle, in Germany, in 1902 (Hanko 1988:9, Heerema 1986:62). The one person, who exerted the most influence on this developing scholar, writes George Stob, was Dr. Martin Kahler at Halle, under whose supervision Janssen submitted his doctoral thesis on textual criticism and the Gospel of John (Stob 1955:301).

Janssen was initially appointed, through the efforts of his pastor Rev. Johannes Groen, to teach exegetical theology at the Seminary Division of Calvin College in 1902. From the start there were differences between Janssen and Professor F. M. ten Hoor, as Stob relates, 'on the question of the relations of theological science' (Stob 1955:301). Ten Hoor believed theology to be the queen of the sciences, but nonetheless under the governance of the church (Stob 1955:301), whereas Janssen did not look kindly on this idea of ecclesiastical oversight. Following Kuyper's lead, and borrowing a great deal from him as well, Janssen believed that theological science should not be subject to the church, but rather exercised 'sovereignty in its own sphere' (Stob 1955:302). These opinions, in addition to using the 'university method' in his teaching, did not serve to increase his popularity with his colleagues in the theological faculty. 'Since he also was not an ordained minister of the gospel,' writes David Holwerda of Calvin Seminary, 'several insisted that he had no right to be a professor of theology, and they feared that his appointment meant that greater significance would now be given to the demands of scholarship and objective research than to the confessions of the church' (Holwerda 1989:11). Since this type of reasoning was widespread, Janssen was generally suspect and his commitment to the Reformed faith was openly questioned, so much so that in 1906 he was not re-appointed to his position on the faculty.

Upon failing re-appointment, Janssen traveled to the Netherlands to study in the Faculty of Theology at the Free University in Amsterdam. G. D. de Jong, in an essay on the early history of Calvin Seminary, wrote that 'Janssen had spent two years (1906-1908) in Europe and the Free University of Amsterdam conferred on him the degree of Doctorandus of Theology. Some of the delegates knew (Janssen's earlier trials), but statements like these: "Dr. Janssen longs to serve the church in which he was born"; "Dr. Janssen has learned a great deal since 1906"—were conducive to lessen the apprehension' (DeJong 1926:41). With this new found support, Janssen was re-appointed to Calvin Theological Seminary as Professor of Old Testament in 1914, a position he held until his dismissal in 1922. Edward Heerema, in his biography of R. B. Kuiper, Janssen's brother-in-law, concludes 'that Janssen was appointed this time in the confidence that his study under Bavinck and Kuyper in Amsterdam had cleared up whatever questions that had emerged in his previous tenure' (Heerema 1986:63). Even though Janssen's second appointment in 1914 coincided with Herman Hoeksema's last year in Calvin Seminary—he graduated in 1915—Hoeksema never mentions him in connection with his study for the ministry. It is probable that Hoeksema did not have any first hand experience with the teachings of Professor Janssen and only became acquainted with them later.

By 1919 Janssen had again become the object of suspicion among his colleagues at the seminary. This was due primarily, as David Holwerda explains, because of certain 'student complaints voiced to certain professors during annual home visitations' (Holwerda 1989:11). He writes:

> One student revealed that he had often thought about leaving the seminary to take up some other occupation because Janssen's instruction had shaken his faith in the reliability and infallibility of the Scriptures. Another felt that Janssen's view of miracle negated any immediate intervention by God. A third confirmed that Janssen taught that the Song of Songs was an eastern love song and that the Pentateuch was not in its entirety from the

pen of Moses. And a fourth student rendered the opinion that Janssen did not present a high view of the Bible. (Holwerda 1989:11.)

As a result of this testimony, in the spring of 1919, Professors L. Berkhof, W. Heyns, F. M. ten Hoor, and S. Volbeda, 'niet om te twisten, maar uit gewetensdrang' (not in order to quarrel, but out of moral constraint) (F. M. ten Hoor, W. Heyns, L. Berkhof, & S. Volbeda [s.a.]:3) as they themselves insist, presented a pamphlet entitled *Nadere Toelichting omtrent de Zaak Janssen* (Further elucidation about the Janssen case) to the Curatorium of the Seminary essentially demanding a full inquiry into the matter. Expanding further on the student's statements from home visitations with the aid of student notes from Professor Janssen's classes, the four professors charged Janssen with: a dubious view of the inspiration of Scripture, a downplaying of the miraculous elements in the miracles recorded in the Scriptures, and a questioning the Mosaic authorship of portions of the Pentateuch (Boer 1972:18). Janssen, appealing to both Kuyper and Bavinck, explained his own views on inspiration without hesitation.

> I hold to that view of the inspiration of the Holy Scriptures which in present Reformed Theology (e.g. Kuyper and Bavinck) is called organic inspiration. This to me implies: 1. that the writers of the Scriptures were infallibly moved and guided by the Holy Spirit, and 2. that the Holy Scriptures are *verbally* inspired, theopneusta, and are credible, infallible and of Divine authority for faith and practice. Strictly speaking, it is only autographa that are infallible. Organic inspiration does full justice to the Divine and human factor. ...But Theol. thought goes on. Continued study of the Scriptures, Exegesis, Biblical Theology, etc. will bring to light new facts.—That is, I take it, in accordance with the promise of Christ, that the Holy Spirit will lead into all truth. Of that new light account will have to be given in the further study of the Locus on Inspiration. How to bring the truths, which Theological study may bring to light, within the definition of Inspiration as Reformed Faith formulates it—that is our task in the future, and that task will be there as long as there shall be a militant church. (quoted by Boer 1972:18.)

According to Herman Hanko, the response of the Curatorium to the four professors' demand for an investigation into the teachings of Professor Janssen was to appoint a committee to consult both with the four professors and with Professor Janssen (Hanko 1988:12). These meetings having been accomplished, the Curatorium proceeded to give Professor Janssen a vote of complete confidence. Specifically, they insisted that the four professors should have gone to Professor Janssen privately before bringing this matter into the public forum, and 'that Professor Janssen has given full assurance that he believed completely and wholeheartedly in the authority, credibility and infallibility of Scripture' (quoted in Hanko 1988:15).

Hoeksema agreed with the decision of the Curatorium in so far as it reprimanded the four professors for not going to Professor Janssen in private. However, he was uneasy with the fact that the Curatorium, while giving Professor Janssen a vote of confidence, failed to investigate the matter beyond the personal assurances given by Professor Janssen as to his own orthodoxy (Hanko 1988:16). So much was Hoeksema's uneasiness over the disposition of the allegations of the four professors against Janssen that he admits he became 'a strong opponent of Prof. Janssen after the Synod of 1920' (Hanko 1988:16).

If Hoeksema was uneasy, the four professors were even more so. They summarily ignored the Curatorium's admonition to privately discuss the matter with Professor Janssen. Instead, as Hanko relates, 'they notified the Curatorium that they were appealing to the Synod of 1920 (Hanko 1988:17). In the interim the Curatorium once again scrutinized the matter, reaffirming their original decision regarding the soundness of Professor Janssen's instruction (Hanko 1988:18).

It seems as if the events of 1920 were pivotal for everyone concerned, the four professors and Hoeksema, as well as Janssen. The four professors renewed their charges against their colleague in Old Testament before the Synod of 1920, which was held in June of that year. Hoeksema, who had been writing under the rubric 'Our Doctrine' for *The Banner*, began the year with a series on 'The Kingdom and the King,' only to interrupt his series to examine the charges against Janssen more closely. After due deliberation, the Synod of 1920 exonerated Professor Janssen of all charges pending against him.

4.2 Contextually Speaking

Before detailing the specific events of 1920, and beyond, I think it pertinent to put things in a bit larger context to gain a better perspective on the events that are about to take place. Recounting the history for this period, George Harinck writes:

> The Neo-Calvinists in the Christian Reformed Church tried to reinforce their position by enabling theologians to study under the supervision of Bavinck and others at the Vrije Universiteit. Their plan worked and several of the theologians who made use of this opportunity, such as R. Janssen, Y.P. de Jong, H.H. Meeter, and S. Volbeda, were appointed at Calvin Theological Seminary of the Christian Reformed Church or at Calvin College. Among ministers who had done graduate work in the Netherlands the idea arose that closer relations with the Neo-Calvinists and a better knowledge of their view of culture might help the Christian Reformed to integrate as Reformed people in modern America. But the counter forces were strong, and tensions grew when Dr. Janssen ... of Calvin Seminary was rejected by his colleagues around 1920. Instead of promoting Neo-Calvinism successfully, his appearance resulted in a serious blow. Following Neo-Calvinists, especially Bavinck, he further developed Reformed theology by presenting fresh reflections on the Bible and culture to his students. He confronted the Christian Reformed Church with the uneasy but unavoidable question: is our Reformed theology fit for modern times? (Harinck 1996:120.)

Others of the Neo-Calvinist spirit within the Christian Reformed Church at the time were, Dr. Henry Beets, Prof. H.J.G. van Andel, and Rev. Gerrit Hoeksema (Harinck 1996:136). These men were of one mind with Professor Janssen on the need for the 'Americanization' of the 'Dutch' Reformed church in America

(Harinck 1996:119). Americanization was understood to mean the development of a more positive attitude towards culture; more specifically overcoming an inherent 'antithetical cultural attitude' by means of the concept of common grace as developed by Kuyper and Bavinck (Harinck 1996:119). This antithetical cultural attitude to Americanization was seen by the Neo-Calvinist followers of Abraham Kuyper in the Christian Reformed Church as no more than certain hesitancy among members in the churches to adopt American culture and thereby loose their Holland roots. By contrast, Herman Hoeksema believed the use of this common grace concept by the Neo-Calvinists to construct a bridge between Christianity and culture was in fact bridging the gap or 'Antithesis' between the church and the world (Bratt 1984:100). According to Bratt, Hoeksema branded Neo-Calvinism as 'Pseudo-Calvinism, which would really have us mingle with the world ... adopt the principles and methods of the world and deny our own' (quoted by Bratt 1984:102). Elsewhere, Hoeksema called the proponents of Neo-Calvinism 'jongeren;' restless young men who adopted the theory common grace because it 'offered them a philosophy that would support their latitudinarian views in the name of Calvinism' (Hoeksema 1947:16). For their insistent opposition in this matter, Hoeksema, and others of like mind, were labeled 'Separatists' and 'Antitheticals' (Bratt 1984:100). H. J. van Andel of Calvin College ridiculed the 'Antithesis' which Hoeksema preached, saying that it was 'neither biblical nor historical. It is simply a product of erring fantasy. (And) the Antithetical's problem involved their mental habits. They were cold and humorless, sterile in their eighteenth-century logic, oppressive with their party line, and arrogant for assuming that their principles described all reality for all time' (quoted by Bratt 1984:100).

I would suggest that the year 1920 was a watershed. The stage was set for a battle to determine nothing less than the future course of the Christian Reformed Church. I also believe that the main issue at stake in this battle was the doctrine of common grace. In this, Christian Reformed historian James Bratt concurs. Bratt perceives that 'by the end of 1920 the stage was set for its discordant enactment ... the definitive lines for the struggle had emerged as the defensive parties joined across the pietist/Kuyperian divide for the decisive battle' (Bratt 1984:104). Bratt also sees the doctrine of common grace as the main issue in both the Janssen affair and in Hoeksema's deposition two years later. He writes: 'at issue in each case was the doctrine of common grace, which, positively or negatively, defined the various streams of the Dutch Reformed tradition and, as the theory relating "the people of God" to "the world," constituted the prime theological metaphor for the question of acculturation' (Bratt 1984:105). Common grace was not, however, immediately perceived by everyone as the main issue, and this includes Hoeksema himself.

While the Synod of 1920 exonerated Professor Janssen of any charges of heresy, it did maintain 'that Dr. Janssen should endeavor to avoid all that has given or might give occasion to misunderstanding' (Stob 1955:312). Synod also decided 'that Dr. Janssen, in the interpretation of Holy Scripture, sometimes has placed too much emphasis on the human factor and on the natural means, so that on that account the special divine factor did not come to its right in the mind of some students' (Stob 1955:312). After being vindicated by both the Curatorium and Synod, any question concerning Professor Janssen's orthodoxy would seem to have been settled. And, if not for the pen of Herman Hoeksema, this probably would have been the case. This is not to say that Hoeksema was solely responsible for the eventual deposition of Professor Janssen. The four professors, Janssen's colleagues, were already pursuing an independent course of action that would have resulted in Janssen's demise regardless of what Hoeksema did. But Hoeksema, by his decision to delve into the matter publicly in his column, did himself a disservice and, at the same time, seriously bungled a matter that would have eventually resolved itself.

4.3 In the Pages of the Banner

Shortly after the Synod of 1920 adjourned, Hoeksema succeeded in getting copies of the student notes that first cast aspersion on the teachings of Professor Janssen. The fact that he had been appointed to the Curatorium of the seminary in July of 1920 undoubtedly aided him in this acquisition (Hoeksema 1969:132, Woudenberg 2001). His editorial column, 'Our Doctrine,' in *The Banner*, underwent a subtle but definite change after Synod adjourned in June of 1920. He spent the whole summer studying the student notes relating to Professor Janssen's classes and preparing his arguments. During these summer months, even though Hoeksema was still writing under the theme 'The New King and His Kingdom,' he now seemed more intent on discussing the historicity of the Old Testament. Finally, on 23 September, he was ready to discuss his findings. Under a revised heading entitled 'Objective Revelation or Subjective Development,' Hoeksema now wants to make clear the relationship of what has gone before to his more recent investigations into Higher Criticism. 'Before I proceed to discuss the question of higher criticism in regard to the Old Testament,' he writes, 'I wish to point out that this apparent digression on my part is closely related to the main subject of our discussion: the development of the Kingdom as presented in the Word of God' (*The Banner* 1920:584).

After this seemingly innocuous token, Hoeksema launches into his discussion, all but forgetting his main subject: the Kingdom. 'The question of higher criticism in regard to the Old Testament,' he argues from the start, 'concerns first of all our conception of supernatural revelation. And in the second place the problem of the historicity of Scripture' (*The Banner* 1920:584). At the outset Hoeksema assures his readers that his purpose in writing on these things is not personal, but then he turns just as quickly to discussing the blunders of the last Synod. While he does not as yet mention Janssen by name, he does accuse the Synod of 1920 of majoring on minors. He forcefully says to the delegates of that Synod that the question is 'inspiration,' pure and simple. In the course of this stinging rebuke to the Synod of 1920, Hoeksema lays out three presuppositions by which he judges higher criticism:

> 1. The Reformed faith always was and still is, that in the Old Testament we have a record of supernatural revelation. God supernaturally revealed himself in paradise, to the patriarchs, in Israel's laws and sacrifices and ceremonies and to the prophets. A supernatural revelation which finds at once its center and climax in Christ, the Word become flesh. And Scripture is the written record of this revelation. 2. This certainly leaves room for development in revelation. God did not, and because of the human and natural factor could not, reveal

himself and the plan of redemption as fully and clearly to Adam as He did to Isaiah. There is, therefore, development in the fullness and clearness of revelation. And accordingly, there is also development in the fullness and clearness of the conception of God and his covenant in the minds of his people. 3. But this leaves no room for development from a wrong to a correct conception of God. The idea of supernatural revelation rules out all possibility of development from polytheism to monotheism, of belief in many gods to the faith in One God, of belief in an immoral to faith in a moral God. Adam, and Noah, and Abraham no more believed in many gods than did Isaiah. I wish to emphasize that the Reformed conception of supernatural revelation absolutely rules out the possibility of such development. (*The Banner* 1920:584-585.)

It is not until his next installment, in the 30 September 1920 issue of *The Banner*, that Hoeksema finally mentions Janssen by name (*The Banner* 1920:600). And even then it is not really what one would have expected from Hoeksema at this point. In point of fact, he is objective, even conciliatory, no doubt expecting the same from his would-be opponent, Professor Janssen. Beginning with his dissatisfaction regarding the actions of the previous Synod, Hoeksema writes:

It is in this connection that I wish to state my first reason for being concerned and uncertain in regard to the action of the last Synod. And I want to state it objectively. In the first place, in justice to Dr. Janssen, whose teachings were called in question before the Synod last June, it must be stated very strongly, that he is no disciple of the Wellhousen school of criticism. Of this he has been frequently accused in private conversation. And lest I leave the impression that this is also my opinion, I want to express myself very positively to the contrary. Proof abundant I would be able to furnish that the professor is always combating on scientific grounds the Grafian theory of the Old Testament. Time and again in the professor's dictations one meets with a presentation of the critical view of a certain matter in order then to be followed by a refusal of this view by Dr. Janssen. Neither, let it be plainly understood, do I underrate the doctor's scholarship. I rather wish to pay my highest regard to his scientific ability and attainment. I do not believe that in regard to knowledge of Semitic languages there is another man that could take Professor Janssen's place. And I would not rejoice, but rather think it a pity if we would have to lose him from our circles. And yet ... I feel uncertain. To my mind the professor in his teaching yields too much to the critical school, so much that it is difficult to harmonize it with the idea of revelation. And I consider it a pity that Synod did not enter into this matter. (*The Banner* 1920:599-600.)

Some feel that what followed, in succeeding issues of *The Banner*, can be construed as nothing less than a calculated attack by Hoeksema on Janssen. Herman Hanko, professor emeritus at the Protestant Reformed Seminary, is of this opinion (Hanko 1988:23). While it is true that Hoeksema's rhetoric continued to build in successive issues, Janssen's comments were no less caustic. Hoeksema was looking for answers and, for him, he was going about it in a rather objective manner. Janssen, however, was looking to deflect blame and, as successive issues prove, in this he was very successful. Additionally, whether Hoeksema actually had the right to pursue this matter in the pages of *The Banner*, independent of Classis or Synod or their appointed representatives, is yet another matter.

4.4 The Rhetoric Escalates

In the 7 October 1920 issue of *The Banner* Hoeksema inquires into certain of Professor Janssen's 'higher critical' teachings saying that 'all these can, to my mind, scarcely be reconciled to the Reformed conception of objective, supernatural Revelation' (*The Banner* 1920:615). At the same time Hoeksema ponders whether Synod's failure to take any disciplinary action against Professor Janssen at this time implies that 'the above views are henceforth to be considered as officially approved by Synod' (*The Banner* 1920:615). Becoming even bolder, in the next paragraph Hoeksema goes so far as to hint at Synod's complicity in the whole matter by conspiring to hide what was taught at the seminary (*The Banner* 1920:615). He ends this rather stinging editorial by pointing to the utter seriousness of the matter, which, in turn, continues to fuel his concern with the decisions taken by Synod in regard to Professor Janssen the previous June. He writes that, 'The seriousness of the matter seemed to me sufficient justification for my lengthy digression from my subject proper. I feel satisfied that I have written without malice, without personal hostility against anyone. I know no such hostility in my heart. But I feel that the Word of God is at stake and nothing less' (*The Banner* 1920:615).

In the last installment for October of 1920, Hoeksema busies himself with discussing the covenant as it relates to Noah. While briefly mentioning common grace, he says nothing about the ongoing debate with Professor Janssen. The 4 November 1920 issue of *The Banner*, however, is of singular interest because in it for the first time we have a reply from Professor Janssen concerning what Hoeksema had written to date. By way of an introduction to Janssen's reply, Hoeksema wrote:

> We are glad to give space to the reply of Dr. Janssen to our criticism of his views. And we just as sincerely hope that the professor may be able to justify himself before our church, which he serves at our school. To personal insinuations we shall give no reply. We would ask the professor to avoid them in the future. They do no earthly good in his case. I do not regard this a personal controversy between Dr. Janssen and myself, but a serious matter concerning nothing less than the very basis of our faith. Let us simply bar them from discussion. In the second place let no one be deceived by the above attack on our view regarding the doctrine of common grace. Of course, we are glad to discuss that doctrine with the professor. But then we must have more than mere statement. However this may be, it is my deepest conviction that there is no relation between our views on common grace and our criticism of Dr. Janssen's views. However, we are anxious to learn what connection the professor has discovered. (*The Banner* 1920:667.)

Janssen's reply turns out to be essentially that which Hoeksema has already deemed a 'personal insinuation,' and to which he promised no further reply. Janssen begins by claiming that Hoeksema's digression into higher criticism in his column over the preceding three months was nothing less than 'an attack on the chair of Old Testament at our theological seminary,' namely, himself (*The Banner* 1920:667). Janssen then reprimands Hoeksema for his use of student notes, or 'dictations,' as the ground on which to base his investigations. The Old Testament Professor states categorically that he 'has not as yet prepared or issued for his classes "dictations"' (*The Banner* 1920:667). In what Hoeksema will undoubtedly construe as only more personal insinuations, Janssen outlines both his complaint and his intent:

> What there is extant is simply student-materials, notes which they have put together. It is, therefore, in the first place, an injustice to represent the material that is subjected to criticism as "the professor's dictations," or to make the public believe that this material is accurate and has the authority of the "professor" back of it. It is, in the second place, an injustice to rush into print with this kind of material, an injustice to both students and professor. …In the third place the Christian Reformed churches have their curators for the Theological School and Calvin College. If Rev. Hoeksema has some "professor's dictations" that he feels like criticizing, he should lodge his complaint with that body. His present method of procedure ignores the curators and our church polity. He is taking the law into his own hands. And fourthly, it is nothing short of astounding that Rev. Hoeksema, the pastor of Eastern Avenue church, the church of which the professor is a member, should never have spoken one word to me about these "professor's dictations," nor have declared to me his intention to write a series of articles attacking me. However, be the methods of the pastor as deplorable as they may be, be furthermore the attempt he makes in his articles to assure his readers that there is no malice on his part and that he is not actuated by animosity, as vigorous as possible, I don't really see as yet why he should come with such assurances to his readers at all,

> why he should repeat the assurance; I don't understand that psychology. I say, be the methods what they may, the fact remains that the attack of Rev. Hoeksema is there, and I purpose to devote a few articles to it and also after that to some other theological questions which, to my mind, deserve to be looked into, questions which it is timely to discuss for general enlightenment. (*The Banner* 1920:667.)

Despite much of what would be said about him over the next two years, Janssen was both intelligent and refined, and he could write. He was also politically astute, and he was not finished with Hoeksema. Whether through honest disagreement or subterfuge, Janssen was unwilling to reply to Hoeksema's accusations forthrightly, instead, he turns the spotlight on Hoeksema's 'denial' of common grace. In his response, Hoeksema was utterly flabbergasted that anyone could make so much of such a minor point. Referring back to many of Hoeksema's previous articles in *The Banner*, Janssen seemed intent on putting an entirely different spin on what Hoeksema had written regarding common grace. Hoeksema, even at this early date, did not like terming any grace 'common.' Grace was grace, and, while it may be multi-faceted, to him it was still grace nonetheless. Trying to distinguish different kinds of grace from God was, for Hoeksema at least, both futile and silly. Not so for the Professor. Janssen, who, with stinging elegance, culls from Hoeksema's articles, both from actual statements and from silence, what he interprets as a pattern of denial of what he considers one of the Reformed Church's most precious doctrines. Janssen argues:

> We are not Roman Catholics, not Lutherans, nor Anabaptists, not Arminians. Calvin is our spiritual father, to his doctrines we subscribe, doctrines that distinguish him from Luther, from Arminius, from the Anabaptists, etc. Now, one of the main doctrines which distinguish Calvin from the Roman Catholics, the Anabaptists, etc., is the doctrine of common grace. In fact, that doctrine was Calvin's discovery. He found it taught in Holy Scripture. That doctrine, from Calvin on, has been an essential part of the Reformed faith. It was a great discovery, this doctrine of Calvin. In the early history of the Reformed

church, it is true, the doctrine was not much further developed. The early Reformed theologians did little more than repeat what Calvin had said about it in the institutes. But the doctrine is here. All the Reformed dogmaticians of the time agree that it is there. The doctrine is there also at the Synod of Dort. Our confession presupposes it. The Canons of Dort point out that the Arminians interpret common grace wrongly, identifying it with the light of nature and making also a wrong use of it. When much later the reawakening comes of the Reformed churches, the doctrine of common grace is in evidence more than ever before. That it is essential and fundamental stands "al seen paal boven water." It is to this doctrine and its further exposition that the Reformed theologians devote themselves. The names of the two great leaders of present day Reformed thought, Kuyper and Bavinck, need only be mentioned to enable one to see what importance is attached to this doctrine of the Reformed faith. But how about Rev. Hoeksema and common grace? You say, he stands foursquare on the doctrines of the Reformed faith and, therefore, undoubtedly holds to this important Reformed doctrine. Let us see what precisely the views of our critic are and find out where he stands. (*The Banner* 1920:668.)

After scrutinizing four more of Hoeksema's editorials from the previous year, Janssen, with more the acumen of a trial lawyer than an Old Testament professor, presents his closing argument:

> Quotations similar to the above, from Rev. Hoeksema's articles, can be multiplied. They all in a variety of ways give expressions to his standpoint that there is no common grace. We can now sum up. Our discovery brings us face to face with a very discouraging fact. The unexpected has happened. In Rev. Hoeksema we are after all not dealing with a critic that is a sound Calvinist. In denying common grace he has broken with true Calvinism and joined ranks with the Anabaptists. He has been found to deny one of the most important doctrines of our Reformed faith. How this unreformed standpoint of Rev. Hoeksema affects his criticism of the

"professor's dictations" we shall see later. (*The Banner* 1920:668.)

Despite the response put forth by Professor Janssen, Hoeksema felt sure that where there was smoke there was fire; that the notes from the students must contain a fairly accurate representation of what was being taught in Professor Janssen's classes, and thus, he continued to probe into the matter. Janssen, for his part, published nothing, hence, the difficulty in judging objectively exactly what was being taught in the seminary. Additionally, while his case against Hoeksema might seem substantive, Janssen actually proved nothing. Janssen assumed both the validity and importance of common grace without ever proving his point. That is to say, he assumed that which needed to be proven, which, in philosophical circles, is known as begging the question.

4.5 *The Exchange Continues*

Hoeksema's rubric in the 11 November 1920 issue of *The Banner*, in addition to a rather substantive response to Professor Janssen, also contains an interesting insight that would prove significant for the future of both combatants. Continuing his exposition of 'The Covenant with Noah' which he began on 28 October, prior to any mention of Janssen, Hoeksema sets about criticizing Kuyper's view of common grace and its effect on the covenant of grace (*The Banner* 1920:683). In the course of his analysis, Hoeksema refers to Kuyper's view as a 'covenant of so-called common grace' (*The Banner* 1920:666). I believe that even at this early date Hoeksema repudiated the idea common grace espoused by Abraham Kuyper in its entirety. While it is true that a few paragraphs later (*The Banner* 1920:667) he says that he would be happy to discuss Janssen's idea of common grace and its relation to his teachings, I do not think this is sufficient reason to conclude that he subscribes to the concept. In fact, in response to Janssen's use of the 'doctrine of common grace' to defend his teachings, Hoeksema writes:

> It is a rather strange coincidence that we are writing on the covenant established with Noah, concerning which we believe that it is the covenant of grace, at the same

time that one of our seminary professors makes that attempt to raise the doctrine of common grace to one of the main doctrines of the Reformed faith. One cannot but stand aghast at the boldness of the statement that the doctrine of common grace constitutes one of the main doctrines which distinguish Calvin from others! Over against it we make the statement that there is room for debate on the question whether Calvin did teach anything at all that did resemble the so-called doctrine of common grace, a debate in which I would be willing to take the negative side. But the matter becomes mockery when the professor knows to say nothing more in regard to one of the essential doctrines of the Reformed faith than that it is "presupposed" in the confession! In the first place I would deny even this. But in the second place does the professor seriously think that one of the most essential doctrines of the Reformed faith would be merely presupposed in the confession? But we will answer these statements in detail when the professor is through with his reply to us. If he wishes to prove nothing but that his views of Scripture as revealed by the dictations I mentioned are rooted in a certain view of common grace, all the worse for that conception of common grace. In the meantime we will continue our discussion of the covenant with Noah. (*The Banner* 1920:683.)

If Hoeksema had stuck with his contention that Janssen's higher critical views were rooted in his concept of common grace, or rather, that Janssen's higher critical views were a direct result of his doctrine of common grace, he might have won the day, but he never mentions it again. He does, however, respond to Janssen's charge of Anabaptism. Hoeksema states categorically: 'Characteristic of Anabaptism is that it separates nature and grace. Nevertheless, we establish a connection between nature and grace, more intimate than any doctrine of common grace can ever do. We believe that not only the souls of a few elect, but the elect organism of the human race as a whole shall be saved by grace' (*The Banner* 1920:684).

From the outset Janssen realizes that, given the intellectual climate in the Christian Reformed Church at the time, there is no way he can defend his views on the Bible in the public forum, so he simply sidesteps the issue. In addition, Hoeksema, by getting involved at all, is simply the one who provides the forum for Janssen to defend himself. Janssen develops his position by means of public debate and he uses the opportunity to scourge Hoeksema on common grace. Effectually, Janssen makes Hoeksema the 'whipping boy' in place of the professors who were after him. It is doubtful whether Hoeksema could see any of this at the time as, according to all who knew him, he was particularly inept in understanding church politics. This fact becomes painfully obvious in that Hoeksema allows Janssen to keep writing and then urges him back when he later quits, instead of branding all Janssen had written as simply irrelevant and refusing to print it. Additionally, Hoeksema simply could not sit down and just speak with Janssen either. Regardless of what Janssen says or does Hoeksema adamantly refuses to get sidetracked, but he gets tarred as a result. Meanwhile, Janssen is not finished.

Janssen's second 'Reply' to Hoeksema is broken up into installments, the first is in the 18 November 1920 issue of *The Banner* and the second is found in the 25 November issue. While the 18 November issue also contains another installment from Hoeksema on 'The Covenant with Noah,' the 25 November issue contains the Janssen response alone. In his first installment, on 18 November, Janssen begins with a recapitulation of both the arguments and conclusions from his previous 'Reply' on 4 November. 'In this weeks article,' he writes, 'I want particularly to examine Rev. Hoeksema's denial of common grace more in detail. ... [After all,] disturb any part of the Reformed system of thought and you disturb the whole system' (*The Banner* 1920:701). From this suggestive beginning, brimming with expectations, Janssen, for the remainder of the 18 November installment, merely laments Hoeksema's denial of God's favor to the reprobate. The second half of Janssen's 'Reply,' contained in the 25 November issue of *The Banner*, looks more substantive, at least on the surface. Janssen begins boldly, saying that it is now time to take the testimony of the 'Reformed authorities' (*The Banner* 1920:716). He begins with Herman Bavinck, a well-known exponent of a 'form' of common grace (see Bavinck's 'rectoral address at Kampen in December 1894, entitled "De Gemeene Genade"' (Van Leeuwen 1989:35)). Janssen follows Bavinck with 'quotes' from John Calvin, Abraham Kuyper, H. H. Kuyper, and A. G. Honig, all of whom seem to substantiate Janssen's contention that universal blessings are indeed bestowed by God upon the world at large. These things are said to be 'most excellent gifts,' yet no mention is made of specifically what they are. And, while he quotes freely from these illustrious authorities, actual, verifiable, references to specific works is sorely lacking. Additionally, one thing becomes abundantly clear; the doctrine of common grace is hindered by a strong view of reprobation. In fact, Janssen almost wants to redefine Calvin's view of reprobation. On this he writes:

> And there are other features of Calvin's doctrine of reprobation to which attention should be called. There is, in the first place, the fact that he says so little about the working of reprobation. The Institutio is a work characterized by great sobriety, wholly free from scholastic abstruseness; it everywhere treats the doctrine of faith in the closest connection with the practice of religion. But of even greater significance is that with Calvin reprobation does not mean the withholding of all grace. Although man through sin has been rendered blind to all the spiritual realities of the Kingdom of God, so that a special revelation of God's fatherly love in Christ and a "specialis illuminatio" by the Holy Spirit in the hearts of sinners here becomes necessary, nevertheless there exists alongside of these a "Generalis Gratia" which dispenses to all men various gifts. If God had not spared man, his fall would have involved the whole of nature in ruin. As it was, God immediately after the fall interposed, in order by his Common Grace to curb sin and to uphold in being the "universitas rerum." (*The Banner* 1920:716.)

While Janssen pays Calvin great tribute in this portion of his 'Reply,' his understanding of Calvin seems to be tempered more by his understanding of Abraham Kuyper than of Calvin himself, the language clearly bears this out. Abraham Kuyper was a great and well-known exponent of common grace, but I am convinced that Kuyper's views on the matter were decidedly not those of the Genevan Reformer (see Ridderbos 1947; Douma 1966 and Hylkema 1911 for a balanced discussion on the matter). (We will consider in greater detail later the specifics of Kuyper's concept of common grace and Hoeksema's response.) Towards the end of his response, Janssen attempts by way of summary to put Hoeksema's denials of common grace into stark relief, which he then contrasts with Kuyper's teachings on common grace. This is rather telling as to where Janssen got his concepts, but beyond that it proves nothing.

4.6 The Rationalist and the Irrationalist

In the 16 December 1920 issue of *The Banner* we have the third 'Reply' of Professor Janssen to Hoeksema. Hoeksema, so it would seem, is either oblivious to or simply does not care about what is happening in his column. I say this because there was absolutely no response on his part to Janssen's second 'Reply,' either the first or second installment. Hoeksema simply continued, on both 2 December and 9 December, with his discussion of the covenant with Noah, seemingly oblivious to Janssen's remarks.

Janssen's third 'Reply' also appears in two installments; the first of which is in the 16 December 1920 issue of *The Banner* and the second in the 30 December 1920 issue. In the 16 December portion Janssen, in a rather offhanded manner, accuses Hoeksema of being an Anabaptist, again (*The Banner* 1920:764). This time, though, in addition to being an Anabaptist, Hoeksema is now a 'fanatic,' and an 'intolerant' one at that (*The Banner* 1920:764). Janssen then succeeds mightily; he labels Hoeksema in a way that would be remembered even to the present day. Janssen, focusing primarily on Hoeksema's method which he compares favorably with the higher critical method he himself stands accused of, now accuses Hoeksema of being a 'rationalist.' He writes:

> This whole procedure of Rev. Hoeksema shows plainly that reason virtually decides that matter for him. The Reformed doctrine of Common Grace is called before the bar of reason. If it cannot stand the test that reason may impose, well that ends it. What here cannot commend itself to reason cannot retain a place in our faith. And as to Rev. Hoeksema's observation ... I would remark that our Reformed theologians knew better than to

give the doctrine of Common Grace a rationalistic basis.
(*The Banner* 1920:763).

The debate, or rather monologue, especially the sweeping, unsubstantiated accusations that flowed so effortlessly from the pen of the esteemed Professor of Old Testament, became an increasing point of contention among the readership of *The Banner*. Appended to the 30 December offering is a letter from several subscribers to the General Editor, Henry Beets, insisting that the writings of Professor Janssen be, in no uncertain terms, ended. The subscribers go on to say that the 'debate,' with its attendant name-calling on the part of the Professor, is an absolute disgrace (*The Banner* 1920:802). Beets avers to Hoeksema as the editor of that specific rubric, only commenting that it is good that both sided are being heard. Hoeksema, however, remained silent.

Under the heading, 'The New King and His Kingdom,' commencing on 6 January 1921, Hoeksema begins a series of several articles on Melchisedec in which he interacts thoroughly with the views of Abraham Kuyper. In the 13 January 1921 installment, Hoeksema refers to Kuyper's explanation of Melchisedec's priesthood as one of 'so-called common grace' (*The Banner* 1921:22). Janssen's fourth 'Reply,' however, which is contained in the same issue, seems to overshadow anything Hoeksema has to say about Melchisedec. Janssen crafts a huge edifice of results, causes and second causes, all of which supposedly flow from Hoeksema's denial of common grace. Janssen's edifice lacks any sort of evidence or proof, but it is replete with all sorts of assumptions. As it really has to be read to be appreciated, I include a rather interesting portion as illustrative. Janssen begins:

> It has been seen that by denying common grace one is committed to much more. The implications of the denial are many and manifold. They affect every article of the Christian faith. They extend to every locus of Reformed dogmatics. If common grace has to go, much more has to go. This has already in a measure been demonstrated and will be demonstrated still more as we go on. Then too, more specifically, there are other consequences resulting from the denial. Force the doctrine of common grace out of the Christian faith and the

necessary distinction between creation and redemption ("schepping en herschepping"), the work of God the Father and the work of God the Son, cannot be maintained. And if the proper distinction cannot be maintained, the relation of the one to the other becomes the wrong relation. Then, likewise, the correct relation between the covenant of grace and the covenant of works, between Israel and the non-Israelitish nations, between Christianity and paganism, between religion and culture cannot be maintained. Take the doctrine of common grace out of the Reformed system and what is left ceases to be Reformed. The doctrine is essential to the system. It is the case here as with the essential attributes of God. Deprive, in your theology, God of one of his essential attributes and your whole theology becomes impossible. If common grace has to go, it is difficult to see what part of our theology will remain unchanged. (*The Banner* 1921:23.)

But, Janssen says that he would be remiss if he were to stop here. Hence, he proceeds in the same manner to develop a positive side to his argument, which, in his estimation, encompasses all of Reformed Theology in its implications. Contrary to his previous, copious references to Calvin, the theology of Abraham Kuyper again looms large in his presentation. Promising to present the 'barest outline' of the 'Reformed' doctrine of common grace, he writes:

> Very briefly stated the Reformed position is as follows, immediately after the fall, when the "foedus operum," i.e., the covenant of works, had been broken, God intervened with his grace, his common grace and his special grace. By his common grace God curbs sin and upholds in being this world of ours. Had God not interposed with his common grace, man's fall would have involved this world in ruin. That grace, therefore, was in character a "bewarende genade." It preserved and perpetuated the ordinances of creation. The presence in man of the remnants of the divine image, the seed of religion, man's god-consciousness—this is to be ascribed to God's common grace. By virtue of this same grace the institutions of marriage, of the home, of society, of the

state either continue to exist or are permitted to develop. As we follow the history of the descendants of the first human couple the working of common grace becomes very manifest. Through a fratricide, Cain's life is spared. In his favor God gives Cain a sign which shall be instrumental in protecting him against the avenger of blood. This murderer becomes, furthermore, the recipient of numerous other gifts of God's common grace. He is permitted to become the father of a race. His race through God's common grace is privileged among other things to build a city and lay the foundations of civilization. In addition to this it is privileged to originate and develop the 'fine arts.' The race of Seth, on the other hand, is permitted through the working of common grace to preserve the knowledge of the true God. After the flood this common grace receives its fixed form in God's covenant that henceforth remains effective in the life of the world. The descendents of Noah, through God's common grace, develop into powerful nations. These nations at different periods in the history of the world become the founders of great civilizations. Babylonia, Egypt, Asia Minor, Greece, Rome, all are centers which at one time or another witness the rise of great empires. In these empires arts and sciences, philosophy and literature, law and medicine, architecture and sculpture, flourish. God does not leave himself in this pagan world without a witness, "doing good to them, giving them rain and fruitful seasons, filling their hearts with food and gladness." These pagan peoples, too, are, to use Paul's own words, "the offspring of God." In Him they live and move and have their being. God is not far from each and every one of them. He giveth them "life and breath and all things." Among them are found men of genius, of high morality, of proverbial virtue, men with a lofty conception of God. Socrates and Plato in all subsequent periods of history have aroused the admiration of the believer. And what holds true of Greece can be said of pagan peoples elsewhere. All of which, goes to show that there is an abundant working of God's common grace in the pagan world. (*The Banner* 1921:23-24.)

From Janssen's perspective, it is difficult to see what if anything does not depend upon common grace. On 20 January, 1921 Professor Janssen abruptly curtailed any further reply to Rev. Hoeksema (*The Banner* 1921:40).

4.7 Hoeksema's Response

Amazed and bewildered, coupled with a measure of sadness, Hoeksema regrets that Professor Janssen has decided to discontinue his articles. Hoeksema is also sorry that the esteemed Professor has seen fit to take any and all criticism as personal attack (*The Banner* 1921:55). Now, under the heading 'Not Satisfied,' Hoeksema finally responds to some of what Janssen has been saying. Hoeksema tries to explain, and in a rather laborious manner at that, that his contention with the Professor's teaching is not a personal matter. In fact, writes Hoeksema, 'synod did not advise the brethren professors to settle the matter between them, but openly discuss the matter and come to a conclusion. Synod did not consider the matter a personal one, but one of general significance for the whole church' (*The Banner* 1921:55). Quoting from the alleged 'dictations,' Hoeksema shows repeated instances where Professor Janssen by his teaching has undermined the historicity of the Word of God. Referring again to these dictations, Hoeksema concludes: 'And it is these that cause my concern. What conception do our future ministers obtain of the Word of God? I assure you that on the basis of such a conception I could be no preacher of the Word of God. And I fail to see how anyone can be. I write this without personal antagonism, but with grave concern about our future' (*The Banner* 1921:56).

Next, Hoeksema seeks to address Janssen's 'absurd' accusations regarding common grace. Aside from viewing any discussion of common grace as a ruse, Hoeksema still, to a certain degree, gets drawn in. Obviously annoyed and responding to what he considers purely an ad hominem argument, Hoeksema comments at some length:

In regard to the matter of common grace, I wish to state that this is not the matter at issue for the present, and I refuse to be thrown off at a tangent in regard to the main question between us. If the professor had shown the connection between this question and common grace and higher criticism, the matter would have been different. He failed to do so, however. A few things of a formal nature I wish to say, nevertheless. First of all, the professor made very serious charges. He called me unreformed. In regard to one of the main doctrines of our confession. Hinging his statement on a single phrase he even intimated that I was a rationalist. I kindly ask the professor to retract these statements or to follow them up. The matter cannot rest here. The professor made mere accusations. He promised to substantiate them by passages from our Reformed Standards. This he never did. Not for once. I publicly ask the professor for proof that the theory of common grace is a confessionally Reformed doctrine. I here deny that it is. All that the professor has shown is that I differ on this subject with Kuyper and Bavinck. As to Calvin's views, we shall again (sic). But remember, I refuse to be called unreformed only because I differ with these great men. Not they, but our standards are the criterion in this case. And that the professor must know as well as any man that a person can hold to my view of common grace and be thoroughly Reformed. In the second place, I would welcome a serious and friendly discussion on this subject at any time. I think it is very unfortunate that Prof. Janssen broached this subject as he did. It was plainly evident that the whole discussion on common grace was marred by the single purpose the professor had in view: to destroy the critic in order that he might destroy the criticism with regard to his teachings. That is deplorable. It accounts for the fact that the whole discussion, even from a purely scholarly point of view was a lamentable failure. (*The Banner* 1921:56.)

4.8 Abraham and the Covenant of Grace

Almost a month passes without any serious discussion of common grace in the pages of *The Banner*, meanwhile; Hoeksema busies himself with his investigation of various Old Testament personages. After a rather long look at Melchisedec, Hoeksema begins a significant series of articles on 'Abraham, the Friend of God' in his column for 10 February 1921. The significance of these articles lies in their treatment of the covenant. The first of these, for 10 February, outlines the pertinent history regarding Abraham, his calling by God and his place in covenant history. The only attention common grace receives in this entire discussion is in a passing reference. 'Thus the representation of this part of sacred history is often given,' contends Hoeksema, that 'before the appearance of Abraham on the stage of history all that is narrated has reference to common grace. Special grace commences with Abraham. This conception is, of course, entirely beside the representation of Scripture. The line of God's covenant of grace commences immediately after the fall' (*The Banner* 1921:79).

Hoeksema's exposition of Abraham and the covenant of grace extends well into the summer of 1921, giving full vent to his contention that the heart of the covenant is friendship between God and man, and not simply a contract governed by mutual obligation. This growing certainty that friendship is the defining characteristic of the covenant is aptly illustrated in a paragraph from the 5 May 1921 column. In it Hoeksema writes:

> First of all it appears that God is Abraham's friend. He will bless Abraham and take his side over against the enemy in the world in which he lives. This is always first in God's eternal covenant of grace. Surely, as also our baptism form has it, in all covenants there are contained two parts. In the covenant of grace the parties are Almighty God and his elect people in Christ. But never should we forget that in this covenant God is always first. His people become a possible party in the covenant only through the powerful operation of his grace in their hearts. God chose his people. God redeemed his people. God delivers his people through his grace. God calls and

prepares his people to be received in his covenant and to be his party in the world. The action always proceeds from God. Thus it is with Abraham. It is God who calls and prepares Abram in order that he may be his covenant friend. God is first of all Abraham's friend, and by making him the object of his grace also prepares Abraham to assume his own part in the covenant of God. (*The Banner* 1921:276.)

In later years Hoeksema would dispense with the language of 'parties' in the covenant stating categorically that 'the relation between God and man can never really be that of an agreement between contracting parties, with mutual stipulations, conditions, and promises' (Hoeksema 1981:4). But even at this early date (1921) I think it is important to understand that, for Hoeksema, the covenant was both established and maintained by God alone; man was merely a recipient of God's goodness. In his understanding of these things Hoeksema betrays a debt to Herman Bavinck, probably going back to his days in seminary.

4.9 The Letter from A. Dykstra

During the course of his discussion of Abraham and the covenant and about a month after the last 'Reply' from Professor Janssen, Hoeksema receives a letter from an A. Dykstra, forwarded to him by *The Banner's* editor-in-chief, Henry Beets. The letter, printed on 17 February 1921, protests strongly the disservice Hoeksema is doing to the church by his repeated denial of common grace. Dykstra believes that 'God's common grace was revealed right at the gates of the lost paradise' (*The Banner* 1921:101), and that it, not redemption, runs as a 'golden thread' throughout the whole of sacred history. Dykstra's position betrays an obvious Kuyperian provenance in his belief that God has a purpose with the development of civilization and culture quite apart from redemption, a purpose which only common grace can assure. Dykstra is particularly adamant that the doctrine of common grace 'is clearly taught in Scripture and is being upheld by the very best and most learned of our Reformed theologians' (*The Banner*

1921:101), and Reverend Hoeksema should be censured for teaching otherwise.

Hoeksema's response to Dykstra gives evidence a genuine pastoral concern for a fellow brother, as well as a willingness to help a brother develop and clarify his own views regardless of how much they may ultimately differ from one another. Hoeksema begins by informing Dykstra that not all opinions concerning common grace are the same. In fact, writes Hoeksema,

> Kuyper differs from Bavinck, and that rather essentially. Kuyper holds that there are two kinds of grace, the one from Christ as mediator of redemption ("special grace"); another from the Mediator of creation or the eternal Word. In this case Common Grace is not based on atonement. But Bavinck holds that there is but one grace essentially that flows from Christ Jesus. And among us there are various conceptions about this matter. Some of our men that hold to Common Grace refute Kuyper's conception of it. Some, moreover, hold that Common Grace is something that concerns only the world outside of Christ; others maintain that it is a grace believers and unbelievers have in common. You see, we do not define the issue by saying that we are talking about Common Grace. (*The Banner* 1921:102.)

Hoeksema also informs Dykstra that his articles 'attacking' common grace were published a year and a half ago, and that when my 'recent critic on this point (Professor Janssen) informed me that he intended to attack my view on Common Grace, he was not even aware of the fact that I had written on the subject in *The Banner*, and I kindly selected *The Banner* numbers for him' (*The Banner* 1921:101). Hence, the current controversy raging in the pages of *The Banner* is not about common grace, in spite of what the Professor may say, it concerns certain teachings propagated at our school by the Professor (*The Banner* 1921:101). Helping Dykstra to gain clarity regarding his own views of common grace in order to make a better case, in addition to giving his most vociferous critic, Professor Janssen, the very articles in which he previously denied common grace demonstrate that, for Hoeksema, common grace was not a doctrine but an opinion open to vigorous debate, something which he relished. In fact, he openly states as much. To Dykstra, he writes:

> I want to reassure you that I would greatly enjoy a friendly controversy on this subject. I believe in healthy controversy. I believe in controversy in public. Not for the purpose of biting and envying one another, but for the sake of developing the truth and to come to a clear understanding of one another. In the Netherlands they are not half so afraid of debates and controversies as we are here. They discuss most anything in the papers. They believe in rubbing elbows. And if you had our Netherlands publications, or some of them, you will know that the controversies in the old country and our Church here in America run somewhat along parallel lines. I welcome your criticism most heartily. And I do wish our people would understand that it is wholly possible to exchange thoughts on certain subjects without running into personalities and bitterness. Hence, once more, I welcome your communication. (*The Banner* 1921:102.)

Hoeksema's frustration remained, as no one wanted to enter the debate.

4.10 Janssen Reenters the Fray

Beginning with the 17 February 1921 issue of *The Banner*, Professor Janssen abruptly takes up his pen again—Janssen's self-imposed silence did not last very long. The editorials that followed, which Hoeksema continued to publish, were little more that a rehash of what had previously been said. Janssen continued to draw all sorts of radical, even bizarre, conclusions from Hoeksema's denial of common grace. Trying to remain gracious, Hoeksema wrote:

> We are glad to hear that Prof. Janssen took up his pen again. When we read the article, however, we were sorry, and that for his sake and for the good of his cause. The professor has nothing new. Still the same method is pursued: to place his critic in a bad light in order to

weaken his criticism. Professor, I deem it below the dignity of a theological professor to come with unproved, unfounded accusations as the above. And I deem it below my own dignity to answer them at length. (*The Banner* 1921:103.)

A week later, after another editorial from the Professor's pen filled with absurd conclusions, vitriol and personal abuse—he calls Hoeksema a liar (*The Banner* 1921:117)—Hoeksema seems as if he is beginning to loose his temper. Still, with more composure than his opponent, Hoeksema responds:

> I really do not care to answer all sorts of personal insinuations. But sometimes it is necessary. I am not dodging anything. I am only refusing to assume responsibility for views that are not my own at all. You distill them out of my writings and try to present them as mine. They are not. And this is the only answer I will ever give to these supposedly erroneously views that are not mine at all. I refuse to be sidetracked. Now, please, professor, write about the subject rather than about me. I did not attack you personally. It is your notes I am attacking. You have not come to the point yet, although you wrote several articles. If I presented your teachings in a wrong light, you shall have a public apology in The Banner. But if I presented them fairly, I maintain that there is no room for them at our school. My person is in no way involved. I am neither excited nor bitter. But I am very serious about this matter. (*The Banner* 1921:119.)

In a sense, this type of reasoning was Hoeksema's fatal mistake. This is why he was effectually blind-sided by Janssen. From the start Hoeksema wanted to discuss Janssen's notes and the higher critical leanings that they betrayed. Janssen, however, was not about to sit still and be questioned about his teachings, rather, his approach was to go on the offensive. While from every angle Janssen was a master politician, Hoeksema, as I have endeavored to show, could not fathom church politics. His attitude was simple: let's discuss it openly. Granted that, for Hoeksema, discussion really meant a knock down, drag out fight, just like when he was a child on the streets of Groningen, except now in print. Add to this Hoeksema's renowned debating prowess and it is understandable that the last thing Janssen wanted was to confront Hoeksema over the issues; hence he decided to take a different tack. So, while Hoeksema is essentially dumbfounded and continues to reply only that 'the professor has not come to the point yet' (*The Banner* 1921:150), Janssen's editorials are being widely read and taken seriously.

Beginning on 24 March 1921, Hoeksema appears to be through waiting, but his first offering actually allows Janssen to determine the terms of the debate. Entitled 'Common Grace,' the 24 March editorial merely laments Janssen's changing the ground of the debate from his own views to common grace. Hoeksema, in what amounts to a rather feeble effort, summarizes his own views on common grace and concludes that: 'In the meantime, let us not forget what I wrote on the notes of Dr. Janssen still stands. That part of our controversy remains separate' (*The Banner* 1921:182).

For the next month Janssen's editorials continued, interspersed with Hoeksema's very technical analysis of Janssen's notes. It is not hard to imagine which editorials were more widely read in the pews. Hoeksema's analysis of Janssen's teaching is highly technical and is written in highly technical language, while Janssen's editorials are designed to have popular appeal. As Hoeksema deals at length with scientific method, Janssen successfully portrays him as an arch heretic. In the final analysis, both men managed to annihilate each other. While Hoeksema managed to bring to light the aberrant instruction that was occurring at the denominational seminary, Janssen, by means of innuendo, wild assertion, and outright falsehood, dealt Hoeksema fatal blow. Hoeksema, however, by his unwillingness to answer Janssen, regardless of the absurdity of the accusation, also did himself a great disservice. He effectually allowed himself to be caricatured. Finally, in April 1921, for the good of the church at large, 'The Publication Committee has decided to discontinue the debate of Prof. Ralph Janssen and Rev. Herman Hoeksema after April 21' (*The Banner* 1921:214).

4.11 The Controversy Widens

In addition to the ongoing debate being conducted in *The Banner*, other denominational periodicals began to follow suit (Hanko 1988:24). The four colleagues of Professor Janssen, who originally sought inquiry by the Curatorium into his teaching, co-authored another pamphlet, again outlining their objections to Janssen's teachings and how these teachings were contrary to both the confessions of the church and the Word of God (Hanko 1988:25). With attention from ever widening circles within the Christian Reformed Church being focused on Janssen, it is no wonder, as Harry Boer laments, that 'the fears of the four professors swept through the church' (Boer 1972:19). Boer goes on to say that 'when the (Curatorium) met again in 1921 there were before it requests from no less than eight (out of thirteen) classes that the views of Janssen be investigated. No one made any charges. There were only "questions" and "unrest" in the church' (Boer 1972:19). Meeting in June 1921, the Curatorium took the following decision: 'Although the Curatorium has never received any definite charges against Dr. R. Janssen, nevertheless, because of the present prevailing unrest the Board decides to make a most thorough investigation of the teaching of Dr. R. Janssen and consider its findings at its next meeting' (Boer 1972:19). Curatorium also decided that, while the investigation was ongoing, all discussion on the matter in church papers or periodicals would effectively cease (Hanko 1988:26, Stob 1955:323). Pending the completion of the investigation, Professor Janssen would be required to take a year's leave with salary (Stob 1955:322). At this point, according to Stob, 'Dr. Janssen protested that this would amount to "accommodation to the unjustifiable propaganda that had been waged against me," and also declared his conviction that "in my teaching I have been advocating the cause of truth," and that in consenting to a leave of absence he would become disloyal to that cause' (Stob 1955:323).

The June 1921 meeting of the Curatorium also saw the appointment of an investigating committee to look into the views of Professor Janssen. Herman Hoeksema was appointed to this committee. One of the first acts of the investigating committee was to secure much needed information. To accomplish this objective, the committee first made a 'formal and public request for both "student notes" and "individual notes." (Hanko 1988:27, Stob 1955:325). Next, the committee formally requested Professor Janssen to submit the notes from which he conducted his lectures. 'Dr. Janssen did not answer the first letter of the committee,' writes George Stob, 'and to the second replied: "Permit me to say that I do not care to be responsible in any way for what may involve the violation of our Reformed Church polity"' (Stob 1955:325). For the duration of the investigation, Stob reports, 'Janssen refused to cooperate in the process of investigation, and withheld himself from the opportunity to witness to the truth to which he was committed' (Stob 1955:326). Janssen remained adamant, throughout 1921 and into 1922, in his judgment that the proceedings against him were contrary to proper Reformed Church order. Prior to the opening of the Synod of 1922, which met in June of that year in Orange City, Iowa, Janssen was requested to explain his opinions to an advisory committee. R. B. Kuiper, Janssen's brother-in-law, relates what was asked of him:

> Dr. Janssen was requested to appear before the advisory committee to correct and complete students' notes of his lectures, before Synod had determined whether the Janssen case came before Synod in the proper way. Synod never asked Dr. Janssen in so many words to explain his views regarding certain specific articles of our confessional standards. He was requested to correct and explain certain students' notes, which of course contain much material on which the confessions say nothing. Dr. Janssen did not refuse under any and all circumstances to give an account of his teaching. He promised to answer all possible objection.... He even asserted that he was anxious for an opportunity to speak. So, while he did refuse to defend himself under the given circumstances, he did not refuse a defense as such. Dr. Janssen's second communication, in which he restated his objections to a trial under the circumstances, was received by Synod as a communication and never considered. (Kuiper 1922:35-36.)

While the war of words, both pro and con, continued, Janssen published a pamphlet in his own defense in February 1922. In it, while addressing himself to the issues in a rather cursory manner, he expends himself in charging his colleagues, the four professors, and that portion of the investigating committee antagonistic to him with being Anabaptists because of their denial of common grace (Stob 1955:327).

The investigating committee produced both majority and minority reports. The majority report, in which Hoeksema had more than a little influence, was adopted by Synod. Janssen, however, was given the opportunity to defend himself on the floor of the Synod of 1922. Edward Heerema, R. B. Kuiper's son-in-law, writes of this crucial moment:

> R. B. Kuiper strongly advised his brother-in-law to speak in his own defense. "If you don't do so," R. B. told him, "you may as well take the next train out of here." Janssen persisted in his refusal to speak. He maintained that there were those at synod who were prosecutors as well as judges, people who had made up their minds about him, people who had spoken or written publicly about him. He said he would be glad to discuss all the points in dispute, but only if his objections to the stacked makeup of synod and the violations of good order were acknowledged. Dr. Janssen was deposed. (Heerema 1986:67-68.)

Three months after Janssen's deposition, R. B. Kuiper wrote in *Religion and Culture* that the whole affair was nothing more than a sham and reeked of politics (Kuiper 1922). David Holwerda writes regarding the proceedings in which Janssen refused so adamantly to take part:

> Even the opponents of Dr. Janssen admitted that the requirements of the Church Order had been violated by the procedures leading to the decisions of 1922, but they defended such violations by asserting that in Reformed theology the Church Order is not a law but a set of prescriptions to be followed in ordinary circumstances. Moreover, the highest law is the welfare of the church, and when the church is threatened, "extraordinary

circumstances demand extraordinary measures." (Holwerda 1989:13.)

Hoeksema would find later, much to his dismay, that this same 'end justifies the means' attitude would prevail in his own struggles with the Christian Reformed Church. He went after Janssen, and Janssen's supporters would do the same to him (see Bolt 2000a). Within two years it would be Hoeksema complaining of procedural abnormalities, and finding those complaints falling on deaf ears just as Janssen's did in 1922.

It is impossible in retrospect to judge whether Janssen was guilty of what he was charged. He wrote almost nothing. What he did write were pamphlets critiquing and condemning the proceedings against him from a procedural perspective (Holwerda 1989:13). The student notes on which his teaching was judged are no longer extant, and any access to their content is now limited to quotations found in the report of the investigating committee (Holwerda 1989:13). Notwithstanding, it seems that, apart from family members such as R. B. Kuiper, all are agreed that Janssen's teaching was to a greater or lesser degree tainted with higher criticism (see Holwerda 1989, Bolt 2000a). But were Janssen's purported higher critical views really the issue in the 'Janssen Case?' Of course he was deposed for his higher critical leanings, still, I do not see this as the main issue for everyone concerned. George Harinck concluded that Janssen was deposed for his Neo-Calvinist perspective, which manifested itself most particularly in his desire to see the Reformed faith made relevant to the modern world (Harinck 1996:120). Janssen himself consistently appealed to both Kuyper and Bavinck (see especially Janssen 1922), and their teachings on common grace, as a precedent for his instruction. According to Holwerda:

> The doctrine of common grace provided Janssen's main line of defense. He rejected out of hand the suggestion that his theology was an exercise based on an unbelieving empiricism; the real fault, he insisted, lay with his opponents' failure to appreciate the rightful place of the sciences God had given us through his common grace. Did not common grace justify an appreciation of the sciences? ...Did not common grace justify the search for

parallels, continuities, and relationships between the history and religion of Israel and the surrounding peoples? ...And did not common grace constitute the broad basis of special grace? Janssen held fast to the belief that common grace warranted an emphasis upon the human agents used by God who brought with them much from their background and environment. (Holwerda 1989:27.)

At what point Hoeksema finally realized that common grace was the main issue in the Janssen case is really open to debate. In *The Banner* editorial for 4 November 1920 Hoeksema did make known both his own disagreement with Kuyper's doctrine of common grace and Janssen's appeal to it in his defense (*The Banner* 1920:666-667). By the later half of 1922, though, the connection was definitely made in Hoeksema's mind (see Danhof and Hoeksema 1922). Hanko writes of this period:

He [Hoeksema with Danhof-PB] admitted that common grace was always the issue. And, while insisting that the issue could be decided on other grounds, he nevertheless prophesied that if common grace was not repudiated, Janssen's views would rise in the church and prevail. It was his considered opinion that if the Christian Reformed Church did not repudiate common grace as taught by Kuyper, and if the church took the position that common grace was basically Reformed and in agreement with the Confessions, Janssen would emerge after all as victorious. (Hanko 1988:189.)

In addition to his editorials in *The Banner*, one of the two other times Janssen accused his detractors of denying the doctrine of common grace was in a pamphlet written in 1922 entitled, *De Crisis in de Christelijke Gereformeerde Kerk in Amerika*. He accused the members of the Curatorium, especially Hoeksema (Janssen 1922:17), of the 'false doctrine of the Anabaptists, (specifically), in their denial of Common Grace' (Janssen 1922:53). 'And why should one object to a view of special revelation rooted in general revelation, or of special grace based upon common grace, or of miracles based upon created nature,' comments David Holwerda on Janssen's accusation, 'unless one has failed to catch the essential unity and compatibility of nature and grace, which is the hallmark of the doctrine of common grace but lacking in the Anabaptist tradition' (Holwerda 1989:27)?

Janssen's legacy to the Christian Reformed Church was that anyone who denied the 'Reformed' doctrine of common grace, was, quite simply un-Reformed, and, as such, would be more properly identified as an Anabaptist: a heretic who was guilty of despising the creation and seeking to flee from it. Reminiscing about the Janssen case, Hoeksema believed that it had been a fundamental mistake for him to have cooperated with the four professors in their opposition to Janssen (Hoeksema 1947:24). In the two years following Janssen's deposition Hoeksema saw an alignment, or compromise, begin to form between the neo-Calvinist supporters of Professor Janssen and the four professors. This confederation would now turn against Hoeksema precisely because of his repudiation of the 'Reformed' doctrine of common grace (Hoeksema 1947:23). In fact, it is very probable that Hoeksema's prolonged exchange with Professor Janssen in the pages of *The Banner* was instrumental in bringing about this confederation. Hoeksema himself was persuaded that:

> The fact that the four professors and others of the opponents of Doctor Janssen could unite with the pro-Janssen faction in their action against the three ministers (Hoeksema, Danhof, and Ophoff) that were deposed in 1924-1925, plainly reveals that, apart from superficial differences, there was a fundamental agreement in principle. There was in the Janssen controversy an underlying principle which, had it not been violently and intentionally forced to the background, would have paralyzed every effort of the four professors to combat Doctor Janssen's views and would have aligned them from the beginning with the pro-Janssen faction against the Reverends H. Danhof and H. Hoeksema. This underlying principle is the theory of common grace! (Hoeksema 1947:23.)

In retrospect, Hoeksema changed his mind about the importance of common grace and its relation to the Janssen case. In the beginning, around 1920, he believed that the issues revolved around the Professor's use of higher critical methods and that common grace was merely 'smoke screen' used deliberately by Janssen in order to obscure the real issues. After witnessing the materialization of an alignment between the former opponents of Professor Janssen and his ardent supporters over against the deniers of common grace, Hoeksema finally understood that the real issue was always common grace. It seems that when Hoeksema allowed himself to get drawn into the dispute with Janssen, he did not realize what he was getting himself into. Granted, Hoeksema started the dispute in the pages of *The Banner*. He should have left it alone. Janssen, because of his views, was doomed anyway. Hoeksema does not seem to have understood this at the time and by the time he did, it was too late.

Janssen's charge of Anabaptism, with its concomitant accusation that denying common grace was un-Reformed, did not fall on deaf ears. I firmly believe that the Christian Reformed Church could not integrate into her ranks one such as Hoeksema who dared deny the Kuyperian basis of Christianity and culture that the neo-Calvinists in her midst were so insistent upon. This ultimately proved to be the case.

4.12 Conclusion

The events of 1924, in which Hoeksema's ouster from the Christian Reformed Church is central, were founded firmly upon the events leading up to and including the Synod of 1922. While Professor Ralph Janssen's expulsion in 1922 from his teaching post at Calvin Seminary was not based primarily on the investigations of Herman Hoeksema, Hoeksema did succeed in bringing this sordid affair before the eyes of the church at large. Additionally, while Hoeksema may not have initiated the furor over Janssen, he surely took advantage of it. Janssen tried to cloud the issue with repeated references to common grace. He tried to weave a huge tapestry of causes and results that would inexorably follow from any denial of this common grace. And while much of what Janssen wrote may have been extreme, nevertheless, he had a substantial following. Common grace, because of Janssen, would eventually become the cause célèbre in the Christian Reformed Church.

I have tried to demonstrate that because of the events surrounding the 'Janssen Affair' Hoeksema himself would eventually be deposed from the ministry of the Christian Reformed Church by Janssen's supporters and fellow Neo-Calvinists. Hoeksema went after Janssen in the pages of *The Banner* in such a way that it instilled a profound fear in many of his contemporaries. His debating prowess, his mental acuity, his logical rigor, and his constant need to be right were sufficient reason that none wanted to face him in open debate over the issues. At the same time, a sizeable contingent in the Christian Reformed Church began to realize that if they did not rid themselves of Hoeksema, he would eventually get rid of them.

Chapter 5

1924 and Beyond

In a decision marked particularly by the speed in which it was taken, the Christian Reformed Church adopted a three-point statement on common grace at the synod of 1924 giving it full confessional status. Herman Hoeksema, along with George Ophoff and Henry Danhof, staunchly resisted these doctrinal amendments and refused to abide by them. For their efforts, all three men were deposed from the office of minister of the Gospel in a manner that, according to Hoeksema at least, was completely illegal and smacked of hierarchy.

As the events of 1924 faded into the background, Hoeksema and his followers gradually organized themselves into a coherent denominational structure called the Protestant Reformed Churches, replete with a rather distinct theological emphasis. Not everything, however, that followed on the heels of 1924 would be either easy or placid. The years of The Depression were especially hard on this small and struggling denomination, and growth was negligible. But, it was during these years, among other things, that Hoeksema would finally answer the charge of 'rationalism' employed so successfully by Professor Janssen a decade earlier.

It was also during the decade of the 1930s that Hoeksema would meet a kindred spirit, so to speak, in the person of the Klaas Schilder; a vigorous theologian and churchman in his own right. Hoeksema's health, however, would preclude any true meeting of the minds.

5.1 The Synod of 1922 and its aftermath

In the wake the Synod of 1922, in which Professor Ralph Janssen was deposed, the editor of *The Banner*, Henry Beets, announced rather matter-of-factly that 'Rev. H. J. Kuiper was elected to edit the department Our Doctrine in the stead of Rev. Hoeksema' (*The Banner* 1922:406). Although this turn of events has aroused suspicions of a possible conspiracy, my own included, I can find no reason to assume that Hoeksema's departure from *The Banner* in 1922 was anything other than a routine changing of the guard. On this matter, biographer Gertrude Hoeksema is strangely silent (Hoeksema 1969:135). It is true that many hard feelings were directed towards Hoeksema for his role in Professor Janssen's deposition, John Bolt of Calvin Seminary calls this rather bitter climate, 'concerted ecclesiastical opposition' (Bolt 2000a:32). Still, the *Acts of Synod* for 1922 give no indication of an organized ecclesiastical front in the matter of his being removed from the staff of *The Banner*. It is also true that Classis Hudson voiced reservations regarding the instruction given in Hoeksema's column, but Synod, at that time, was not of a mind to deal at any length with Classis Hudson's concerns (*Acta der Synode* 1922:45). In the several pages following Classis Hudson's questions, nominees are submitted to head-up every departmental rubric covered in both *The Banner* and *De Wachter*, Hoeksema's name was simply not among them (*Acta der Synode* 1922:47 also p. 48). One name does appear, however, that gives one pause, Reverend G. Hoeksema. This pastor, no relation to Herman Hoeksema, would later involve himself in writing a protest against Herman Hoeksema, to be delivered by others, under their names, to the Consistory of Eastern Avenue Reformed Church. In fact, it was Rev. G. Hoeksema's protest which effectively began the spiral of events of 1924. Still, I can find no evidence that any of this had anything to do with Herman Hoeksema being removed from the staff of *The Banner*. Knowing Hoeksema, if he had been subject to any disciplinary measures from the Synod and subsequently removed as the editor of 'Our Doctrine,' he most certainly would not have kept silent on the matter. From the time Synod concluded in June 1922, during which he was voted off *The Banner* staff, until his last installment as editor of 'Our Doctrine' on 31 August 1922, Hoeksema's columns dealt exclusively with the letters to the seven churches of Asia Minor as detailed in the opening chapters of the Book of Revelation.

In a recent article revisiting the events of 1924 and those leading up to it, John Bolt poses the question: If Hoeksema had savored his victory in the Janssen case and 'not insistently pushed for a wholesale repudiation of common grace...would the events of 1924 and the subsequent history of the CRC have turned out differently' (Bolt 2000a:14)? This query by Bolt presupposes that Hoeksema continued to agitate against common grace after Janssen's deposition in June 1922. This was simply not something that Hoeksema did. It is true that eventually he got drawn into a pamphlet war over common grace, but this was not at Hoeksema's instigation. If he had chosen to militate against common grace after Janssen's disposition, what would have been his outlet? The only forum Hoeksema had at his disposal for disseminating his views was his rubric in *The Banner*. And since he was voted off the staff of *The Banner* at the same Synod that deposed Janssen, his only forum quickly disappeared. In fact, from the time he was voted off the staff of *The Banner* in June 1922 until his last column in August of that year, he mentioned common grace only once and this in connection with the historic Anabaptist movement of the sixteenth-century. Hence, with the possible exception of sermons which would have had a strictly limited influence, there is no evidence to support the contention that Hoeksema, in an unprovoked manner, continued to militate against common grace in the months following the conclusion of the Janssen affair.

While Herman Hoeksema did not seek to provoke a confrontation over the issue of common grace, this confrontation, however, eventually found him. Picking up where Professor Janssen left off, Reverend Jan Karel van Baalen, a Christian Reformed minister in Munster, Indiana (Bolt 2000a:15), was determined not to let the matter rest. Hoeksema followed the chronology of the events in his own inimitable way:

> The friends of Doctor Janssen, realizing that their idol had been irrevocably cast down, and his foes, acting from a subconscious motive of fundamental agreement with the underlying principle of the instruction they had opposed, now combined their attacks upon the two ministers (Hoeksema and Danhof-PB) that had performed the lion's share of the work in the Janssen controversy and borne the brunt of the battle. The Reverend Jan Karel Van Baalen published a pamphlet entitled: *Loochening Der Gemeene Gratie, Gereformeerd of Doopersch?* (Denial of

Common Grace, Reformed or Anabaptistic?), to which the two ministers replied with another pamphlet bearing the title: *Niet Doopersch Maar Gereformeerd* (Not Anabaptistic but Reformed). Professor Berkhof wrote an article in *The Witness* under the deceiving heading: "Genade Voor De Onbekeerden" (Grace for the Unconverted). The two ministers personally approached the professor with the direct question, whether he had thus written in ignorance or intentionally. And the professor promised to make amends, the attempt to do which made matters worse. Van Baalen followed up his first attack by the publication of *Nieuwigheid en Dwaling* (Innovation and Error), to which as well as to other attacks the accused pastors replied in the brochure: *Langs Zuivere Banen* (Along Straight Paths), which was very soon followed by still another pamphlet entitled *Om Recht en Waarheid* (For the Sake of Justice and Truth). They also published their chief work of that period: *Van Zonde en Genade* (Of Sin and Grace). And in the meantime formal protests had been filed against the two pastors and legal action had been started. The battle that had apparently been won at the synod of 1922, for the salvation of the Christian Reformed Churches, was fundamentally and hopelessly to be lost for those churches at the Synod of Kalamazoo. (Hoeksema 1947:25-26.)

The Holland Sentinel (November 22, 1923) called this new turn in the discussion of common grace the 'Battle of the Books.' Acknowledging that the present battle grew out of the Janssen Case, the editorial concluded that 'the attack and counter attack are for the most part in regard to the doctrine of common grace, which doctrine is said to be rejected completely by the authors of *Sin and Grace*, and which is affirmed by the other parties in the controversy' (Hoeksema 1992:19). Those who represented the opposition or 'other parties,' as the *Sentinel* referred to them, were, almost to a man, adherents of what was commonly known in Christian Reformed circles as Neo-Calvinism (see Harinck 1996, especially pages 124 and 136, for a partial listing).

James Bratt, in his history of the Christian Reformed Church as a distinct subculture, outlines what he believes were Hoeksema's major doctrinal errors. He insists that Hoeksema denied that there is any grace of God for humanity other than the elect. In close association with this major thesis, Hoeksema also denied that, what many consider to be the good gifts of God, namely, good health, sunshine and peace, are in any way grace to the unbeliever. Moreover, these 'good gifts' only contributed to the unbeliever's ultimate damnation. Additionally, Hoeksema, following from the first premise, denied that unbelieving humanity in general produces any neutral good such as might be seen in the political or social spheres of life (civic righteousness). In fact, writes Bratt, according to Hoeksema, all of humanity's best attempts merely cloak 'evil as good' (Bratt 1984:111). What Bratt is proposing is that anyone who emphasized particular grace, as did Herman Hoeksema, to the total exclusion of common grace, could not help but exclude the 'world' from every facet of the life of the 'elect' (Bratt 1984:112).

My own feeling is that Hoeksema contemporary and rival, Reverend J. K. van Baalen, put Hoeksema's distinctives in bolder relief when he described Hoeksema's theology as '"single-track" theology where the Bible laid out a "double-track" theology' (Bratt 1984:112). Actually, Van Baalen's criticism of Hoeksema was two-pronged in and of itself. He accused Hoeksema of holding a single tracked theology and of being a rationalist, all in his 1922 pamphlet *De Loochening der Gemeene Gratie: Gereformeerd of Doopersch* (The Denial of Common Grace: Reformed or Anabaptist). I mention the charge of rationalism at this point simply because it became a staple in almost all subsequent criticism of Hoeksema's position, and that Van Baalen simply mimicked Janssen in his use of it (see Chapter 6).

In building his case for a two tracked theology and by implication repudiating Hoeksema's single tracked theological position, Van Baalen, following Abraham Kuyper's lead, appealed to God's covenant with Noah (Van Baalen 1922:12-23). Echoing Kuyper, Van Baalen argued that God's covenant with Noah was a covenant of common grace with humanity and not a covenant of particular grace in Christ (Van Baalen 1922:12-13). Hoeksema recast Van Baalen's thesis in the course of responding to the question: To what does Kuyper point as the basis for his operation of common grace?

To the covenant God established with Noah after the flood. This covenant, according to Kuyper, is not to be regarded as the covenant of grace in Christ, but as a covenant of universal friendship with the entire and fallen human race as such. Its blessings are temporal, are only for this present life and are intended for the entire human race. In and through this covenant the natural and totally depraved man becomes God's friend and ally over against the devil and fights on God's side for the maintenance and development of a positively good world-life. (Hoeksema 1947:313.)

Responding from a distinctly Protestant Reformed perspective, Herman Hanko writes that 'by a "two-track" theology van Baalen meant that theology runs on two parallel tracks which never meet. ...theology consists of two lines of truth which cannot be harmonized. Common grace is one of these lines; other doctrines in the Reformed faith which seem to contradict common grace are the other line' (Hanko 2000:200). I think what Hanko writes is true as far as it goes, but he fails to take into account the whole of the Neo-Calvinist program.

James Bratt writes that Kuyper's Neo-Calvinism can be explained 'as a logical whole, using the theological or philosophical categories of common grace and antithesis, sphere sovereignty and the Lordship of Christ, presuppositional epistemology and the Christian cultural mandate' (Bratt 1996:99). David Holwerda, in the course of analyzing Ralph Janssen's Neo-Calvinism, adds additional categories such as general revelation and special revelation and, especially, the unity of nature and grace, which he concludes is a 'hallmark' of 'common grace but lacking in the Anabaptist tradition' (Holwerda 1989:27). These categories, represented as they are by apparent polar opposites, constitute the substance of the two-tracked theology of Neo-Calvinism. Hoeksema, however, did not use the designation 'two-tracked,' but preferred to speak of categories such as 'two spheres' or 'dualistic' (Hoeksema 1947:310-311).

Hoeksema understood the basis of what he called 'Neo-Calvinist dualism' as originating in the activities of God after the fall. In speculating about Kuyper's purpose in developing the ideal of common grace, Hoeksema wrote, that 'he sought to show that there still is a positively good world-life and development of the human race in connection with all created things and by the theory of common grace he offered an explanation of the positively good in the world in connection with the fact of the fall and the curse of God in the world and the total depravity of the natural man' (Hoeksema 1947:309). After the fall of man, wrote Hoeksema summarizing Kuyper's position, if God had not intervened with common grace all things would have come to an ignominious end in the garden (Hoeksema 1947:309), and 'as a result there would have been no room for the establishment and development of God's covenant of grace in Christ' (Hoeksema 1947:309). Thus, concluded Hoeksema on the nature of Kuyper's two-track theology:

> [God-PB] by His common grace…intervened, the universe did not suffer destruction, man did not immediately die and the original divine idea and ordinance of creation can be and is realized in the history of this world. At the same time a sphere is created for the realization and development of special grace in Christ Jesus. He, therefore, conceives of the work of God in a dualistic way. God has an original purpose with creation, the normal development of all things under man as their king. This purpose is apparently frustrated by the temptation of the devil and sin. But through the operation of common grace God carries out the original idea and brings about a positively good development of the human race in connection with the earthly creation. But, on the other hand, God also carries out His purpose of predestination in the redemption of the elect and the damnation of the reprobate. (Hoeksema 1947:310.)

According to Hoeksema, Kuyper's two-tracked theology had to do essentially with God's purpose in and for the world. God had two separate and distinct purposes in mind with regard to the world of humanity. One of which was with Adam and the creation mandate to go forth and subdue the creation for the benefit of mankind. Even though God's purpose with Adam was frustrated by the fall, God still had a purpose for this world that sprang from the creation mandate, namely, the creation and spread of culture. God still desired that the world develop culturally, and it was essentially a denial of God's goodness not to find good in it. Hence, it follows, that there were also two kinds of revelation, general revelation and special revelation, or the creation and Scripture, respectively. Two deposits of divine revelation, both of which must be taken into account since both are functions of God's grace, one from common grace and the other from special grace. The result of all this, as Hoeksema saw it, was that these two 'revelations' would become equal, both open to man's interpretation, i.e. rationalism. In repudiating the whole concept of common grace and by implication the whole of Neo-Calvinism's two-tracked theology, Hoeksema wrote that 'in so far as he [Kuyper-PB] ascribes the preservation and development of created things after the fall to God's common grace, he certainly calls grace what is merely God's providential care and government' (Hoeksema 1947:310). Years later, reflecting back on the events of 1924, Hoeksema quipped 'that the CRC Kalamazoo Synod of 1924 could not tell the difference between the Holy Spirit and a policeman' (Engelsma 2001:294).

5.2 The Beginning of the End

While the concluding months of 1922 and all of 1923 were taken up with the writing of pamphlets for and against common grace, it was at the very outset of 1924 that things began in earnest. The new year was to be a time of protests and legal wrangling, all of which began promptly on Saturday morning 19 January 1924. On this morning three members of the Eastern Avenue Christian Reformed Church appeared in Herman Hoeksema's parlor to discuss certain objections that they had to the content of his preaching and writing (Hoeksema 1947:28). Hoeksema readily admitted that he saw all this merely as subterfuge on their part. The three men had committed their complaints to writing and said they wanted to present them to their pastor, which they did. Hoeksema, observing that the document containing the complaints was formally addressed to the consistory and not to him alone, refused to either receive or discuss the complaints, suggesting rather that they be presented to the consistory. The men, realizing their mistake, quickly amended the protest. At that point, Hoeksema offered to discuss the matter with each man individually. Only one of the three complied; the other two refused to discuss anything unless they were permitted to do so together. Hoeksema recounted that the one who opted to speak with him in private seemed unfamiliar with the contents of his own protest (Hoeksema 1947:29). Since the other two would not discuss their concerns individually, Hoeksema also refused to entertain their objections, believing 'that none of the three protestants was the final author of the written document they had delivered, and, if at all possible, the author ought to lured from his hiding-place and called to account' (Hoeksema 1947:29). In this instance Hoeksema's suspicions proved to be correct. It was later discovered that 'none of the three protestants had composed the protest. Much later, through a forced testimony in a worldly court, one of the protestants revealed that his brother, a neighboring pastor, the Reverend G. Hoeksema, was the writer of that first protest' (Hoeksema 1947:29).

Seeing their way thwarted, the three men decided to change their course of action. Thus, shortly thereafter, they lodged a protest directly with the consistory of the Eastern Avenue Christian Reformed Church, charging their pastor, Herman Hoeksema, with public sin in regard to the content of his preaching (Hoeksema 1969:143). The consistory strongly disagreed 'and after trying to persuade the three men to retract their protest, without success, the consistory censured them as proper objects of church discipline' (Hoeksema 1969:143).

Was it wise or indeed proper for the consistory, led by Hoeksema, to put these men under church discipline for protesting the preaching of their pastor? Hoeksema vigorously defended the actions taken by the consistory in this matter in his history of the Protestant Reformed Churches (Hoeksema (1947: 30 also p. 32). However, in a rather protracted discussion on Article 31 of the Church Order of Dordrecht, which guarantees the believer the right of appeal to a broader church assembly if the decision of a consistory does not adjudicate a matter, Herman Hanko, an emeritus Protestant Reformed professor, believes the consistory of Eastern Avenue acted improperly (Hanko 2000: 59 also p. 102-103). Basing his argument on a lengthy series of articles written by the late George Ophoff, Hoeksema's colleague at the Protestant Reformed Seminary, and printed in the *Standard Bearer* in the 1920s, Hanko concludes that the three men:

should not have been put under censure for challenging the Reformed character of the preaching and finally appealing their case to a broader assembly. If the broader assemblies had decided in favor of the consistory, then indeed the protestants would have been required to retract their accusations. And if they still refused, discipline would have been necessary. But the fact of the matter is that synod waffled, declaring their accusations to be essentially true, but also affirming the Reformed character of their pastor. The point is that the censure should not have been imposed prior to the adjudication of their protests. Eastern Ave.'s consistory was wrong in its censure of the protestants. (Hanko 2000:103.)

In addition to the outstanding protest of the three members of his own congregation, there were also protests against Hoeksema's teaching from Reverend van der Mey, a minister without a charge who was also a member of Eastern Avenue Christian Reformed Church, Reverend J. K. van Baalen, and Reverend M. Schans. After the publication of Hoeksema and Danhof's *Van Zonde en Genade* (Of Sin and Grace), writes the former President of Calvin Seminary, John Kromminga:

> Agitation on this point [i.e., Hoeksema's denial of common grace-PB] reached such a pitch that several classes found it necessary to send overtures on the matter to the Synod of 1924. Classes Hackensack, Sioux Center, Hudson, and Muskegon all asked for a thorough study of the problem, with a view to clearer formulation of the matter. One of these classes declared that the denial was contrary to the Formulas of Unity (the three Confessional Standards), while another asked Synod to declare that such a denial was contrary to Scripture and Reformed Doctrine. (Kromminga 1949:83.)

Even though a committee of pre-advice appointed by Synod compiled a list of eleven disputed points gleaned from the many protests sent to Synod, attention seemed to focus on three matters to the exclusion of all others. These were, according to Kromminga, 'the gracious disposition of God towards all men, and not alone towards the elect; the restraint of sin in the life of the individual and in the life of society; and the performance of so-called civic righteousness by the unregenerate' (Kromminga 1949:83-84). There were many at the Synod of 1924 who urged caution, believing that the Synod was ill prepared to issue any definitive statement on these matters. Kromminga relates that there was even a proposition discussed 'which advised that Synod be content with instructing the churches to make a basic study of this matter' (Kromminga 1949:84). This proposition, however, along with all others urging caution, was summarily rejected. At this point, writes Kromminga, Synod proceeded to adopt, by official motion, those propositions which became forever after known as 'The Three Points of Common Grace' (Kromminga 1949:84). In addition to its adoption of the Three Points, Synod concurrently declared the writings and teachings of the Reverends Hoeksema and Danhof 'to be out of harmony with the Bible and the Confessions on those points, although it recognized the fact that these men desired to be nothing but Reformed, and basically were Reformed, with a tendency to one-sidedness' (Kromminga 1949:84). Synod also admonished the Reverends Hoeksema and Danhof to henceforth abide by the decisions of Synod in their teaching and writing.

Henry Danhof, who was himself a delegate to Synod, made it plain to all present that he had no intention to abide by the Three Points, and that he fully intended to militate publicly against what he saw as an erroneous decision by Synod. Hoeksema, while not a delegate to Synod but in attendance anyway, was tried and convicted along with Danhof almost in absentia. It began with the committee of pre-advice, which neither notified nor summoned the Reverends Hoeksema or Danhof to appear in their defense, and ended with the same committee condemning them, as Hoeksema later wrote, 'without having heard them or given them an opportunity for self-defense' (Hoeksema 1947:70). Synod did essentially the same thing. In retrospect, Hoeksema wrote that 'common decency and justice would have prompted synod…to summon him, to invite him to its meetings, to examine him if necessary, to offer him an opportunity to defend his views. Synod, however, was utterly negligent in this respect' (Hoeksema 1947:70).

As the first session of the Synod wore on, Hoeksema broke the rules of order and insisted he be given a chance to speak, this as the Synod deliberated on his case while he sat in the gallery. His request was summarily refused. As the Synod proceeded with a discussion of the proposed Three Points, Hoeksema again violated the rules of order, arose in the audience, and requested the evening session to present a defense of his own views. In order to induce Synod to respond favorably to his request, Hoeksema wrote later that 'he foolishly promised that he would not ask to speak again' (Hoeksema 1947:72). The request was granted and 'at the evening session before a packed auditorium and deeply interested audience, the pastor expounded his views before synod' (Hoeksema 1947:72). In a later session, when Synod was involved in debate over the First Point of Common Grace, Hoeksema, not being able to restrain himself, again requested the floor. 'Synod refused,' Hoeksema later wrote, 'giving as the ground of their refusal, that the Reverend Hoeksema had promised not to ask for the floor a second time' (Hoeksema 1947:72). At this point Hoeksema promptly left the gallery and attended no more sessions of the Synod of 1924. Reflecting back on the events of 1924, John Bolt ponders 'whether the whole business could not have been handled with less haste and with greater propriety and charity. The impression is overwhelming that the assault on Hoeksema was well-orchestrated and hurried, a kind of ecclesiastical blitzkrieg' (Bolt 2000a:17-18).

While the Synod of Kalamazoo in 1924 may have adopted the Three Points of Common Grace, and while it may indeed have admonished the Reverends Hoeksema and Danhof to refrain from any dissent on the matter (Bolt 2000a:30), as Hoeksema maintained, 'the conclusions of synod were too ambiguous to settle anything' (Hoeksema 1947:99). Part of this ambiguity was its 'failure' to deal specifically with the protest from the members of the Eastern Avenue Church. Hence, the three protestants from the Eastern Avenue Christian Reformed Church who sometime earlier had accused their pastor of 'public sin,' though partially vindicated by the decisions taken at Synod, were still under censure in their own church. Another facet of this ambiguity, writes John Bolt, was that it failed to stop 'the concerted ecclesiastical opposition to Hoeksema' (Bolt 2000a:32). As this ecclesiastical opposition continued its sustained attack in the denomination's official publications (Bolt 2000a:32), Classis Grand Rapids East, meeting on 20 August 1924, decided that the censure against the original protestants 'should be lifted as soon as possible, on the ground that synod had sustained the accusation of these protestants against the pastor' (Hoeksema 1947:109). 'Needless to say,' Hoeksema remembered with mixed emotions, 'the advice of the Classis was of such as nature that it was strictly impossible as well as morally wrong for the consistory to heed it. And for this reason this decision was plainly the beginning of the end' (Hoeksema 1947:110). Not wishing to face Hoeksema on any of the matters concerned, Classis requested that the consistory of Eastern Avenue Church write down their decisions and submit them to Classis and Classis would, in turn, respond accordingly (see Hoeskema 1947:168-263 for copies of this correspondence). Concerning these final days, John Bolt writes:

> When Classis Grand Rapids East met again in a number of sessions from November 19, 1924 to December 12, 1924, the die was cast. Neither side would budge from its position. The classis insisted that Hoeksema submit to the three points, and he naturally refused. After much ecclesiastical wrangling, a civil court case ensued, primarily over the disposition of Eastern Avenue CRC's property, and by early March 1925, Hoeksema and his supporters were ousted from the church. (Bolt 2000a:33.)

Although Hoeksema, Danhof, and their respective consistories, as well as George Ophoff and his consistory, appealed the decision of Classis to the next Synod, they had to wait almost two years for a decision. When the Synod of 1926 finally met, it decided that the protest was inadmissible since the protestors were already outside the denomination (Hoeksema 1992:92-93). Thus, the split was complete.

5.3 The Twenties and Thirties

The decades of the Twenties and Thirties were not easy for Hoeksema's small, fledgling denomination. Problems were large and friends were few. Gertrude Hoeksema relates many instances in which there was not enough money or fuel to visit prospective groups and, as a result, growth was slow. Henry Danhof, stalwart in his defense of Hoeksema and equally staunch in his repudiation of common grace, became contentious and bitter after the split from the Christian Reformed Church. 'The three Danhofs,' writes Gertrude Hoeksema, '—the Reverends Henry, and his nephews Ralph and also student Ben—had become disillusioned, dissatisfied, and troublesome' (Hoeksema 1992:95). In the end, The Danhofs went their separate ways. Herman Hoeksema, commenting on the Danhof matter, wrote: 'Always there is bright sunshine and there are gloomy shadows' (Hoeksema 1947:257). During the remaining years of the 1920s, churches struggled to find places to meet until proper accommodations could be built. Growth was slow but steady; much of which was of a spiritual nature. The 1930s saw more churches established in the Grand Rapids area, as well as further a field, such as Belflower, Redlands and Los Angeles, all of which were in California. The denomination called its first missionary in 1936 and 'his first call for help was from Edgerton, Minnesota; and in 1938 the group was organized as a Protestant Reformed congregation' (Hoeksema 1992:100). A similar story held true for all the congregations organized during the decade of the Thirties.

It was also in the decade of the Thirties that Herman Hoeksema met what he considered a kindred spirit in the person of Klaas Schilder. Hoeksema met Schilder for the first time in 1939 when the latter was invited by some within the Christian Reformed Church to tour North America speaking in her churches (Vander Kam 1996:52). This meeting would later prove to be one of the high points and, at the same time, one of the low points in Hoeksema's theological career. The two men were very similar in many ways. Both were theologians of note and both endured much for their respective causes. Still, Hoeksema thought he had found a kindred spirit, and because of this perception the eventual disappointment was most severe.

Klaas Schilder was born in Kampen, in the Netherlands, in 1890. Recognized early as one of uncommon ability (Knight 2000:27, De Klerk 1990:4), Schilder was assured a place in both the local gymnasium and at the Theological School through the early efforts a primary school teacher (De Klerk 1990:4). After graduation on the eve of World War I, he was ordained into the ministry of Gereformeerde Kerken in Nederland (GKN), proceeding to serve six congregations between 1914 and 1930 (De Klerk 1990:5). During the course of his last pastorate in Rotterdam, a colleague,

Rev. R Zijlstra, offered to loan him the money needed to undertake doctoral studies. For Schilder, this was a dream come true (Vander Kam 1996:32-33). The Free University was the obvious and the logical choice, but Schilder had crossed swords with members of the faculty there both in person and in print before (Vander Kam 1996:33). And, as John Knight records, Dr. V. Hepp, 'Bavinck's successor at the Free University, insisted that Schilder take his introductory course in dogmatics as the condition for pursuing his studies at the Free University. Schilder felt insulted and instead enrolled at the University of Erlangen in Germany' (Knight 2000a: 25). For the next two years Schilder studied at the Friedrich-Alexander University at Erlangen; graduating in 1933 with highest honors for a thesis on 'paradox' entitled, *Zur Begriffsgeschichte des "Paradoxon" mit besonderer Berücksichtigung Calvins und des nach-Kierkegaardschen "Paradoxon"* (De Klerk 1990:5)—a subject that was also of interest to Hoeksema at the time and to which he would return later in connection with the 'Clark Case' in the Orthodox Presbyterian Church in the early 1940s. Shortly after his graduation early in 1934, Schilder was installed as professor of dogmatics and ethics to succeed Professor A. G. Honig at the Theological School of the Gereformeerde Kerken in Kampen (Vander Kam 1996:37).

Klaas Schilder was a prolific writer with a sharp pen (De Klerk 1990:11). With it he made many uncomfortable, even angry. So much so that, in 1938 when Schilder received the invitation to lecture in the United States, 'Rev. H. J. Kuiper, the editor of *The Banner,*...wrote in his column that he thought it would be far better if K. S. would not come at this time. He feared that Schilder might bring the theological differences that were being debated in Holland to the United States—especially his position on common grace' (Vander Kam 1996:52). Undeterred, Schilder issued a press release that his intent was to be in America for the months of January and February 1939 (Dee 1990:85).

Schilder arrived in the United States in the fall of 1938, where he received a warm welcome from fellow ministers in the Christian Reformed Church in New York and New Jersey (Vander Kam 1996:53). Henry vander Kam goes so far as to say: 'It can honestly be said that he took the East by storm' (Vander Kam 1996:53). Having spent the Christmas Holiday in the East, Schilder arrived in Grand Rapids, Michigan in January of 1939. He preached the following Sunday to a packed crowd at the Eastern Avenue Christian Reformed Church, Hoeksema's old church. John Piersma, minister emeritus in the Christian Reformed Churches, who was present on this occasion, said it was one of the most remarkable sermons he had ever heard, and that this was also the consensus of those present at the time (Piersma 2002).

Schilder was not one to mince words; neither was he given to avoiding difficult or controversial subjects (Vander Kam 1996:56). According to biographer Rudolf van Reest, Schilder wanted all debate out in the open (Van Reest 1990:168-169). Believing that everything had to be clear and true (Vander Kam 1996:43), Schilder did not hide his openness, nor was he given to straddling the fence on important issues (Vander Kam 1996:37). I believe this is one of the reasons why Hoeksema believed he saw in Schilder a kindred spirit. Yet there are many more similarities between these two men. Both men were polemicists; fighters who would not yield an inch if either believed he was right (Vander Kam 1996:42-44). Both saw worldliness engulfing the Church of Christ and strove to combat it whatever the costs (Vander Kam 1996:19, also p.44). And later, 'that Hoeksema and Schilder had a great deal in common in terms of what they had experienced at the hands of the churches that ordained them is clear,' writes Rudolf van Reest, 'and this was no doubt part of the reason for the kinship they felt' (Van Reest 1990:421). Reverend Woudenberg adds yet a further dimension to this commonality. After his departure from the Christian Reformed Church, Hoeksema was not able to attract a following of seasoned, experienced ministers to fill the pulpits of his fledgling churches. Henry Danhof, who was deposed by the Christian Reformed Church along with Hoeksema, ultimately went his own way and established an independent Reformed church. Especially in the early years, the Protestant Reformed Churches greatly needed trained ministers, and it was incumbent upon both Hoeksema and George Ophoff to train them. By the time of Schilder's visit to the United States in 1939, the ministry of the Protestant Reformed Churches was made up exclusively of young men trained by Hoeksema and Ophoff, many of whom had no previous college education. It would be easy to see how Hoeksema could become starved for theological fellowship in such an environment. Theologically speaking, both Hoeksema and Schilder were head and shoulders above many of their contemporaries. Thus, I believe Hoeksema saw in Schilder one like himself, one with whom he could converse as an equal on any subject (Woudenberg 2001).

Against this backdrop, on the eighth of February 1939, Dr. K Schilder 'entered the auditorium of the First Protestant Reformed Church of Grand Rapids to deliver his lecture on the subject of Common Grace' (Hoeksema 1939b:243). While the actual text of the address has not survived the intervening years, Hoeksema's summary of its contents along with a few remarks was printed in the next *Standard Bearer*.

The question concerning "common grace" deals with the problem of "nature and grace", a problem that in our day attracts universal attention and is worthy of our earnest consideration and study. The antithesis is not one between "nature and grace", but between "sin and grace". Scripture abundantly testifies that God loves and preserves His creature. He loves the works of His hands, sun, moon and stars, the trees of the forest, and flowers, the beasts of the field, the birds of the air, the fish of the sea. And also what is His own work in man, even after the fall, the "remnants of His image", the "natural light", man as His own creation, He loves. This does not mean that He loves man as a sinner, outside of Christ. For, He is gracious to the sinner in Christ only. But His own work in man He loves. The fact that, after the fall, man still exists, is not yet in hell, receives many things, such as rain and sunshine, food and drink, clothing and shelter, gifts and talents, does not warrant the conclusion that there is a gracious disposition (gezindheid) in God towards him. Things are not grace. The speaker used the illustration of a man that is condemned to death, but the execution of whose sentence is delayed because things are not yet ready for the severe form of punishment that is intended for him. Such a man cannot justly conclude from that fact, that he still has a few days to live, to a gracious disposition towards him on the part of the judge. The same is true of the sinner, that receives many things, but who is prepared for eternal damnation. Common grace cannot mean that there is a gracious disposition in God towards the reprobate ungodly. This truth was emphasized more than once in the lecture. There is a reining (beteugeling), retardation, restraining of sin, even as there is a retardation (beteugeling) of grace. The end does not come at the beginning. Beginning and end are separated by an historic process, in which God preserves all things to serve as understructure for the realization of His purpose of election and reprobation, salvation and damnation, sin and grace. In this historic process man, even fallen man, is confronted by the "common mandate", to multiply and fill the earth and develop the powers of creation and to do this in the love of God. (Hoeksema 1939b:244-245.)

Concerning the free offer of the Gospel, Schilder is reported to have said:

There is no objection to speak of an "offer" (aanbod) of grace, provided we understand by it that in a pedagogical sense the gospel, with its promise and demand, is presented to the rational, moral consciousness of all men promiscuously. However, this "aanbod" is no ground for the conclusion that in the preaching of the gospel there is a gracious disposition (gezindheid) in God. Through it God accomplishes His own purpose, both of election and reprobation, salvation and damnation, life and death. (Hoeksema 1939b:245.)

Hoeksema's editorial on the lecture expressed his hearty agreement with many things Schilder said; concluding with approval that Schilder also differs substantially from the *Three Points* as adopted by the Christian Reformed Church in 1924. Hoeksema, referring to the fact that Schilder denied any favor on the part of God for the ungodly, wrote: 'to my mind, this is the very heart of the question' (Hoeksema 1939b:244). Though there were questions that he would like to have asked Dr. Schilder, Hoeksema sincerely believed that they were in substantial agreement (Hoeksema 1939b:245).

In his address Schilder did not dwell on his conception of the 'cultural mandate' and its relation to common grace; had he done so, more areas of disagreement between him and Hoeksema would have inevitably surfaced. In his scheme, Schilder essentially replaced 'common grace' with the 'cultural mandate. 'By this,' writes Walter Campbell-Jack, 'he means that the continuance of fallen creation and sinful humanity and the cultural development which we witness within creation are not to be understood as being grounded in a general operation of God. Schilder's understanding of creation and cultural activity are instead understood as being based upon the divine determination that man as a covenant creature fulfill his created cultural function as expounded in the cultural mandate of *Genesis 1:28* to fill the earth and subdue it' (Campbell-Jack 1992:106). Contrariwise, for Hoeksema, any pursuit of the cultural mandate in a fallen world is merely part of the organic development of sin (Hanko 2000:254-255). 'I do not have to call special attention to the patent fact' Hoeksema insisted, 'that grace does not change this situation as long as we are in this world. The Christian lives in the same world as the ungodly, and he must work with the same material. Even as sin could not and did not fundamentally and essentially change the world, so grace does not renew and regenerate it' (Hoeksema 1977:13-14).

Another difference between Hoeksema and Schilder was on the nature of the covenant of grace. Writing on this aspect of Schilder's thought, Walter Campbell-Jack points out that, for Schilder, the presentation of the gospel is always 'within the context of the covenant' (Campbell-Jack 1992:108). Additionally, 'Hoeksema speaks of unconditional promises which are always particular whilst Schilder speaks of the covenant promise and the gospel promise as conditional inasmuch as he wishes to emphasise human responsibility in response' (Campbell-Jack 1992:108). Though these differences were not at issue during Schilder's visit in 1939, they would become more noteworthy on Schilder's second American visit in 1947.

5.4 Reunion?

Prior to the visit by Klaas Schilder to the United States in 1939, Hoeksema had sought several times unsuccessfully to initiate a conference between the Christian Reformed Church and the Protestant Reformed Churches in order to discuss the issues that separated them (Woudenberg 2000:9). With the coming of Schilder, however, 'the Christian Reformed came; they could hardly deny the doctor' (Woudenberg 2000:9). As current Protestant Reformed Professor of Dogmatics, David Engelsma, records, it was an 'all-day conference in the old Pantlind Hotel, now the Amway Grand Plaza, in Grand Rapids, Michigan on March 29, 1939' (Engelsma 2000:4). Especially for this conference, Herman Hoeksema took a week off from his regular work in order to craft a speech worthy of the event (Engelsma 2000:6). Entitled *The Reunion of the Christian Reformed and Protestant Reformed Churches*, Hoeksema's speech runs some 46 pages in its English translation. Present at the conference were sixteen Christian Reformed men and fourteen Protestant Reformed (Engelsma 2000:4-5). Hoeksema was the first to address the gathering, Schilder followed emphasizing 'the need for unity' (Vander Kam 1996:56-57).

Intending to get to the heart of the matter without delay, Hoeksema stated unequivocally: 'now I come to the question which faces this gathering, be it not in an official sense: Is it required that the breach be healed? Is it possible? And is it desirable?' (Hoeksema [s.a.]:16). Citing Klaas Schilder's emphasis on unity and its importance, Hoeksema declared himself willing to put aside any personal animosities and grievances in order to get at the issues (Hoeksema [s.a.]:16). Unity, however, in Hoeksema's mind was ultimately dependent upon standing 'together upon the basis of the reformed confessions.... The question of the truth must govern, dominate this discussion. And that implies that we must discuss thoroughly the issue of common grace, which also includes the three points adopted in 1924' (Hoeksema [s.a.]:17). Without doctrinal unity, according to Hoeksema, there is simply no unity. Thus, any differences must first be discussed in detail, with either side yielding to the one found to be in possession of the truth (Hoeksema [s.a.]:17). As Hoeksema stipulated:

> If they succeed in convincing us, we will acknowledge that we erred and that we must unite with them upon the basis of the three points. If we succeed in convincing them, they must acknowledge that they erred in 1924 then the three points will presently be recalled, and then they will stand with us upon the same confessional basis. Only in this manner may we proceed. Any other way is the way

of compromise, which I continue to refuse. (Hoeksema [s.a.]:17-18.)

After laying the ground rules which he assumed would be acceptable to all the participants, Hoeksema entered into a long, detailed discussion of the issues and where the specific differences lay (Hoeksema [s.a.]:19-46). Even so 'the meeting was a failure,' writes David Engelsma (Engelsma 2000:5). According to Henry vander Kam, 'the conference failed to produce agreement because the Christian Reformed ministers did not appear to be interested in settling differences' (Vander Kam 1996:57). David Engelsma also attributes the failure of the conference to Christian Reformed representatives, who 'refused to discuss the issues. …Nothing availed. They all were determined to sit as "silent listeners." Two of them were at pains to advertise their complete disinterest by ostentatiously reading the newspaper' (Engelsma 2000:5). Hence, 'the conference came to a sorry end,' Engelsma writes, 'the last three hours were a wrangling, whether the group should discuss the doctrine of common grace. Common grace was never discussed' (Engelsma 2000:5). It should also be mentioned that none of the professors from Calvin Seminary were present at the conference.

One of Hoeksema's distinctives, as seen so vividly in his *Banner* articles, was that he wanted to discuss even the most controversial issues openly. While he just assumed that everyone else wanted the same, the opposite was most often the case; Hoeksema was the only one who wanted to talk. His opponents often viewed him as the problem, and, rather than discuss difficult issues, it was just easier to get rid of him. In seeking parallels between Hoeksema's deposition in 1924 and Schilder's in 1944, Rudolf van Reest reveals a sordid and sinister side of the events of 1924, where Herman Hoeksema was indeed seen as the problem. He writes:

> Reluctantly the church let go of Dr. Janssen: in the face of the overwhelming abundance of evidence assembled by Rev. Hoeksema, it simply *had* to be done. But the doctrine of common grace was beautifully suited to get rid of Hoeksema as well. "He must be put out," wrote a well-known minister in those days, "but how are we going to accomplish it?" Kuyper's construction

regarding common grace could be of service here. (Van Reest 1990:419.)

If Hoeksema was a problem in 1924, my own feeling is that he was still viewed by the Christian Reformed Church as a significant threat, even in 1939.

5.5 Schilder and Hoeksema in the 1940s

When Schilder returned to the Netherlands, Europe was on the verge of war. That very same year Germany would successfully invade and conquer Poland. Under the able command of Hitler's foremost expeditionary general, Sepp Dietrich, soon the Netherlands was occupied territory as well. 'Shortly after German forces occupied the Netherlands in May 1940,' writes John Knight, 'Schilder was arrested' (Knight 2000:26). For four months he was held in relative isolation, separated from friends and family, although he was allowed to send and receive letters. His work, his editorials, however, just stopped (Vander Kam 1996:68). When he was finally released in December of 1940, writes John Knight, 'he was placed under a gag order. He could no longer publish his opinions, at least not openly' (Knight 2000:26).

After his release, Schilder remained in hiding; constantly moving to avoid further arrest, or something worse (Vander Kam 1996:70). When he left the United States, Hoeksema and Schilder 'parted as close friends, determined to maintain contact with each other and to support each other in their future battles' (Woudenberg 2000:5). 'All through the war,' recounts Reverend Woudenberg, 'Rev. Hoeksema tried to maintain contact; but little other than greetings and expressions of concern could get through. Eventually, however, the war was over, and as quickly as possible plans were in the making for another visit of Dr. Schilder to the United States, this time at the invitation of the Protestant Reformed' (Woudenberg 2000:9).

Meanwhile, in war-torn Holland, Schilder had pressing matters of his own to contend with. While still in hiding in 1944, Schilder found himself first suspended and then deposed both as a minister and professor, in abstentia, from the Gereformeerde

Kerken in Nederland by its National Synod (Knight 2000:26). Even though this decision was the result of a long chain of events stretching back as far as 1936, its propriety was suspect by many. Viewed in this light, the support he received from the people in the churches during his ordeal was truly extraordinary. Primarily in response to this outpouring of support, Schilder proceeded to found his own churches, hereafter known as the Liberated. This series of events brought one more commonality to the bond between Schilder and Hoeksema. Van Reest sees this commonality in the way both men were treated by the respective churches from which they were deposed, for Hoeksema it was the Christian Reformed Church and for Schilder it was the Gereformeerde Kerken. He writes of the 'striking parallels between the battle waged by Rev. Hoeksema and his followers against the hierarchy of the Christian Reformed Church, on the one hand, and the battle of the "protesters" against the hierarchy of the Churches in the Netherlands, on the other' (Van Reest 1990:417-418). When the decision reached Schilder of what the National Synod of the GKN had done, he was dumbfounded. He apparently could not fathom, as Vander Kam relates, 'that this decision was made "from above" and without consulting local ecclesiastical bodies' (Vander Kam 1996:72). In the events of 1924 Hoeksema was confronted with essentially the same situation; he steadfastly maintained that a 'higher' assembly had usurped the powers delegated specifically to the consistory, and thus, the presumed illegality of the whole affair. Herman Hanko, in his doctrinal history of the Protestant Reformed Churches, expounds a view to which I believe both Hoeksema and Schilder would have subscribed (see Vander Kam 1996:76 also p. 83-84 for changes in the church order in the GKN between 1938 and 1942). Hanko writes that:

> It is Reformed to maintain firmly, as the PRC does, the autonomy of the local congregation, while at the same time giving the broader assemblies their right to exercise judicatory authority in the federation in order to preserve the unity of the denomination. But such exercise of authority must never usurp the right of the local church to preach God's Word, administer the sacraments, and exercise discipline. (Hanko 2000:118.)

In August of 1947 Schilder made his second trip to the United States. A very different set of circumstances prevailed this time in contrast to his previous visit in 1939. In 1939 he was still attached to the GKN and, as a result of the sister church relations that existed between the Gereformeerde Kerken Nederlands and the Christian Reformed Church in America, the CRC pulpits were opened to him. This time, writes Calvin College Librarian, Peter de Klerk, 'the Synodical Committee placed a notice in *The Banner* that the CRC had no sister relationship with the Liberated Churches. Schilder was therefore not allowed in the CRC pulpits' (De Klerk 1990:16). This was not true of the Protestant Reformed Churches, whose pulpits were open, just as they had been on his previous visit. This, concludes Peter de Klerk, 'prompted Schilder upon his return to the Netherlands to write, that the Protestant Reformed Churches were the only churches where the members of the Liberated Churches immigrating to North America could feel at home' (De Klerk 1990:16 & 17); a statement which Schilder would later come to regret.

5.6 The Stroke

Two months before Dr. Schilder's expected visit, Herman Hoeksema, while vacationing with his wife Nellie, daughter Jeanette, and her husband Bill in Sioux Falls, South Dakota, suffered a massive stroke that left his right side paralyzed and his power of speech gone (Hoeksema 1969:257-258). Because of this unfortunate occurrence, even though the May 1st issue of *The Standard Bearer* gave Dr. Schilder a warm welcome, Hoeksema was physically unable to enter into any sustained discussion with his friend from the Netherlands on areas of doctrine where there were acknowledged differences (Hoeksema 1969:282). On the effects of Hoeksema's stroke and Schilder's 1947 visit little is actually said beyond what is chronicled by Herman Hanko (Hanko 2000) and Gertrude Hoeksema (Hoeksema 1969).

Concerning what significance Hoeksema's stroke and Schilder's 1947 visit had on each other is not discussed; moreover, any substantive connection between the two is seldom made. Hence, the following explanation regarding the significance of these events is a summary of many conversations with Reverends Bernard Woudenberg and John Piersma; the latter having left the Protestant Reformed Churches for the Christian Reformed Church in the late 1940s. When the Protestant Reformed Churches were formed in the mid-1920s it became incumbent upon both Herman Hoeksema and George Ophoff to train the future Protestant Reformed ministers. By the time of Schilder's second visit in 1947, several of the first generation of Protestant Reformed ministers, such as Cornelius Hanko, would have been actively in the ministry for up to twenty years. Many of these, as I said before, were fresh out of high school when they first began their ministerial instruction under the tutelage of Herman Hoeksema. In many cases, all they knew was 'Protestant Reformed.' Additionally, they were, in most instances, country ministers not critical scholars. When Schilder toured the Protestant Reformed Churches in October and November of 1947, even holding a two-day conference from November 4-6, it was with these men that he conversed. With Hoeksema unable to present the Protestant Reformed position, the sheer force of Dr. Schilder's presence swayed many. This force was not just the persuasiveness of his theological argumentation, but primarily in the strength of his rhetoric. In addition to being an accomplished rhetorician, Schilder also had a commanding and inspiring personality. Many of the ministers and elders who met with him were flattered by the attention he gave to them. Besides preaching in the churches, Schilder met with many of the Protestant Reformed ministers in their homes on a very personal basis. Schilder talked with them, listened to them, and made them feel important and appreciated and an integral part of the theological scene. The days following Dr. Klaas Schilder's visit to the United States,' recalls Reverend Wouderberg with fondness, 'were exciting days.

> A new sense of enthusiasm seemed to fill the churches. After all, being visited by Dr. Schilder, a man who so recently had been the most noted theologian in the Netherlands, gave to our churches a degree of recognition, which we had long been denied. And even more, with the promise of a new flood of post-war immigration, it seemed altogether likely that those who came from the Liberated churches would be joining ours. Then at last we might have the kind of growth for which

we had long hoped but never known. All of this was stimulating, and a resurgence of interest in church and theology began to take place. But not everything was as positive as it might have seemed. Some of what was happening, at least to the more discerning, did not forebode good; and that for a number of reasons. Perhaps the most evident of these was the rise of voices within our churches in defense of conditional theology. (Woudenberg 2000:7.)

I would like to suggest, that it was a combination of Schilder's commanding personality together with his growing popularity in the eyes of many in the Protestant Reformed Churches that caused his ideas, especially his ideas on the covenant, to be adopted. Schilder returned to the Netherlands in December, just prior to Hoeksema's departure for California for much needed rest and recuperation (Hoeksema 1992:146). It is said that a stroke accentuates a person's worst characteristics. This was definitely true in Hoeksema's case, and it is, no doubt, one of the reasons why his popularity in his own churches declined so suddenly. Additionally, because of the incapacitation brought on by the stroke, Hoeksema's son, Homer, took over many of the duties once reserved for his father. Herman Hoeksema was forced to rely on his son in many areas, and his son took him in directions both theological and ecclesiastical that the elder Hoeksema probably would not have ventured on his own.

In the aftermath of Schilder's 1947 visit, amid the rather all-pervasive positive outlook for the future, voices of dissent began to assert themselves. Over the next five years this dissent became deafening. Finally, in 1953, the Protestant Reformed Churches suffered a severe rupture. Many who left at this time eventually found their way back to the Christian Reformed Church, while a smaller percentage dispersed into other Reformed and Presbyterian churches. Prior to this split in 1953 the Protestant Reformed Churches, never what one would consider a large denomination, had approximately six thousand members. After the split that number was reduced to approximately three thousand and it was not until the mid 1960s that the Protestant Reformed Churches regained numerically the membership they had before the split of 1953. Hoeksema, however, did not live to see this development. After his stroke, from which he never fully recovered, his involvement in his own denomination began to diminish even as that of his son, Homer, increased. It was during this time that Hoeksema wrote his dogmatics, completing it in 1956, but for the most part his productive years were over. His wife of almost sixty years died in September 1963 leaving him a profoundly lonely man (Hoeksema 1969:353). During the next two years Hoeksema suffered a series of small strokes which had the effect of weakening him all the more. Finally, two years after the death of his wife, on 2 September 1965, Hoeksema passed away quietly as he slept (Hoeksema 1969:355).

5.7 Conclusion

During the course of this chapter I have tried to show the dependency of the events of 1924, in which Hoeksema and his associates were deposed from the ministry of the Christian Reformed Church, on earlier events leading up to and including the Synod of 1922. Professor Ralph Janssen's expulsion in 1922 from his teaching post at Calvin Seminary and the denomination at large was to a good measure brought about by *The Banner* articles which Hoeksema authored. And, while Hoeksema may not have initiated the furor over Janssen, he certainly seems to have advantage of it. I have tried to demonstrate that, for his troubles Hoeksema was himself dismissed from the Christian Reformed Church by Janssen's supporters and fellow Neo-Calvinists. Hoeksema went after Janssen with a vigor that instilled a profound fear in many of his contemporaries. His debating prowess, his mental acuity, his logical rigor, and his constant need to be right at any cost were the reasons none wanted to face him in open debate over the issues. At the same time, a sizeable contingent of ministers in the Christian Reformed Church realized that if they did not rid themselves of Hoeksema, he would eventually get rid of them. Because of both his theological acumen and his faith in the correctness of his own opinions, his detractors, instead of doing battle face to face outflanked him politically. This is essentially what happened in 1924. Both Janssen's supporters and his own enemies united to rid themselves of a common and greater threat: Herman Hoeksema.

Hoeksema, frustrated and a bit baffled, went down complaining of procedural anomalies and aberrations just as Janssen before him.

The Synod of 1924, however, did bring the concept of common grace to the fore, especially in its adoption of the Three Points. In a decision marked by its alacrity, the Christian Reformed Church gave confessional status to widely held opinions without due consideration of the ramifications. Hoeksema said just this. He also predicted that one of the results of this decision by the Christian Reformed Church was a bridging of the antithesis, which for him meant letting the world into the church.

Hoeksema's appeal of his deposition to the Synod of 1926 was really just a formality. For all intents and purposes, the Protestant Reformed Churches had already gotten under way. Hoeksema's new denomination, contra the Christian Reformed Church from which he came, was built upon a foundation that repudiated any notion of a common grace of God as outlined in the Three Points.

The next two decades were very difficult for Hoeksema and his followers and growth was, for all intents and purposes, negligible. Still, a high point in Hoeksema's career came in the 1930s in the person of Klaas Schilder. Schilder first came to the United States in 1939 and preached in both the Christian Reformed and Protestant Reformed Churches. Hoeksema and Schilder became fast friends, primarily because both denied common grace as detailed in the Three Points adopted by the Christian Reformed Church in 1924. Hoeksema saw in Schilder a kindred spirit. But, by the time of Schilder's second visit in 1947, both men's lives had changed significantly. Schilder had been expelled from his former church and had started a new one and Hoeksema had suffered a debilitating stroke. As a result of Hoeksema's diminished capacity, Schilder's time was spent with other Protestant Reformed ministers. With his magnetic personality, his scintillating rhetoric, and his simple willingness to listen, Schilder won many Protestant Reformed ministers to his position. Hoeksema never fully recover from his debilitating stroke and, as a result, his son Homer took over more and more of the denomination's daily operations; tasks which Hoeksema had previously reserved for himself. Homer took Herman and the denomination in a decidedly different direction, but by this time the distinctives of Hoeksema's theology was already complete.

Chapter 6

The Rationalist

Because the charge of 'rationalism,' or its relative 'rationalist,' always seems to hold pride of place in any discussion of Hoeksema's thought, in the following chapter I would like to investigate this matter.

6.1 J. K. van Baalen

J. K. van Baalen, in his 1922 pamphlet entitled De Loochening der Gemeene Gratie: Gereformeerd of Doopersch (The Denial of Common Grace: Reformed or Anabaptist) (Van Baalen 1922), simply mimicked Professor Ralph Janssen who first charged Hoeksema with rationalism a year or so earlier. I say mimicked, because it seems Van Baalen offered no more by way of proof of this charge than did his predecessor; in fact, any justification of the charge just seemed to be assumed at the outset. His critique of Hoeksema's 'rationalism,' is confined exclusively to a discussion of common grace and Hoeksema's denial of it and it is from this critique that his charge of rationalism subsequently flowed. Reading Van Baalen's critique, however, one is struck by his consistent misunderstanding and misstatement of Hoeksema's position.

6.2 A. Kuyper Jr.

The next one to charge Hoeksema with rationalism was Dr. A. Kuyper Jr. This came about when a series of articles that were originally published in *The Standard Bearer* were issued in book form under the title: *Een Kracht Gods Tot Zaligheid of Genade Geen Aanbod* (A Power of God unto Salvation or Grace No Offer) (Hoeksema 1996). Originally published in 1931, these articles comprised a lengthy debate between Herman Hoeksema in *The Standard Bearer* and a Reverend H. Keegstra in the Dutch weekly *De Wachter* (The Watchman) on the subject of common grace. When the articles were finally published as a collection they were reviewed from various quarters, one of which was published in the *Gereformeerde Kerkbode* (Reformed Church Messenger) of Rotterdam by Dr. A. Kuyper Jr. (Hoeksema 1996:54-66).

Initially, Hoeksema was elated to have an esteemed colleague from the Netherlands take such as interest in his work. He wrote that: 'We have eagerly awaited the day when men of prominence and position in the Netherlands would let themselves be heard in regard to the issues that occupy our attention' (Hoeksema 1996:54). This initial euphoria, however, was to be short lived. Dr. A. Kuyper's review of *A Power of God unto Salvation* extended over the course of three installments, but by the end of the second article Hoeksema's enthusiasm had waned substantially. 'When I read this article (#2),' Hoeksema lamented, 'I was deeply disappointed. Now that the conclusion of Kuyper's discussion of my brochure has reached me and I have read all of it, I am even more disappointed' (Hoeksema 1996:59). He regretted his decision to publish Kuyper's critique of his book in *The Standard Bearer*, along with his own comments because, as he said later, 'they are not worth it' (Hoeksema 1996:60). It seems that Hoeksema's one desire was that 'finally we would actually discuss the issue' (Hoeksema 1996:60). He was clearly not satisfied with the outcome. In fact Hoeksema's disappointment was precipitated by some rather severe criticism on the part of Dr. A. Kuyper. Kuyper wrote concerning Hoeksema's position on common grace:

> We cannot say that we find the reasoning of Rev. Hoeksema to be logical; it appears to us to be more *rationalistic*. He builds a rationalistic system upon a Reformed foundation. ...Seemingly this reasoning of Rev. Hoeksema is logical. But this is nothing more than sham. The Germans would call it *conzequens-macherei* (sic). (quoted in Hoeksema 1996:55.)

Elsewhere in his review, Kuyper referred to Hoeksema's reasoning as both 'hyper-logical' (Hoeksema 1996:59) and 'one-sided' (Hoeksema 1996:64). By the end of the third installment,

Hoeksema's ire was kindled; this is evident from the tone of his response. In a rather gruff manner he wrote:

> Why does he [Kuyper-PB] not do justice to my reasoning and then in a manly manner answer argument with argument, instead of assuming that he can brush us aside with a few texts? No, Dr. Kuyper has done his work poorly. He does not enter into any of my arguments. He acts as if they do not exist and as if I as a rationalist had put my own reason on the foreground. Is that the way the leaders in the Netherlands deal with their opponents? (Hoeksema 1996:63.)

Hoeksema then continues:

> The esteemed writer [Kuyper-PB] expresses as his opinion that my reasoning appears to be logical, but in reality is illogical. This accusation as such does not disturb me very much, although naturally I readily agree that reasoning must remain logical. But it does interest me that, if somewhere I have made myself guilty of an error in logic, I be straightened out in this regard, so that I can correct it. In other words, Dr. Kuyper should have brought the error in my logic out into the open. That he did not do. And, therefore, let him take no offense: I do not accept it. I accept absolutely nothing from any persons purely upon their authority. Therefore Dr. Kuyper will be compelled to point out my error. Otherwise I maintain that my entire reasoning is completely logical and no *conzequenze-macherei* (sic). The accusation of rationalism is more serious. Rationalism wants to exalt reason above the Scriptures. May the Lord protect me from that! But again Dr. Kuyper offers no proof. He in no way shows how I in my brochure attack the Holy Scriptures or would want to exalt my human reasoning above its authority. It is probably not asking too much that I expect Dr. Kuyper will still prove this, or at least withdraw this last accusation. (Hoeksema 1996:58.)

Hoeksema went on to say that all he really wanted was for Dr. Kuyper to have entered into the contents of the book and analyzed it, pointing out any inconsistencies in either reasoning or argumentation along the way. He was at a loss to explain Kuyper reticence in this matter. 'There remains but one possibility,' concluded Hoeksema, 'the articles of Dr. Kuyper offer to us the very best that can be offered in defense of a so-called general offer of grace. At least they offer to us the best that Dr. Kuyper can give us' (Hoeksema 1996:60).

While the exchange with Dr. Kuyper is very interesting to read, it gives little insight as to why Kuyper would have charged Hoeksema with rationalism, and/or faulty reasoning, in the first place. Hoeksema may have worn his frustration and disgust on his sleeve as he commented on Kuyper's last two installments, but he did not imagine the distinct lack of proof that attended much of Kuyper's criticism. Additionally, while Hoeksema requested that proof beginning with his comments on Kuyper's first installment, none was forthcoming. Even though Kuyper may not have provided any explanation for his charges, I think some inkling may be gleaned from another controversy several years later on which Hoeksema commented extensively.

6.3 The Clark Case

In the early 1940s the Orthodox Presbyterian Church was rocked by a dispute over the ordination of Dr. Gordon H. Clark by the Presbytery of Philadelphia. In addition to a charge of rationalism, Clark was also criticized for his denial of the 'Free Offer of the Gospel' as well as his questioning of the prevailing view, in the Orthodox Presbyterian Church, of the incomprehensibility of God (see Klooster 1951). Because of the issues involved, Hoeksema followed the course of what came to be known as 'The Clark Case' with intense interest. While I do not intend to enter into every facet of this case, I would like to discuss several aspects that are pertinent to question at hand.

The first point of contention involved the question of the incomprehensibility of God. It was alleged that Clark denied this particular facet of 'Reformed' doctrine. The opposition, led by the faculty of Westminster Theological Seminary under the leadership of Cornelius van Til, asserted that God's knowledge is not just quantitatively different than man's knowledge but qualitatively different in every respect. Desiring to maintain the 'creator/creature' distinction, the opposition claimed that man's knowledge is 'analogical' to God's knowledge, but their use of the word 'analogy' is mitigated by their insistence that man's knowledge and God's knowledge do not correspond at any single point (Robbins 1986:33-34). Clark, on the other hand, understood incomprehensibility to mean that human knowledge, while not as comprehensive as God's knowledge, is still true, as far as it goes. Clark said time and again that God understands the relation of every proposition or truth to every other proposition; his knowledge is infinitely higher than that which is possible to humanity. Hoeksema, whose suspicions were aroused by the dictates of the opposition, did not miss this fact. He commented:

> even now one begins to wonder whether the real question in this controversy is not whether *God*, but whether his *revelation* to us in the Scriptures, is comprehensible, that is, can be logically understood by the mind of man. Dr. Clark's position is that all Scripture is given us that we might understand it, that all of it is adapted to our human mind, so that, even though there be many things in that revelation of God which we cannot *fathom*, there is nothing in it that is *contrary* to human intelligence and logic. And the opponents appear to deny this. ...Either the *logic* of revelation is *our logic*, or there is no revelation. (Hoeksema 1995:8.)

This spirited defense of Clark's position points to Hoeksema's own views on revelation, language and logic. He believed, first and foremost, that there are no contradictions or inconsistencies in the Holy Scriptures whatsoever. Flowing naturally from this premise, Hoeksema also believed that the Scriptures were given for the express purpose of being understood, in their entirety. While there are undoubtedly difficult verses and passages, the problem is not with the language or the logic, in that regard they are perfectly capable of being understood, no, the problem is with humanity's lack of a desire to study and understand.

Clark's opposition used their conception of incomprehensibility to justify the acceptance of 'paradox,' 'contradictions' and/or 'apparent contradictions' in Scripture. In fact they demanded, as evidence of piety, that these contradictions be accepted as part and parcel of the Reformed faith. The leader of the opposition, Cornelius van Til, believed that all knowledge inevitably involved a paradox. 'Now,' declared Van Til, 'since God is not fully comprehensible to us we are bound to come into what seems to be a contradiction in all our knowledge. Our knowledge is analogical and therefore must be paradoxical' (Van Til 1967:44). Writing on this matter, Hoeksema, drawing a comparison between the events at hand and those of 1924, maintained that the whole purpose of this reasoning is:

> to persuade the Orthodox Presbyterian Church to adopt the Arminian doctrine of the Christian Reformed Church as expressed by the Synod of Kalamazoo in 1924, particularly the view that God is gracious to the reprobate, and that the preaching of the Gospel is a well-meaning offer of salvation on the part of God to all men—in other words, the doctrine that God sincerely seeks the salvation of those whom He will not save—this first point is quite important. For this Christian Reformed doctrine, itself a plain contradiction, is based on the contention that there are contradictions in Scripture, and that it is possible for faith to accept contradictions, that is, you understand, contradictions for man's mind, not for God. And in that light one can understand that the complainants must maintain the position: *A proposition does not have the same meaning for God as for man.* (Hoeksema 1995:11.)

Clark found himself afoul of the denominational leaders from Westminster Seminary precisely because he refused to accept the contradictory, and went about developing a solution. Herein, I believe, lies the basis for the charge of 'rationalism.' Hoeksema, comparing the charge against Clark to 'the language of the Christian Reformed leaders since about 1922-1924' (Hoeksema 1995:23), commented that:

> The accusation of rationalism is based on the contention that Dr. Clark tries to solve problems, paradoxes, and contradictions, particularly the problem of the relation between divine sovereignty and human responsibility Anyone who makes an attempt to solve this

problem, who tries to harmonize these two, who claims that this solution is possible—and especially he who is ready to offer his solution of this problem—is, according to the complainants, a rationalist. (Hoeksema 1995:22.)

As to the whole idea of contradictions in Scripture, Hoeksema writes:

> As to "contradictions," I maintain that there are no such things in the revelation of God in Scripture, for the simple reason that the Scripture teaches everywhere that God is One, and that he cannot deny himself. His revelation, too, is one, and does not contradict itself. No, but the complainants would say, there are no real contradictions, but there are *apparent* contradictions in the Bible nevertheless, and them we must leave severely alone, without even making an attempt at solution. We must simply and humbly accept them. I most positively deny all this. By *apparent* contradictions the complainants mean propositions or truth that to the human mind, and according to human logic, are contradictory. I deny that there are such propositions in the Bible. If there were, they could not be the object of our faith. It is nonsense to say that we must humbly believe what is contradictory. This is simply impossible. The complainants themselves cannot believe contradictions. Contradictions are propositions that mutually exclude each other, so that the one denies the truth of the other. ...I challenge anyone to point out that there are propositions in the Bible that violate [the] fundamental principles of logic. I challenge anyone to prove that it is possible for a believer to accept such contradictions, or that it is Christian humility to claim such faith. (Hoeksema 1995:26-27.)

That the type of thinking Hoeksema attacked in the 'Clark Case' was also present in the Christian Reformed Church is evidenced by a bit of autobiographical material from Herman Hanko. Hanko recalled that R. B. Kuiper, Ralph Janssen's brother-in-law and also a professor at Westminster Theological Seminary during the years of the 'Clark Case,' gave a graduation address entitled 'The Balance that is Calvinism' at his graduation from Calvin College in May

1952. 'He was at great pains,' Hanko recalled, 'to demonstrate that the genius of true Calvinism was its ability to hold in proper balance doctrines that were, as far as we could tell, mutually contradictory and, therefore, mutually exclusive of each other. Such doctrines were man's responsibility and God's sovereignty, and the well-meaning offer of the Gospel and God's decree of election and reprobation, etc.' (Hanko 2000:200-201).

6.4 Conclusion

Based on the above evidence I am persuaded that Herman Heoksema was not guilty of the rationalism wherewith he was charged. On the contrary, Hoeksema followed closely in the line of Bavinck and Ten Hoor, from whom he learned so much. His method, I am convinced, was radically biblical, and thus, he was logical to a fault. That he was familiar with philosophy, I could hardly dispute. But, to charge Hoeksema with rationalism because he would not subscribe to contradictions in Scripture, apparent or otherwise, seems to me to be rather odd indeed. More than likely, I suspect, the charge was made because he refused to submit to the current thinking on common grace. Rationalism was just the most convenient brush with which to tar him. Hence, I am convinced that those who would level the charge of 'rationalism' or 'rationalist' are themselves confusing rationalism with rationality.

Part Two

The Three Points Of Common Grace

The Three Points of Common Grace

Acts of Synod, 1924, pages 145-147

Twenty-Sixth Session, Monday Evening, July 7
Article 132

I. De Synode overwogen hebbende dat deel van het *Advies der Commissie in het Algemeen*, hetwelk voorkomt onder punt III onder het hoofd: *Behandeling der Drie Punten*, komt tot de volgende conclusies:

A. Aangaande het eerste punt, rakende *de gunstige gezindheid Gods jegens de menschheid in het algemeen, en niet alleen jegens de uitverkorenen*, spreekt de Synode uit dat volgens Schrift en Confessie het vaststaat, dat er, behalve de zaligmakende genade Gods bewezen alleen aan de uitverkorenen ten eeuwigen leven, ook een zekere gunst of genade Gods is, die Hij betoont aan Zijn schepselen in het algemeen. Dit blijkt uit de aangehaalde Schriftuurplaatsen en uit de Dordtsche Leerregels II, 5, en III en IV, 8 en 9, waar gehandeld wordt van de algemeene aanbieding des Evangelies; terwijl het uit de aangehaalde uitspraken van Geref. Schrijvers uit den bloeitijd der Geref. theologie bovendien blijkt, dat onze Gereformeerde vaderen van oudsher dit gevoelen hebben voorgestaan.

B. Aangaande het tweede punt, rakende *de beteugeling der zonde in het leven van den enkelen mensch, en in de samenleving*, verklaart de Synode dat er volgens Schrift en Confessie zulk eene beteugeling der zonde is. Dit blijkt uit de aangehaalde Schriftuurplaatsen en uit de Nederlandsche Geloofsbelijdenis, Art. 13 en 36, waar geleerd wordt dat God door de algemeene werkingen Zijns Geestes, zonder het hart te vernieuwen, de zonde in haar onverhinderd uitbreken beteugelt, waardoor de menschelijke samenleving mogelijk is gebleven; terwijl het uit de aangehaalde uitspraken van Geref. schrijvers uit den bloeitijd der Geref. theologie bovendien blijkt, dat onze Gereformeerde vaderen van oudsher dit gevoelen hebben voorgestaan.

C. Aangaande het derde punt, rakende *het doen van zoogenaamde burgerlijke gerechtigheid door de onwedergeborenen*, verklaart de Synode dat volgens Schrift en Confessie onwedergeborenen, hoewel onbekwaam tot eenig zaligmakend goed (Dordsche Leerregels, III, IV, 3), zulk burgerlijk goed kunnen doen. Dit blijkt uit de aangehaalde Schriftuurplaatsen, en uit de Dordtsche Leerregels, III en IV, 4, en de Nederlandsche Geloofsbelijdenis, Art. 36, waar geleerd wordt, dat God zonder het hart te vernieuwen zoodanigen invloed op den mensch oefent, dat deze in staat gesteld wordt burgerlijk goed te doen; terwijl het uit de aangehaalde uitspraken der Gereformeerde schrijvers uit den bloeitijd der Geref. theologie bovendien blijkt, dat onze Gereformeerde vaderen van oudsher dit gevoelen hebben voorgestaan.

The English translation of the Three Points was made by Herman Hoeksema and printed in *A Triple Breach in the Foundation of Reformed Truth: A Critical Treatise on the "Three Points"*, adopted by the Synod of the Christian Reformed Churches in 1924, pages 13, 20, 22 and 23

I. Synod, having considered that part of the Advice of the Committee in General, which is found under point III under the heading: Consideration of the Three Points, comes to the following conclusions:

A. Relative to the first point, which concerns the question of *a favorable attitude of God towards humanity in general*, and not only towards the elect, synod declares it to be established according to the Scripture and the Confessions, that, apart from the saving grace of God shown only to those that are elect unto eternal life, there is also a certain favor or grace of God which He shows to His creatures in general. This is evident from the Scriptural passages quoted and from the Canons of Dordrecht, II, 5 and III, IV, 8 and 9, which deal with the general offer of the Gospel, while it also appears from the citations made from Reformed writers of the most flourishing period of Reformed Theology that our Reformed fathers from the past favored this view.

B. Relative to the second point, which is concerned with *the restraint of sin in the life of the individual and in the community*, the synod declares that there is such a restraint of sin according to Scripture and the Confessions. This is evident from the citations from Scripture and the Netherlands Confession. Articles 13, 36 which teach that God, by the general operation of the Spirit, without renewing the heart of man, restrains the unimpeded breaking out of sin, by which human life in society remained possible; while it is also evident from the quotations from Reformed writers of the most flourishing period of Reformed theology, that from ancient times our Reformed fathers were of the same opinion.

C. Relative to the third point which is concerned with the question of *civil righteousness as performed by the unregenerate*, synod declares that, according to Scripture and the Confessions, the unregenerate, though incapable of doing saving good, can do civil good. This is evident from the quotations from Scripture and from the Canons of Dordrecht, III, IV, 4, and the Netherlands Confession Art. 36, which teach that God without renewing the heart so influences man, that he is able to perform civil good; while it also appears from the citations from Reformed writers of the most flourishing period of Reformed Theology, that our Reformed Fathers from ancient times were of the same opinion.

Chapter 7

Point One: The Favor of God to the Unregenerate

Relative to the first point, which concerns the question of *a favorable attitude of God towards humanity in general*, and not only towards the elect, synod declares it to be established according to the Scripture and the Confessions, that, apart from the saving grace of God shown only to those that are elect unto eternal life, there is also a certain favor or grace of God which He shows to His creatures in general. This is evident from the Scriptural passages quoted and from the Canons of Dordrecht, II, 5 and III, IV, 8 and 9, which deal with the general offer of the Gospel, while it also appears from the citations made from Reformed writers of the most flourishing period of Reformed Theology that our Reformed fathers from the past favored this view.

'Let us consider, first of all,' writes Herman Hoeksema, 'the chief proposition of the first point. It is, evidently: there is a grace of God over His creatures in general' (Hoeksema 1942:14). Writing specifically on the well-meant offer of the Gospel as contained in the writings of Herman Hoeksema and Klaas Schilder, A. C. de Jong agrees that this point of common grace revolves around the favorable attitude of God towards all (De Jong 1954:11). This all, or better, humanity in general, would encompass both those who have been elect of God from before the foundation of the world and those whom we might also classify as reprobate. Or, as De Jong puts it, the debate concerns 'the attitude or disposition of the God of the Divine Decree towards those whom he decreed to pass by with the redemptively efficacious operations of divine favor' (De Jong 1954:11). Both Hoeksema and De Jong agree that calling this attitude or disposition of God 'favorable' or 'gracious' is the heart of the rub. For De Jong, unless one can consider the attitude of God towards all those who hear the Gospel as one of favor and grace then preaching, among other things, will suffer greatly (De Jong 1954:101-102). Contrariwise, Hoeksema's position, as De Jong readily admits, is that God is 'never favorably disposed towards those human beings whom he decreed to pretermit and condemn'

(De Jong 1954: 11). Hence, while De Jong believes that grace is general both in its scope and application, for Hoeksema grace is, always and everywhere, strictly particular. But what exactly do these men mean by 'grace'?

7.1 Grace

'To arrive at an accurate conception of the operation of the will of God,' insists Hoeksema, 'we cannot proceed from the meaning of the word grace in our everyday usage of the term, nor even from its usage in Holy Scripture' (Danhof & Hoeksema [1923] 2003:164). Further, we must study all the terms with great care so as not to create a concept of our own choosing; giving to God a quality as it exists in the creature, an anthropomorphism if you will. Rather, 'we must work theologically. God Himself determines the character of His will, grace, love, hate, wrath, and so forth' (Danhof & Hoeksema [1923] 2003:164). But, how is this to be done? First, we must examine the Biblical record in detail for all occurrences of the word. 'But this is by no means sufficient to reach an accurate concept of the grace of God,' Hoeksema warns. 'Indeed, we are not dealing with the use of the *word* grace, but with the *idea* of grace—grace as it is in God' (Danhof & Hoeksema [1923] 2003:165). After searching the Scriptures thoroughly, our findings must, therefore, be compared with other translations of the Scriptures, the Confessions of the church, liturgical forms and the works of other theologians as well as the many related words (Danhof & Hoeksema [1923] 2003:165). 'This comparative study,' Hoeksema concludes, 'will enable us to see that the same concrete idea is expressed by all these words, and many others, even though it is true that each of these words, some with interchangeable meanings, usually shows us the rich grace of God from a particular viewpoint and in a special relationship' (Danhof & Hoeksema [1923] 2003:165-166). Even here, we are still not finished. Delving deeper, Hoeksema concludes:

> All of this must be elucidated and interpreted in connection with God's counsel and eternal purpose. We are dealing here with what God wills. That will cannot be explained by something *apart from* God. The main reason for God's will must be sought *in God Himself*. God's will reveals itself in connection with man's sin. That sin did

not take God by surprise, did not occur in creation apart from His counsel and will. Thus, we are concerned with the study of God's will of electing grace and reprobating wrath as works which, in the end, must be ascribed to God. God's grace and disfavor are not determined by one or another attribute in God, but by God Himself—or if we may express ourselves in this manner—by the fullness of God. We must even diligently guard ourselves against separating the attributes of God. God attributes are in a certain sense to be distinguished, but are not essentially different from the essence of God, neither individually nor collectively. We are dealing with God Himself: God's grace and disfavor, His love and His hatred. Election and reprobation are His—God's. He finds reasons in Himself for His will. This is true whether we understand it or not, whether we will it or not. (Danhof & Hoeksema [1923] 2003:166.)

Hence, in defining grace, Hoeksema starts specifically with God and 'as an attribute of God, grace is that divine virtue according to which God is the perfection of all beauty and loveliness, and contemplates Himself as such with infinite delight' (Hoeksema 1966:112). Expounding further on the idea of grace as an attribute of God, Hoeksema writes:

> Now Scripture emphasizes everywhere that God is gracious. He is the God of all grace, the all-gracious God. He is gracious in Himself, apart from any relation to the creature. For also here we must remember that God is the independent, the Self-existent, the Self-sufficient One. He is not in need of the creature. He does not become richer through the existence of the creature. In and through the creature He only reveals Himself and glorifies Himself in His riches, that also the creature may glorify Him. And thus all the virtues of God are in Him independently and absolutely. This also applies to the virtue of grace. God is eternally a God of all grace. He is grace. Graciousness is an attribute, or perfection, of His very Being. Grace belongs to God's holy name. ...In and of Himself God is gracious. And here we must remember the fundamental meaning of the word "grace." It is the virtue of being

pleasant and attractive, beautiful and graceful, and that too, with a beauty that is rooted in and based on ethical perfection. In this sense one can readily understand that God is gracious. For He is the Holy One. He is the implication of all goodness, of all ethical perfections. Goodness is His very Being. He is a light, and there is no darkness in Him at all. He is righteousness, justice, and truth, peace, and love, and life. He is the only Good. For that reason God is also infinitely beautiful, charming, pleasant, and attractive. Even as the ethically corrupt is repulsive and ugly, so the ethically perfect is truly beautiful and pleasant. In the absolute sense of the word, therefore, grace in God is the beauty of His infinite perfections, the charm of His divine goodness. (Hoeksema 1966:111.)

Following from his conception of grace as first and foremost an attribute of God, Hoeksema then seeks to draw out the implications for 'the believer;' he writes: 'Objectively, then, the word "grace" denotes beauty or gracefulness; subjectively, it denotes a gracious disposition or favorable attitude towards someone' (Hoeksema 1966:109). Still, Hoeksema is quick to point out that this attitude of graciousness or undeserved favor is never separated from God's sovereignty and freedom (Hoeksema 1966:109). In fact, it is primarily because of God's sovereignty and freedom, i.e. in election, that grace is shown to the creature at all. 'Grace, then, in this sense,' Hoeksema further elaborates, 'is such a favorable disposition or friendly attitude of God as is revealed even to those that are wholly undeserving in themselves, yea, have wholly forfeited His kindness and favor, and are worthy of wrath and damnation' (Hoeksema 1966:109). On the same page Hoeksema is quick to contrast grace with works.

It is interesting to note that, of all the proponents of common grace, William Masselink is only one of a handful that attempt to ground a particular view of common grace in God. David Engelsma of the Protestant Reformed Churches believes that if anyone is going to attempt a defense of common grace, a firm grounding is an absolute necessity. In fact, Engelsma contends, 'many defenders of common grace are woefully weak here. They make much of a common grace of God in history that has no source in God's eternal plan and no goal in God's everlasting purpose' (Engelsma 2003:75). While Masselink may seek his ground elsewhere, within the 'ontological trinity' (Masselink 1953:190) to be exact, the fact that he seeks to ground his doctrine in God rather than in a simple historical setting is, by Engelsma's criterion, surely commendable. On his decision to ground his doctrine in the very being of God, Masselink writes:

> The ontological trinity as it expresses itself in God's ontological qualities is the source of all common grace, and to understand this rightly we must have correct views of *Divine qualities*. We deem the designation qualities to be more correct than other terms used such as, attributes, perfections, virtues, and the like; because the term quality always expresses a definite relationship to God's essence or being. (Masselink 1953:190.)

Other than the reference to common grace, Hoeksema would agree wholeheartedly with the above. Building on his choice of the word 'quality,' Masselink further contends that *'a quality of God is a relationship to His essence or being*. Strictly speaking there is only one quality in God identical with His being, but there is a multiplicity of qualities in connection with God's various relationships' (Masselink 1953:190). That is to say, while we may observe only one quality within the Godhead, this one quality separates, as through a prism, into a plethora of different relational qualities. Masselink says as much. 'On the one hand,' he writes, 'we maintain that there is in God strictly speaking only one quality identified with His essence; and on the other hand there exists a multiplicity of qualities in connection with God's various relationships' (Masselink 1953:191). Masselink further believes that the one observable quality within the ontological Trinity is love (Masselink 1953191). Yet, despite his assertion of being able to discover the concept of common grace in the relationship of love observable between the persons of the Godhead, i.e., within the ontological Trinity, Masselink actually accomplishes no such thing. In fact, he merely asserts that the quality of love observable within the ontological Trinity translates into common grace for the creature. From my reading of Masselink, I suspect he conceives of common grace as existing in a germinal, embryonic or typological form in this quality of love as it occurs within the ontological trinity. If my assessment is correct, common grace is really nothing more than the development in history of that which only exists in a potential form in God. It would have been helpful and allayed much speculation had Masselink worked out his theory in more detail, with considerably more to substantiate his position.

7.2 Grace and the Covenant

For Hoeksema, God's attitude of favor, kindness, and grace could only be found within the covenant of grace. It is not discussed outside of the covenant of grace, which is why he can turn around and describe the covenant, as we have seen in the previous sections, as the bond of friendship and love between God and His elect. It is also why, for Hoeksema, there is no covenant of works. When you speak of the covenant you are speaking of grace not law. This covenant, contra the views of Klaas Schilder and Wilhelm Heyns, was not a conditional covenant. It was not made with each individual within the church head for head. The covenant God made was with Christ and with the elect as they are in Christ. That is to say, the covenant was made with Christ and by implication with those who are the elect. This covenantal relationship God had within Himself from all eternity, which is why Hoeksema stresses grace as an attribute of God. And it is this same inter-Trinitarian relationship between the members of the Godhead that was expanded to include a body of believers, those whom He has chosen from before the foundation of the world (Ephesians 2) and upon whom He could bestow grace, this attitude of favor and love, because of what Christ has done. Hence, Christ is the focal point, the matrix if you will, by which this favor and love come through God to the elect, i.e. those whom He has chosen.

Since Grace is first and foremost an attribute of God, and since it is found as an integral part of the inter-Trinitarian relationship, and since believers become partakers of this grace as it is in God, for Hoeksema, dividing up or distinguishing grace into various kinds of grace becomes an almost futile exercise. In this regard Methodist Episcopal theologian Charles Buck writes that 'there have been many distinctions of grace; but as they are of too frivolous a nature, and are now obsolete, they need not a place here' (Buck 1826:202). Buck is not exaggerating when he states that there are many other distinctions of grace. Richard Muller, a historical theologian of some note most recently associated with Calvin Theological Seminary, in his *Dictionary of Latin and Greek Theological Terms* for example, lists eighteen different types of grace, with what seems to be multiple sub-categories for each (Muller 1985:129-133). Taking what amounts to a more conservative approach to grace, Ferdinand Deist of the University of South Africa lists only seventeen different varieties (Deist 1992:107-108). For Hoeksema, grace is grace just as God is God and seeking to distinguish grace into multiple sub-categories is rather pointless. On this matter Hoeksema writes:

> Thus it is to be explained that not only all unbelievers, but also a great mass of Christians, do not want the doctrine of God's free grace. That God's grace is made dependent upon sinful man is a common error. Men are not opposed to God's grace if the disposal of it pleases man. Naturally, if this latter were true, man would, by grace, triumph over God. Therefore, men try to change God's grace into a work of man. They make all kinds of distinctions and speak especially of conditions. They speak of baptismal grace, preparatory grace, helping grace, covenant grace, and lastly now also of a common grace that our human race enjoys, and whereby in the so-called sphere of natural life, men are enabled to live a life that is pleasing to God, although only particular grace is saving. Mostly they speak of an objective grace, of which the subjective application is dependent upon sinful man. All these distinctions have actually no other purpose than to maintain something in the sinner over against God—a certain capability for natural or spiritual good, a certain claim upon something in God, even though that be nothing more than God's compassion. (Danhof & Hoeksema [1923] 2003:172-173.)

Hoeksema goes on to say that this type of thinking is nothing more than a vain and wicked attempt, and, what is more, an impossibility. (Danhof & Hoeksema [1923] 2003:173).

In Hoeksema's mind the covenant of grace is one and simply cannot be divided up. Maybe this is why Hoeksema also never spoke of various covenants. To him there is one covenant and that is the covenant controlled by sovereign, irresistible grace. Hence, he repudiated entirely the traditional notion, espoused by many Reformed theologians, of a covenant of works (Hoeksema 1966:217-221). In fact Hoeksema does not speak of the covenant apart from grace and he does not conceive of grace outside of the covenant. They go together. Therefore, neither is a means to an end. As Hoeksema writes of God's covenant with Adam: 'this covenant relation is not to be conceived as something incidental, as a means to an end, as a relation that was established by way of an agreement, but as a fundamental relationship in which Adam stood to God by virtue of his creation. It is not essentially an agreement, but a relation of living fellowship and friendship' (Hoeksema 1966:222). The covenant of grace is, therefore, the end, in and of itself. While Hoeksema certainly is not the only Reformed theologian to speak of grace, he is, at least to my knowledge, the only one to speak solely of particular grace and that within the context of the covenant. There are others who speak of grace within the covenant, but then they speak of grace also in a general manner as well. These general ways include but are not exclusive to sunshine and rain, etc. Those who propound the idea of common grace also use these categories. In this regard, most theologians do speak of grace in ways that are not part of the covenant of grace. By contrast, speaking of grace solely within the context of the covenant, and speaking of grace as particular, seems to me to be exclusive to Hoeksema. Many who speak of the covenant apart from grace also speak of a covenant of works. As already mentioned, Hoeksema would have none of this either, since the covenant is the ground of grace, not of works. On the grounding of grace in the covenant Hoeksema explains:

> The Reformed usually designate God's glory as the purpose of this will. Formerly we have sought to define this more accurately by speaking of covenant fellowship or friendship. The concept of God's glory is very abstract and has no content for our thinking. This becomes somewhat different when we consider that God is the fully Blessed One in Himself. He is fully blessed as one who lives His life of love as the triune, covenant God. God is the God of the covenant. He is that not only according to the counsel of His will in relation to the creature, but He is that, first of all, in Himself, by virtue of His nature. The family life of God is a covenant of friendship between Father, Son, and Holy Spirit. Indeed, God is one in essence, three in persons. The three persons all possess alike the

same divine essence. In their individual independency they are also alike. But in their individual, personal attributes they are different. Their oneness of essence gives them harmony; the equality of persons requires agreement, while the possibility for most intimate fellowship and cooperation lies in the diversity of their individual personal attributes. Oneness and diversity give harmony. The love-life of God, welling up from the unsearchable depths of His being, willed by the Father, Son, and Holy Spirit, and streaming forth in the many forms of the individual attributes, reveals in a glorious, variegated display the full riches of the eternal friendship of the Trinity. That divine love-life in God has become, as we see it, the basis for the fellowship and covenant relationship between the Creator and the creature, and between the creatures mutually. That covenant idea is willed by God. He seeks a reflection of His life of friendship in the creature. That is not a cold concept. Nor is there any evidence of insensibility or hardness in it. It is truly an essentially free and sovereign act of God's will. Its essential character is glorious. The life of love and friendship in the family of God is divinely good and beautiful. To cause His creature to share in it is good and beautiful. This sovereign will of the God of the covenant is the will to reveal and glorify that which is divinely good and glorious. The life and friendship of the Trinity is thus completely enveloped in the glow of love and grace. (Danhof & Hoeksema [1923] 2003:166-167).

7.3 Conditional versus Unconditional

A. C. de Jong, in the section of his thesis evaluating Hoeksema's views on the 'the gospel offer and the sinner's response' (De Jong 1954:73), turns immediately to the concept of the covenant. While he quotes Bavinck on the importance of the covenant for religion, his real concern is with the covenant concepts of Professor William Heyns as they relate to Hoeksema. After giving a bit of history detailing the relationship of Professor Heyns to Hoeksema, De Jong contends that Hoeksema's covenant views were solely the result of a backlash against, or 'sharp reaction to,' the theories espoused by Professor Heyns (De Jong 1954:73). De Jong and Hoeksema are both agreed that Professor Heyns did have considerable influence as a professor and that as a result his views on the covenant are 'generally accepted by ministers in the Christian Reformed Church' (De Jong 1954:73). They are also agreed that 'Hoeksema saw shades of Heyns in the covenantal views of many Liberated [i.e., followers of Klaas Schilder in the Netherlands] Dutch immigrants who sought affiliation with the Protestant Reformed Church' (De Jong 1954:73; Hoeksema 1969:275-276; Faber 1996:47).

Having taught for many years at what eventually became Calvin Theological Seminary, Professor William Heyns had a rather large sphere of influence. As a theologian Professor Heyns focused a good portion of his energies both in research and writing on the idea of the 'covenant.' He described the Covenant of Grace as: 'that special institution for the salvation of man in which the Triune God binds Himself with a covenant and an oath to the believers and their seed, to be their God: their Father, their Redeemer, and their Sanctifier, and binds them to Himself to be His own and to serve Him, thus insuring their salvation, unless they break the Covenant by unbelief and disobedience, Gen. 17:7, Heb. 3:18, 19' (Heyns 1926:125). Hence, for Heyns, the essence of Covenant of Grace is 'the promise of salvation in the form of a covenant' (Heyns 1926:125). Elsewhere, in his discussion of the Covenant of Works, Heyns brings the inherent conditionality in his conception of both covenants into sharper focus. Heyns wrote: 'Even in the Covenant of Works the condition of obedience was not a condition for being taken into the Covenant, but for keeping the Covenant and for gaining its reward. In the same way faith and obedience are conditions for keeping the Covenant of Grace and for inheriting the promise, Heb. 6:15, whereas unbelief and disobedience make the Covenant member a Covenant breaker, who shall not enter in: Heb. 3:18-19' (Heyns 1926:131). Professor Jelle Faber of the Canadian Reformed Church, in a rather lengthy article on *William Heyns as Covenant Theologian*, is at great pains to show how 'Heyns was afraid of Arminianism' (Faber 1997:303). For this reason, writes Faber, 'when he preferred to call faith and obedience not conditions but obligations of the covenant, Heyns showed how perceptive he was to the danger of Arminianism' (Faber 1997:303). For all Faber's insistence on the importance of Heyns's use of the word 'obligation' instead of 'condition' when speaking of the covenant, it seems rather that Professor Heyns perceived no such gravity in the distinction. There is only one place that he uses both terms together, and he does express a preference for 'obligation.' In speaking of the covenant as 'unconditional,' Heyns writes that 'the condition of obedience was not a condition for being taken into the Covenant, but for keeping the Covenant and for gaining its reward' (Heyns 1926:131). While Heyns is adamant that there is no 'condition' for getting into the covenant, there is most certainly one or more conditions—here he mentions two: faith and obedience (Heyns 1926:131)—for remaining in it. Only near the end of his exposition does he remark: 'it might be preferable to call faith and obedience not conditions but obligations of the covenant' (Heyns 1926:131). It seems more likely that Heyns is just pondering aloud the usage of the two words rather than prescribing hard and fast rules for their usage.

On the 'front end' of the covenant relationship, if you will, De Jong delineates an objective-subjective scheme in Heyns's covenant thinking. 'Heyns operated theologically with this objective-pole (God), subjective-pole (man) schematism' writes De Jong. 'On the one hand God *gives, offers, presents, invites* – this is the objective pole. On the other hand man must accept' (De Jong 1954:76). While Heyns does admit that man is indeed dead in trespasses and sins, even so he can still insist that the Gospel is an offer that humanity must choose to accept (De Jong 1954:76-77).

One possible reason for this insistence on the part of Professor Heyns is his strong belief that the covenant is in no way controlled by eternal election (Faber 1996:37). Contrary to Herman Bavinck, who held that 'when the covenant of grace is separated from election, it ceases to be a covenant of grace and becomes again a covenant of works' (Bavinck 1956:272), Heyns, as well as others of the 'American Secession Theologians' (Faber 1996:37), wanted no relation between the covenant of grace and election whatsoever. Hoeksema, following Bavinck, insisted that the covenant of grace was for the elect alone, primarily because it was God who both established and maintained His covenant as a bond of friendship and love with His own (Hoeksema 1966:323-325). This being the case, there could indeed be, for Hoeksema, no talk of conditions for entry into the covenant, and this holds true for the 'back end' of the covenant as well. Heyns, however, readily admitted, as quoted above, that it was up to the believers to keep the covenant, or to keep themselves in the covenant. Obedience here was the key; without it one was a covenant breaker. According to Michael Eaton, in his evaluation the importance of good works in both Arminianism and Calvinism and their relation to salvation, 'In some respects these two theologies are similar. Both assume that salvation and good works are tied together. In one case salvation requires good works; in the other salvation inexorably and irresistibly produces good works. In both theologies salvation and good works stand and fall together' (Eaton 1995:38). For Heyns, unless good works were present, in some unspecified amount, a believer could forfeit the covenant. Maybe this is why Bavinck was so insistent that if one separates the Covenant of Grace from election one is left with a covenant of works once again. This certainly seems to be true in the case of Professor Heyns's view of the 'unconditional' covenant.

7.4 Professor Heyns's Judgment

Professor Heyns was also insistent that unless one accepts both aspects of his covenant scheme, one is guilty of rationalism. He wrote: 'If we do not wish to accept both, we are guilty of a rationalism which either rejects predestination as do the Arminians, or rejects that fact that the free offer of grace is well-meant and general as does ultraorthodoxy. The error may lead both parties in opposite directions, but it is essentially the same error; in both instances it is Rationalism which places its own judgment above the Scriptures' (Heyns 1926:199). Nowhere, at least that I am aware of, does Hoeksema comment specifically on this passage from Heyns. But, knowing Hoeksema, it would undoubtedly have brought a smile to his face.

In his running commentary on the 'Clark Case,' which unfolded in the Orthodox Presbyterian Church in the early 1940s, Hoeksema analyzes a dilemma which very closely resembles the one posed by Professor Heyns above. Hoeksema writes at some length concerning the 'well-meant' or 'general offer of the Gospel' in this controversy:

Now, you might object as also Dr. Clark does, that this involves a direct contradiction: God sincerely seeks the salvation of those whom He has from eternity determined not to save. Or: God would have that sinner live whom He does not quicken. Or: God would have the sinner, whom He does not give faith, to accept the Gospel. Or: God would have that sinner come to Christ whom He does not draw and who cannot come. You might object that this is not rational. But this objection would be of no avail to persuade the complainants of their error. They admit that this is irrational. But they do not want to be rational on this point. In fact, if you should insist on being rational in this respect, they would call you a "rationalist," and at once proceed to seek your expulsion from the church as a dangerous heretic. The whole *Complaint* against Dr. Clark is really concentrated in and based on this one alleged error of his: he claims that the Word of God and the Christian faith are not irrational. According to the complainants, to be reasonable is to be a rationalist. They write that the trouble with Dr. Clark is that "his rationalism does not permit him to let the two stand unreconciled alongside each other. Rather than do that he would modify the Gospel in the interest of reprobation. [This, you understand, is a slanderous remark.—H.H.] Otherwise expressed, he makes the same error as does the Arminian, although he moves in the opposite direction. The Arminian cannot harmonize divine reprobation with the sincere divine offer of salvation to all who hear; hence, he rejects the former. Neither can Dr. Clark harmonize the two, and so he detracts from the latter. Rationalism accounts for both errors". To accuse the complainants of irrationalism is, therefore, of no avail as far as they are concerned. They openly admit—they are even boasting of—their irrational position. To be irrational is, according to them, the glory of a humble, Christian faith. …even though the complainants themselves insist on being irrational, we will have to deal with them according to the rules of logic. If they refuse to be treated rationally, they really forfeit the right to present a complaint to any assembly of normal Christians. And treating them as rational human beings, we must insist that they do not and cannot possibly accept the proposition: God sincerely seeks the salvation of those whom he has sovereignly from eternity determined to be damned. In other words: I know that they claim to believe this, but I deny their claim; I do not accept it. Hence, I must try to rationalize their position for them. How can any man, with a show of rationality, insist that God sincerely seeks the salvation of the reprobate? Only when they define reprobation as that eternal act of God according to which He determined to damn all those whom he eternally foresaw as rejecting the Gospel [A. C. De Jong holds a very similar position (De Jong 1954:106)—PB]. In other words, I insist that the position of the complainants, as soon as you reject their claim to irrationalism, is purely Arminian. And their irrationalism is only an attempt to camouflage their real position. (Hoeksema 1995: 36-38.)

So then by extrapolation, according to Hoeksema, the choice which Professor Heyns advances above is not between Arminianism and ultraorthodoxy, but rather between two positions both of which are Arminian. It is interesting to note at this juncture that Hoeksema was not alone in this thinking. Richard Muller, describing the views of the seventeenth-century Dutch Reformed theologian Leonard Riissen, put it thus:

The "neo-Pelagian" Arminians, however, understand the antecedent will of God as prior to the acts of the creature; and the consequent will they rest not on this voluntas antecedens, but on the will of the creature that precedes it in time. God, thus, antecedently wills salvation of all people and consequently wills salvation only for those who have chosen to believe. God from eternity wills the salvation of Judas, while at the same time knowing that Judas will disbelieve, and on the basis of that knowledge, permits Judas to remain in his infidelity and perish. Who, questions Riissen, would be so foolish as to attribute such wills to God? According to this doctrine God genuinely wills that which he knows will never happen, indeed, what he wills not to bring about. (Muller 1995:273-274.)

Still expositing Riissen, Muller does not stop here. In fact, he takes the argument right back into the heart of Heyns's kind of covenant view. He writes: 'In this view, the covenant of God with human beings depends entirely on the human will and, indeed, only those who have chosen God through faith and repentance will be chosen or elected by God' (Muller 1995:274). Hoeksema, in his volume entitled *Believers and Their Seed*, also concludes that Heyns's covenant view is nothing more than 'Arminianism injected into the Covenant' and 'that the presentation of Prof, Heyns is nothing else than the old Pelagian error applied to the covenant' (Hoeksema 1971:20).

There is one more matter, however, to which Professor Heyns alludes that needs further investigation. The word 'ultraorthodoxy' is used by the Professor to set up the horns of the dilemma which, in turn, gives his argument a sense of urgency. This term, however, is nowhere defined by Professor Heyns, leaving the reader to attach to the word whatever mental or emotional connotations come to mind. I bring this up because De Jong equates Hoeksema's views with this term 'ultraorthodoxy' (De Jong 1954:77). In fact, he does so without any stated rationale whatsoever. Maybe he feels he does not need any, as if it has all been done before. Another word with which Hoeksema has been tarred and which continues to plague the Protestant Reformed Churches to this day is 'hyper-Calvinism.' In a sense, these two terms could almost be used interchangeably. One may have even been the forerunner of the other. Both terms, by their use of the prefixes 'ultra' and 'hyper,' are meant to convey a sense of the extreme. If the prefixes are removed, one is simply left with 'Calvinism' and 'orthodoxy.' Hence, the prefixes are meant to take the words beyond 'Calvinism' or 'orthodoxy.' Since 'ultraorthodoxy' is left undefined, I feel that it is used by Professor Heyns more for its emotional effect than to further clarify a theological position. However, since I am not aware of anywhere else Professor Heyns uses the term 'ultraorthodoxy' in alluding to Hoeksema's position, I want rather to take a closer look at its relative 'hyper-Calvinism,' which I will do shortly in connection with the call of the Gospel.

7.5 De Jong's Criticisms

There is one paragraph in DeJong's discussion to which I would like to turn briefly because it expresses clearly the characteristics of the discussion. In his summary of the views of Herman Hoeksema and William Heyns with respect to the covenant and common grace, De Jong concludes:

We believe that Hoeksema's theological reflections concerning God's covenant with man and concerning common grace are tragically lucid examples of theological reflection in reaction. In Hoeksema's reaction against what he calls "Heynsian common grace," and "Kuyperian common grace," he theologizes so logically and speculatively that he fails to do full justice to various facets of Biblical truth. In fact his reaction to Heyns and Kuyper is so extreme that he arrives at a practical repudiation of some of the very truths he confesses. Because he is essentially a theologian in reaction he becomes speculative. His speculations are logically correct but the very formal correctness of his syllogistic reasoning silences the concrete revelation of Scripture. (De Jong 1954:79.)

This paragraph speaks volumes, but not about Hoeksema. In my opinion, this summary is rather a very carefully constructed assault on someone who is simply disliked. I do not mean to be caustic or defensive in my critique, but this is how this paragraph appears to me. Through the use of allusion, innuendo and loaded words, aspersion is cast on one with whom no substantive fault can be found, at least none is stated. In the first sentence: 'Hoeksema's theological reflections ... are tragically lucid examples of theological reflection in reaction.' Here the word 'tragically' is a weasel word. It appears to be used simply to prejudice the reader against Hoeksema's theological reflections, nothing more. If we simply eliminate it we are left with: 'Hoeksema's theological reflections ... are lucid examples of theological reflection in reaction.' That is to say, Hoeksema's theological reflections are clear examples of a theological position, or positions, set against a position or positions with which he disagrees. In other words, his analysis is clearly understandable. Additionally, in the next sentence: 'In Hoeksema's reaction ... he theologizes so logically and speculatively that he fails to do justice to various facets of Biblical truth.' I have already dealt at some length with Hoeksema's opinions on the use of logic, or being reasonable in the thinking process. The only alternative really would be to be unreasonable or illogical in the thinking process, but then communication, for all intents and purposes, would effectively cease. But what about the word 'speculatively'? De Jong gives no examples of Hoeksema's alleged speculations, but in the last sentence of the quotation he admits that Hoeksema's 'speculations are logically correct.' I guess, given De Jong's definitions, we could just substitute 'logically correct' for 'speculatively' in the second sentence. In which case the second sentence would then read: 'In Hoeksema's reaction ... he theologizes so logically and correctly that he fails to do justice to the various facets of Biblical truth.' Does De Jong really mean to pit Biblical truth against logic? The final sentence seems to indicate that this is indeed the case. Here, De Jong seems to say that logical thinking 'silences the concrete revelation of Scripture.' Hoeksema's response to De Jong's line of reasoning would undoubtedly be that 'either the *logic* of revelation is *our* logic, or there is no revelation' (Hoeksema 1995: 8).

De Jong, it seems, is not the only one who does theology in this manner. In an article revisiting the history and theology of the of the First Point of Common Grace issued by the Synod of 1924, Raymond Blacketer of the Canadian Reformed Church takes Anthony Hoekema of Calvin Seminary to task for similar reasons. Blacketer writes:

> Hoekema asserts that there are two rationalistic solutions that must be avoided: the Arminian proposal of universal, sufficient grace, and the ostensibly hyper-Calvinist contention that the call does not imply God's desire to save the reprobate. We must continue to hold both election and the well-meant offer, "even though we cannot reconcile these two teachings with our finite minds." We cannot "lock God up in the prison of human logic." Hoekema appeals to what he calls the "Scriptural paradox," by which he means that we must believe that apparently incompatible theological statements are in fact somehow resolved in the mind of God. Hoekema appeals to Calvin to justify this method—but not to Calvin himself. He cites Edward Dowey's neo-orthodox interpretation of Calvin as a dialectical theologian, a Barthian before Barth. On this basis, Hoekema contends that Calvin "was willing to combine doctrines which were clear in themselves but logically incompatible with each other, since he found them both in the Bible." But his interpretation of Calvin's methodology is wholly untenable; it cannot be squared with the way Calvin actually operates, particularly in his theological treatises. Calvin argues with opponents by pointing out the logical inconsistencies in their arguments, and demonstrating *both* the biblical faithfulness *and* the logical coherence of his own. Our theological concern, Hoekema concludes,

"must not be to build a rationally coherent system, but to be faithful to all the teachings of the Bible." This sentiment, however, is at odds with the Reformation and pre-Reformation conviction that God's revelation is not only reasonable, but accessible to reason, and capable of a coherent systemization. The fact that not everything is revealed to us, and that our theology is limited by our human capacities, does not give us permission to advance an incoherent system of theology. We may not set faith over against logic or confession over against understanding. (Blacketer 2000:50-51.)

Blacketer, however, is not finished. It has been said that 'every theology stands or falls as a hermeneutic and every hermeneutic stands or falls as a theology' (Eaton 1995:32), and this is where Blacketer now brings the brunt of his criticism to bear. He takes his criticism of the 'incoherent,' as it is seen in the system of theology, back to what he believes is a faulty methodology, undoubtedly believing that the method and its product stand or fall together. Picking up where he left off, it is the pitting of 'logic against faith' and 'the confession against understanding' that is characteristic De Jong's thesis on the well-meant offer as well. Blacketer concludes:

> This is the problem in De Jong's *Well-Meant Offer*. De Jong, following Berkouwer, employs an existentialistic methodology of correlation that is hostile to the concept of a coherent theological system. Thus he can argue that Calvin speaks "from the viewpoint of faith and not in terms of logical objectivity" (p. 112). Divine sovereignty and human responsibility "is confessed and not explained, for if it could be explained it would no longer be confessed" (p. 99). Like Berkouwer, he argues that the concept of causality is qualitatively different when applied to God than it is when predicated of creatures (p. 98). This assertion is not biblically based, but founded in the Kantian distinction, and insuperable divide, between the noumenal and phenomenal realms—a distinction that renders the reliability of God's revelation suspect. While De Jong criticizes Hoeksema's methodology in terms of its ostensible "competitive polarity motif," his own

methodology also constitutes the imposition of an extra-biblical conceptual construct, namely, the dialectical "both/and" of the correlation motif. One could easily argue that the "either/or" motif is in fact more dominant in Scripture. (Blacketer 2000:51.)

The views here criticized by Blacketer were in many ways the same issues that made up the Clark Case in the Orthodox Presbyterian Church in the 1940s and about which Hoeksema commented so heavily. In the course of the Clark Case, it was primarily Cornelius van Til, John Murray, and Ned Stonehouse of Westminster Theological Seminary who were the complainants against Gordon Clark's ordination by the Orthodox Presbyterian Church. Clark was accused of denying the incomprehensibility of God. In point of fact, both Clark and his detractors readily admitted to believing in God's incomprehensibility (Hoeksema 1995:6-12). The difference was in what each party meant by 'incomprehensibility.' For Clark, 'Man can never know exhaustively and completely God's knowledge of any truth in all of its relationships and implications; because every truth has an infinite number of relationships and implications and since each of these implications in turn has other infinite implications, these must ever, even in heaven, remaining exhaustible for man' (Hoeksema 1995:10). That is to say, for Clark, God's knowledge is quantitatively different than human knowledge; God simply knows more.

For his detractors, especially Cornelius Van Til, this conception of the incomprehensibility of God was wholly inadequate. For Van Til and the others, God's knowledge was qualitatively different from that available to humanity. That is to say, for Van Til, 'a proposition does not have the same meaning for God as for man' (Hoeksema 1995:11). In order to protect what he termed 'the Creator/creature distinction' (Frame 1976:37; Van Til 1967:32 ff.), Van Til conceived of all of human knowledge as 'analogical' (Van Til 1967:39). But, for Van Til, analogical means that 'God's knowledge and Man's knowledge "do not coincide at any single point"' (Robbins 1986:33). De Jong is also concerned to maintain this same Creator/creature distinction. He writes that 'we must remember that causation when predicated of God is qualitatively different from causation when predicated of the creature. In our logical categories we must keep the

Creator/creature relationship inviolate' (De Jong 1954:98). Elsewhere, De Jong writes that 'at root of all Hoeksema's argumentation against a well-meant offer of grace lies a misconstruction of the dynamic and reciprocal fellowship which exists between God and man' (De Jong 1954:72). This misconstruction De Jong terms 'Hoeksema's competitive polarity motif' in which Hoeksema supposedly pits God over against man, and in which he not only 'incorrectly applies the categories of human logic to God's decreeing activity, but he also inaccurately conceives of this decree in temporal terms.... This in turn compels Hoeksema to view the elect as a number of chosen individuals who live in a dualistic-antithetic relationship to other individuals whom God sovereignly reprobates' (De Jong 1954:83-84). It is interesting that De Jong's emphasis on this 'polarity motif,' which bears striking resemblance to what he elsewhere refers to as the 'Creator/creature distinction,' is somehow responsible for Hoeksema's viewing humanity along antithetical lines.

It is also because of this Creator/creature distinction that Van Til believes Christians must 'not attempt to "solve" the "paradoxes" involved in the relationship of the self-contained God to his dependent creatures' (Robbins 1986:28). 'Now since God is not fully comprehensible to us,' writes Van Til, 'we are bound to come into what seems to be a contradiction in all our knowledge. Our knowledge is analogical and therefore must be paradoxical' (Van Til 1967:44). Hence, the use of human logic, 'the demand for non-contradiction when carried to its logical conclusion reduces God's truth to man's truth' (Robbins 1986:5, from an interview in *Christianity Today*, December 30, 1977). John Frame, in his discussion of Van Til's belief that 'theological concepts are "limiting concepts"' takes the argument for the origin of Van Til's thought right back to the discussion of the 'noumenal world' as it appears in Immanuel Kant (Frame 1976:34).

While Raymond Blacketer sees the problems inherent in De Jong's *Well-Meant Offer* stemming from G. C. Berkouwer, I have quoted the events and ideas surrounding the Clark Case to show that these same ideas were prominent on this side of the Atlantic as well. Hoeksema wrote extensively on the Clark Case pointing out the irrationalism that surrounded it; then a decade later, De Jong criticizes Hoeksema severely in his thesis, using many of the same ideas and terms Hoeksema exposed in the Clark Case as irrational.

Additionally, throughout his analysis of Hoeksema's views on the covenant and common grace, De Jong constantly refers to Hoeksema's theology as 'reactionary' in one way or another. One has only to read Hoeksema's treatment of the covenant of grace to see that this is not the case. God's covenant is established and maintained by God. God covenant is a bond of friendship and love with the elect. God's covenant is controlled by sovereign, eternal election and as such is for the elect in Christ alone. Hence, entrance into the covenant, as well as remaining in it—as if it were even possible to fall out of it somehow as Heyns maintains—is solely a function of God's sovereign, particular grace. Everywhere Hoeksema speaks of what the covenant 'is' and what grace 'is,' not what they 'are not.' If his theology was indeed so reactionary, would it not be characterized by negativity? But this is certainly not the case. His exposition of these concepts is entirely positive. Where then, I ask, is the reaction? If Hoeksema used the concepts provided by Professor Heyns, as well as others, to develop his own positive concepts, how is this to be considered reactionary theology? Is this not how theology is done?

It is interesting to note that Hoeksema's own review of De Jong's thesis in *The Standard Bearer* is less than one quarter of a page and ends with the question: 'What grace do the reprobate receive in and through the preaching of the gospel?' (Hoeksema 1954:439).

7.6 *Hyper-Calvinism and the Call of the Gospel*

Hyper-Calvinism, although it may seem to be a very precise technical term which accurately describes an aberrant form of Calvinism, is in reality a term about which there seems to be no agreement as to precise definition. I bring this up because the Protestant Reformed Churches in general, and Hoeksema specifically, have been accused of hyper-Calvinism repeatedly over the years, primarily due to their denial of the free offer of the Gospel, and that always, it seems, in a rather off-handed manner. The Protestant Reformed Churches respond to the charge by saying that hyper-Calvinism is just another way to label those who maintain a staunch Calvinism. Additionally, they maintain that hyper-Calvinism refers rather to a particular view of the external call of the Gospel, i.e. the preaching. David Engelsma of the Protestant Reformed Churches testifies that:

> "Hyper-Calvinism" is a term of reproach and condemnation. It is the charge that a theological teaching which claims to be Calvinism has, in fact, so exaggerated and distorted Calvinism that it is not genuine Calvinism at all. The body of doctrines described as hyper-Calvinism is accused of having gone beyond true Calvinism so that, although it has a semblance of Calvinism, it is, in reality, a perversion of Calvinism. Indeed, the seriousness of the epithet "hyper-Calvinism" is that it alleges a theological position to be false doctrine. In Calvinistic circles, it is common to blacken with this brush all those who deny "the offer of the gospel." Since the Protestant Reformed Churches are known to deny the offer, we are dismissed, often out-of-hand, as hyper-Calvinists. This is persistently done by some who know better. The Christian Reformed magazine, *The Banner*, repeated the old canard in its issue of September 28, 1973, when it stated that the Christian Reformed Church opposed the "doctrinal deviation" of "hyper-Calvinism in the Common Grace controversy." (Engelsma 1980:1.)

There is, however, precedent for the Christian Reformed Church using the term in this manner and it is not necessarily as sinister as Engelsma makes out, although I am sure this does not apply to all who employ the term. Curt Daniel, in his massive study on the oft-described 'hyper-Calvinism' of the eighteenth-century English Baptist John Gill, quotes Jay Green, the publisher responsible for the reissuing of Gill's *Body of Divinity* in the 1950s, to the effect that there is no such thing as hyper-Calvinism, and that the term is nothing more than a term of approbation to be used on the enemies of Calvinism (Daniel 1983:756). Daniel himself, however, does not see it this way. Contrariwise, he considers the denial of the free offer of the Gospel to be a constituent part of any definition of hyper-Calvinism. 'Surely Engelsma,' Daniel believes, 'and anyone else who studies the history of Calvinism must be aware that there are varieties of Calvinism. That most of those who deny the doctrine of the free offer also reject the label "Hyper-Calvinist" is obvious, for to accept it is virtually tantamount to admitting that one is either in error or that he has gone beyond Calvin' (Daniel 1983:756-757). After several hundred pages of historical investigation, Daniel offers us the following definition of hyper-Calvinism:

> Hyper-Calvinism is that school of Supralapsarian "Five Point" Calvinism which so stresses the sovereignty of God by over-emphasizing the secret over the revealed will and eternity over time, that it minimizes the responsibility of Man, notably with respect to the denial of the word "offer" in relation to the preaching of the Gospel of a finished and limited atonement, thus undermining the universal duty of sinners to believe savingly with the assurance that the Lord Jesus Christ died for them, with the result that presumption is overly warned of, introspection is overly encouraged, and a view of sanctification akin to doctrinal Antinomianism is often approached. (Daniel 1983:767.)

Daniel wishes to differentiate yet further:

> This could be summarized even further: it is a rejection of the word "offer" in connection with evangelism for supposedly Calvinistic reasons. In all our researches, the only real tangible thing which differentiates the Hyper from the High Calvinists is the word "offer." The Supralapsarians were brought to the very door of Hyper-Calvinism but those who accepted free offers failed to enter into the realm of the most extreme variety of Calvinism that the history of Reformed theology has yet seen. (Daniel 1983:767.)

Daniel is good enough to spell out carefully his definition, and I think it is one which could even be distilled a bit further. On the last page Daniel says that a hyper-Calvinist is one who has simply gone beyond Calvin. This is clear enough. In the above quotes the denial of the word 'offer' as it relates to the preaching of the Gospel seems to hold sway. If we put these two concepts together, a clearer picture of the hyper-Calvinist seems to emerge. Hence, a hyper-Calvinist is one who has gone beyond Calvin by denying the free offer of the Gospel. Here we seem to have a standard, or measure by which to determine who is and who is not a hyper-Calvinist. Daniel is not alone in defining hyper-Calvinism in this way. K. W. Stebbins, minister of the Presbyterian Reformed Church of Australia and author of the book *Christ Freely Offered*, concurs wholeheartedly. While his purpose in writing is different, Stebbins refers to what 'is normally called the hypercalvinist controversy, in which the free offer is denied on the grounds of man's inability' (Stebbins 1978:6).

In much of the writing done on the free offer, the offer of the Gospel and the call of the Gospel are just assumed to mean the same thing. Hoeksema insisted that these terms and the concepts they represent were not the same, while his detractors said they were. Raymond Blacketer comments on the debate over these terms as it occurred in the Christian Reformed Church in 1924:

> There are numerous historical and logical errors in both the synodical report and Berkhof's defense of the well-meant offer. The most glaring logical jump is that which the synod and Berkhof make from the concept of *call* to that of *offer*. In the synodical material and in Berkhof's defense of the three points, these two terms are used synonymously and interchangeably. Berkhof states that "this calling of the Gospel, or this offer of salvation, is, according to the synod, *universal*." The position of Hoeksema and Danhof, however, was precisely that the nature of the call was not that of an offer, particularly in the modern sense of the term. To use call and offer interchangeable, therefore, begs the question. (Blacketer 2000:40.)

The one assumption made by both Daniel and Stebbins in their formulation of the hyper-Calvinist is that Calvin subscribed to the free offer of the Gospel as outlined in 1924. If Calvin did not subscribe to the free offer of the Gospel, then the charge of hyper-Calvinism is an empty one. Further, it is shown to be, as Jay Green and David Engelsma both maintain, nothing more than a term of approbation with which to tar one's enemies.

7.7 *Calvin and the Free Offer*

In deciding whether to enlist Calvin in our arsenal to defend any particular doctrine or opinion it is important, as Herman Hanko reminds us, that we 'not attempt to interpret the Reformers and their views in the light of our modern times and modern theological controversies' (Hanko 1989:20). I say this because many think, even today that to enlist the great name of Calvin is somehow to sanctify the subject. The famous nineteenth-century Scottish Theologian, William Cunningham, rightly warned us against just such an approach (Cunningham 1979:400-401). Furthermore, according to Herman Hanko:

> Calvin himself never faced specifically and concretely the question of the free offer of the gospel any more than did Luther. …the nature and character of the preaching was not an issue between the Reformers and the Romish church. Although there are innumerable passages in Calvin's writings which make use of the word "offer," …the actual theology of the free offer was a question which Calvin did not face. The issue arose over a half century later. …it is clear from all Calvin's writings that he militated against all the ideas which have become such an integral part of the free offer theology. (Hanko 1989:27.)

Given Hanko's direction, I think it profitable to identify those ideas, or doctrines which have become associated with the free offer theology, and thus distill the free offer to its essence.

First of all, I would like to examine the difference of opinion surrounding the use of the word 'offer.' According to David Engelsma, 'It is of no consequence, therefore, that the term "offer" appears in Calvin, in other Reformed theologians, and in such Reformed creeds as the Canons of Dort and the Westminster Confession of Faith. The word "offer" had originally a sound meaning: "serious call," "presentation of Christ"' (Engelsma 1980:81). Also with respect to the word 'offer,' Reverend Barry Gritters, also of the Protestant Reformed Churches, writes:

> It must be noted that Calvin wrote his *Institutes* in the Latin language. The word translated "offer" in English is,

not surprisingly, *offere* in Latin. But this word did not necessarily have the same connotations then as it does in English today. The word *offere* primarily means "to present, to bring towards, to thrust forward, to show, to exhibit." Our word *offer* has broader connotations and implies the ability to accept or reject, as well as a desire on God's part that the offer be accepted. (Gritters 1988:33.)

While I agree that the Latin 'offere' may not be an exact synonym for the English 'offer,' I would not be willing let the matter stand or fall on the basis of the origin of this one word. Besides, *Cassell's Latin-English Dictionary* defines 'offero' as: 'to carry or bring to, place before, present, produce, offer' (Cassell's 1959:380).

The real question surrounding the free offer of the gospel is not the origin of the word 'offer,' but the theology behind the 'free offer.' According the book *The Free Offer of the Gospel*, put out by the Orthodox Presbyterian Church, strong exponents of the free offer, 'it would appear that the real point of dispute in connection with the free offer of the gospel is whether it can properly be said that God **desires** the salvation of all men' (Murray & Stonehouse 1948:3). In his commentary on the 'Clark Case,' also within the Orthodox Presbyterian Church, Hoeksema writes at some length concerning this desire of God to save all men:

> According to the complainants the preacher is called to proclaim to all his hearers *that God sincerely seeks the salvation of them all*. If this is not their meaning when they write: "in the gospel God sincerely offers salvation in Christ to all who hear, reprobate as well as elect," their words have no meaning at all. According to Dr. Clark, however, the preacher proclaims to all his hearers promiscuously *that God sincerely seeks the salvation of all the elect*. The elect may be variously named in the preaching: those who repent, they that believe in Christ, that hunger for the bread of life, that thirst for the water of life, that seek, knock, ask, that come to Christ, etc. etc. But they are always the elect. We may define the issue still more sharply, and limit it to God's intention and attitude in the preaching of the Gospel *with regard to the reprobate*. For it is

more especially about the reprobate and their salvation that the complainants are concerned. Strange though it may seem, paradoxical though it may sound, they want to leave room in their preaching for *the salvation of the reprobate*. For the sake of clarity, therefore, we can safely leave the elect out of our discussion. That God sincerely seeks their salvation is not a matter of controversy. To drag them into the discussion of this question simply confuses things. The question very really concerns the attitude of God with respect to the reprobate. We may limit the controversy to this question: What must the preacher of the Gospel say of God's intention with respect to the reprobate? And these, too, may be called by different names, such as, the impenitent, the wicked, the unbelievers, etc. The answer to this question defines the difference between Dr. Clark and the complainants sharply and precisely. The complainants answer: The preacher must say that God sincerely seeks the salvation of the reprobate through the preaching of the Gospel. (Hoeksema 1995:35.)

While some may insist that Hoeksema distills the concerns of the complainants a bit too far, it is interesting to note that the Christian Reformed Synod of 1924 and Calvin Seminary Professor of Theology, Louis Berkhof, both believed 'that God genuinely offers salvation to all who hear the gospel, including the reprobate—those whom he has decreed to leave in their state of rebellion and to withhold from them "saving faith and the grace of conversion"' (Blacketer 2000:41).

At this point, I would like to ask the question: How are we to understand this doctrine of reprobation? Harry Boer, foreign missionary and teacher for the Christian Reformed Church and no friend of reprobation, writes concerning election and reprobation:

> The fact that God "leaves" the non-elect to their own wickedness may give the impression that reprobation simply means non-election. The casual reader may be left with the thought that God overlooked the reprobate *without* having the deliberate *intention* of abandoning them to their wickedness, and therefore without taking any positive steps to effect their reprobation. Such a reading of

the decree, however, Dort utterly excludes. ...the driving power in God by which, according to Dort, he effected the reprobation of the non-elect *is the same* as that which effected the salvation of the elect. At this point we wish only to note that reprobation has a *purpose*, a rationale if you will, of the same magnitude as the purpose that underlies the decree of election. The latter is "the demonstration of His mercy" (Art.7); the purpose of reprobation is "the declaration of his justice" (Art.15). (Boer 1983:11.)

Harry Boer, because of his work as a missionary, did not like the message the doctrine of reprobation constrained him to preach. A. C. De Jong, in his thesis on Hoeksema, is not remiss to register his dislike for the doctrine also (De Jong 1954:114). 'Why not,' writes Boer, 'write it off as an antiquated piece of rationalistic theology long since left behind?' (Boer 1983:viii). Boer knew better. He knew that the doctrine was much too potent for that. There were other concerns, Boer writes: 'to repudiate reprobation while retaining a numerical conception of election leaves wide open the problem of the "non-elect"' (Boer: 1990:105). Hence, in 1977 he submitted a 'Gravamen' to the Synod of the Christian Reformed Church protesting the doctrine of reprobation as unsound. His protest, after much consideration, was rejected.

Harry Boer, despite his dislike of the doctrine of reprobation, shows clearly that God has a purpose in it. It is not incidental to election. It is decretal in nature and, as such, part of God's counsel with respect to the world and its disposition. The free offer of the Gospel, by contrast, makes reprobation incidental, an after thought on God's part. This trivializes reprobation to the point where one may wonder whether God has any definite plan with respect to the reprobate. Only if God has no definite plan with respect to the reprobate may they be thought of as objects of God's favor and, hence, objects of a free offer of the Gospel in which God sincerely desires their salvation. But, according to Hoeksema, God has a definite plan with regard to the reprobate in history. This plan is for 'those who are presently to be damned must for a time serve the salvation of the elect, be it in an antithetical manner. In this sense reprobation is a divine necessity. In this sense, the reprobate exist for the sake of the elect' (Hoeksema 1993:9-10).

That is to say, reprobation serves election. The reprobate are used, according to the providence of God, to mold and to sanctify the elect in this world. And, while their actions towards the elect may be either good or evil, God uses it all for the good.

What does Calvin say about God desiring the salvation of all people, especially the reprobate? Since the charge of hyper-Calvinism lodged against Hoeksema hinges upon just this point, I wish to quote from Calvin at some length.

In Book III Chapter 22, Section 10 of the *Institutes*, Calvin writes:

> Some object that God would be contrary to Himself if he should universally invite all men to him but admit only a few as elect. Thus, in their view, the universality of the promises removes the distinction of special grace.... I have elsewhere explained how Scripture reconciles the two notions that all are called to repentance and faith by outward preaching, yet that the spirit of repentance and faith is not given to all. Soon I shall have to repeat some of this. Now I deny what they claim, since it is false in two ways. For he who threatens that while it will rain upon one city there will be drought in another [Amos 4:7], and who elsewhere announces a famine of teaching [Amos 8:11], does not bind himself by a set law to call all men equally. And he who, forbidding Paul to speak the word in Asia [Acts 16:6], and turning him aside from Bithynia, draws him into Macedonia [Acts 16:7 ff.] thus shows that he has the right to distribute this treasure to whom he pleases. Through Isaiah he still more openly shows how he directs the promises of salvation specifically to the elect: for he proclaims that they alone, not the whole human race without distinction, are to become his disciples [Isaiah 8:16]. Hence it is clear that the doctrine of salvation, which is said to be reserved solely and individually for the sons of the church, is falsely debased when presented as effectually profitable to all. (Calvin 1960:944.)

In Book III, Chapter 24, Section 1, Calvin writes:

> But to make the matter clearer, we must deal with both the calling of the elect and the blinding and hardening of the wicked. Of the former I have already said something, when refuting the error of those who think that the universality of the promises makes all mankind equal. Yet it is not without choice that God by his call manifests the election, which he otherwise holds hidden within himself; accordingly, it may properly be termed his "attestation." (Calvin 1960:964.)

Calvin also shows that the preaching of the Gospel in itself is not to be considered 'grace' to all, especially the reprobate. In fact, in the next section, he has a very different view of the preaching than the proponents of the free offer. In Book III, Chapter 24, Section 8, Calvin writes:

> The statement of Christ "Many are called but few are chosen" [Matt 22:14] is, in this manner, very badly understood. Nothing will be ambiguous if we hold fast to what ought to be clear from the foregoing: That there are two kinds of call. There is the general call, by which God invites all equally to himself through the outward preaching of the word—even those to whom he holds it out as a savor of death [cf. II Cor. 2:16], and as the occasion for severer condemnation. (Calvin 1960:974.)

Again, dealing with effects of the outward call, the preaching of the Gospel, Calvin writes in Book III, Chapter 24, Section12:

> As God by the effectual working of his call to the elect perfects the salvation to which by his eternal plan he has destined them, so he has his judgments against the reprobate, by which he executed his plan for them. What of those, then, whom he created for dishonor in life and destruction in death, to become the instruments of his wrath and examples of his severity? That they may come to their end, he sometimes deprives them of the capacity to hear his word; at other times he, rather, blinds and stuns them by the preaching of it. (Calvin 1960:978.)

In Book III, Chapter 24, Section 15, Calvin comments on the passage in Ezekiel 33 so often appealed to by those who advocate the free offer:

> But our opponents are in the habit of quoting in opposition a few Scripture passages in which God seems to deny that the wicked perish by his ordination, except in so far as by their clamorous protests they of their own accord bring death upon themselves. Let us therefore briefly explain these passages and prove that they do not conflict with the foregoing opinion. A passage of Ezekiel's is brought forward, that "God does not will the death of the wicked but wills that the wicked turn back and live" [Ezek. 33:11 p.]. If it pleases God to extend this to the whole human race, why does he not encourage to repentance the very many whose minds are more amenable to obedience than the minds of those who grow harder and harder at his daily invitations? Among the people of Nineveh [cf. Matt. 12:41] and of Sodom, as Christ testifies, the preaching of the gospel and miracles would have accomplished more than in Judea [Matt. 11:23]. If God wills that all be saved, how does it come to pass that he does not open the door of repentance to the miserable men who would be better prepared to receive Grace? Hence we may see that this passage is violently twisted if the will of God, mentioned by the prophet, is opposed to His eternal plan, by which He has distinguished the elect from the reprobate. Now if we are seeking the prophet's true meaning, it is that he would bring the hope of pardon to the penitent only. The gist of it is that God is without doubt ready to forgive, as soon as the sinner is converted. Therefore, in so far as God wills the sinner's repentance, he does not will his death. But experience teaches that God wills the repentance of those whom he invites to himself, in such a way that he does not touch the hearts of all. Yet it is not on that account to be said that he acts deceitfully, for even though only his outward call renders inexcusable those who hear it and do not obey, still it is truly considered evidence of God's grace, by which he reconciles men to himself. Let us

therefore regard the prophet's instruction that the death of the sinner is not pleasing to God as designed to assure believers that God is ready to pardon them as soon as they are touched by repentance but to make the wicked feel that their transgression is doubled because they do not respond to God's great kindness and goodness. God's mercy will always, accordingly, go to meet repentance, but all the prophets and all the apostles, as well as Ezekiel himself, clearly teach to whom repentance is given. (Calvin 1960:982-983.)

In his answer to Pighius, in *The Eternal Predestination of God*, Calvin concludes:

Now let Pighius boast, if he can, that God willeth *all men* to be saved! The above arguments, founded on the Scriptures, prove that even the external preaching of the doctrine of the doctrine of salvation, which is very far inferior to the illumination of the Spirit, was not made of God common to *all men*. (Calvin 1950:104.)

Or, in the words of William Cunnungham:

Calvin consistently, unhesitatingly, and explicitly denied the doctrine of God's universal grace and love to all men,—that is, *omnibus et singulis*, to each and every man,—as implying in some sense a desire or purpose or intention to save them all; and with this universal grace or love to all men the doctrine of a universal or unlimited atonement, in the nature of the case, and in the convictions and admissions of all its supporters, stands inseparably connected. (Cunningham 1979:398.)

I think it abundantly clear from the preceding quotes from Calvin that he did not hold to a free offer of the Gospel in the sense that is it held in this day and age. Calvin is emphatic that God does not desire the salvation of the reprobate, as He is the one who reprobated them. After all, is not the assertion that there is a desire on God's part for the salvation of all at the very heart of the 'well-meant offer of salvation to all'? I think that the above quotes from Calvin demonstrate conclusively that there is no desire on the part of God for the salvation of all of humanity, and the preaching of the Gospel is in no way 'grace' to all those that hear it.

I think it is equally clear from Calvin's words that Hoeksema, in his writings on common grace as it relates to the free offer of the Gospel, did not depart from the doctrine of the Genevan Reformer in any way. If, therefore, Hoeksema did not go beyond Calvin in his denial of the free offer of the Gospel, I conclude then the charge of hyper-Calvinism is thoroughly unfounded.

David Engelsma, however, has a slightly different definition of hyper-Calvinism, a definition that came into its own in 1924 and that is more a variant to the one which we have been discussing. It is really the more common, the less technical, of the two definitions. Engelsma writes:

> But hyper-Calvinism is the denial that God, in the preaching of the gospel, calls everyone who hears the preaching to repent and believe. It is the denial that the church should call everyone in the preaching. It is the denial that the unregenerated have a duty to repent and believe. It manifests itself in the practice of the preacher's addressing the call of the gospel, "repent and believe on Christ crucified," only to those in his audience who show signs of regeneration, and thereby of election, namely, some conviction of sin and some interest in salvation. (Engelsma 1980:11.)

Practically, what this means is that a minister can only preach the Gospel to the elect, or at least only to those who give sufficient evidence of possibly being elect. In his book, *Hyper-Calvinism and the Call of the Gospel*, Engelsma says that this concept actually took hold in certain quarters in seventeenth and eighteenth-century England. Evidence of this position can, according to Engelsma, be found in ministries of Joseph Hussey, John Brine, John Gill and others (Engelsma 1980:11). Engelsma bases his study of hyper-Calvinism on Peter Toon's *The Emergence of Hyper-Calvinism in English Nonconformity, 1689-1765* (Toon 1967). I have read Toon's book and I can find no evidence this practice was anywhere accepted. Curt Daniel, in his study of hyper-Calvinism, has this to say on the matter: 'Among other remarkable things is that Engelsma relies so heavily upon Toon, with whom we are in basic agreement. To our knowledge, Toon does not suggest that Gill or Hussey felt that ministers should preach the Gospel only to the elect' (Daniel 1983:766).

Still, it does seem that Hoeksema was accused of this variety of hyper-Calvinism also. Louis Berkhof, formerly Professor of Theology at Calvin Seminary, seems to be the culprit here, writes Raymond Blacketer:

> It is an unfortunate fact that Berkhof demonstrates very little familiarity with the actual views of Hoeksema and Danhof, and he frequently mischaracterizes their position. He accuses the ministers of preaching only to the elect, and ridicules them for attempting something that only Christ himself could do (since only he knows who the elect are), and that in fact did not do. (Blacketer 2000:40.)

Hoeksema was, however, exonerated of holding this variety of hyper-Calvinism as well. A. C. De Jong wrote:

> The preacher need not concern himself about the particular character of his audience, the collectivity with an elect kernel and a reprobate husk. We mention this since Hoeksema was frequently accused of forcing the preacher into an impossible situation [preaching only to the elect-PB]. But Hoeksema would never bow to this objection. The preacher, according to him, preaches to everyone, but his preaching is so used by God to save the elect kernel and to increase the responsibility of the reprobate husk, which does not believe the truths proclaimed by the preacher. (De Jong 1954:47-48.)

7.8 G. C. Berkouwer

While not mentioning hyper-Calvinism specifically, Professor G.C. Berkouwer of the Free University also believes that, for Hoeksema, given his denial of the free offer, 'the "joyful" message, the good news, can really be addressed only to the elect' (Berkouwer 1977:98). This seems to me, allowing for the different expressions, to be the same criticism that Professor Berkhof also leveled against Hoeksema. On the same page, Berkouwer also says that for Hoeksema, 'if the gospel is universally preached, it is possible and meaningful only in the sense that no one knows who the elect are' (Berkouwer 1977:98). Responding to the first of Berkouwer's statements, Hoeksema's son, Homer, wrote: 'If Hoeksema ever mentioned this idea, it was usually in reply to the false charge that he preached only to the elect—a thought which to him was utterly ridiculous for its impossibility' (Hoeksema 1975:44). Berkouwer's second statement assumes that the preaching of the gospel, aside from a general offer of salvation, holds no specific purpose for the reprobate. Hoeksema emphatically denied this. As his son writes:

> One could without difficulty point to a dozen passages in Hoeksema's writings which give the lie to this claim of Berkouwer. The fact of the matter is that Hoeksema rarely made mention of this fact of our not knowing who the elect are. He certainly never taught that this was what made the general proclamation of the gospel possible and meaningful. And still more certainly, he never taught that this general proclamation was possible and meaningful only because of this. Numerous times Hoeksema emphasized that it was God's sovereign good pleasure that the gospel also be proclaimed to the reprobate—not that this was due merely to the preacher's inability to identify the elect. Numerous times Hoeksema emphasized that the preaching of the gospel has a positive purpose also with respect to the reprobate, namely, the manifestation of the sinfulness of sin, the hardening of the reprobate, and thus the historical realization of God's counsel of reprobation, and ultimately theodicy. I dare say that as often as Hoeksema expounded this subject of election and reprobation in relation to the preaching of the gospel, he emphasized this. And almost as often as he spoke or wrote on the subject of preaching and its purpose, he made mention of the fact of the two-fold purpose and effect of the preaching. (Hoeksema 1975:44-45.)

The reason I bring Berkouwer into the discussion at this point is because of his importance as a theologian and because he himself states that it was Hoeksema who exercised great influence on his thinking about election and reprobation in a discussion stemming from the free offer of the gospel (Berkouwer 1977:98). 'When I met Hoeksema in 1952' Berkouwer recalls, 'I was impressed anew that his manner of thinking about election was impossible' (Berkouwer 1977:98). The 'impossibility' to which Berkouwer refers is any reconciliation between the free offer of the gospel and the decree of election and reprobation. He writes that 'in view of the a priori decree of election and reprobation, universal proclamation is not possible, so long as the seriousness and genuinely intended offer of grace is concerned' (Berkouwer 1977:98).

Earlier it was Professor Heyns who insisted that it was a sign of rationalism if one did not hold these two concepts, election and the free offer, in tension. De Jong considered Hoeksema a rationalist because he rejected the free offer as inconsistent with election. By Heyns's definition, the case could be made that Berkouwer also qualifies as a rationalist since he redefines election and reprobation in favor of the free offer of the gospel. On this matter Homer Hoeksema comments at some length:

> Berkouwer denies double predestination. He has stated this forthrightly in connection with a recent visit to the synod of the Hervormde Kerk at the time when the Testimony of Faith (forerunner to a new confession) was presented there.... What is of even greater significance is the fact that Berkouwer here confirms what we have always claimed in connection with the error of the general well-meant offer of grace, namely: that theological consistency (in the light of scripture and the confessions) forces one to choose between the well-meant offer of grace and the truth of sovereign (double) predestination. In the past many theologians have attempted to follow a double-track theology, with the practical result that while they did lip-service to the truth of sovereign predestination, they actually forgot that "track" and concentrated on the well-meant offer "track" in their preaching and teaching. Bear in mind that the alternatives

are emphatically <u>not</u> the general, or promiscuous, <u>proclamation</u> of the gospel and double predestination.... But the alternatives are the general, well-meant <u>offer</u> and double predestination. These, we have always insisted, are mutually exclusive. But Berkouwer has at last—and consistently—chosen for the general offer and has denied double predestination. His position is dead wrong and constitutes a break with the Reformed tradition, but it is at least consistent. And by this open and consistent choice he has confirmed what we have always maintained in this regard. Would that everyone who wants to maintain the general, well-meant offer of grace were as consistent as Berkouwer. Then, at least, we would all know where we stand in relation to one another. (Hoeksema 1975:41-43.)

It seems that for all his theological acumen, Berkouwer's choice of the free offer of the gospel over against election and reprobation, and by contrast, his criticism of Hoeksema's position, is based on a misunderstanding. Berkouwer, as with Hoeksema's critics in 1924, maintains that the free offer of the gospel and the promiscuous preaching of the gospel are the same (Berkouwer 1977:98-100). This criticism, as is evident at the outset, sets the stage for the charge of hyper-Calvinism. After all, if the gospel message is not an offer which God graciously meant for all to accept, then why preach to all except the elect? In fact, preaching to any others than the elect is at worse an insult and in the very least a cruel joke to the non-elect. The confusion here results from identifying the external call of the gospel with a well-meant offer of grace. They are not the same.

Raymond Blacketer, whom I quoted earlier in his dealings with the events of 1924, castigates Louis Berkhof, one of Hoeksema's detractors in 1924, for his 'glaring logical jump ... from the concept of *call* to that of *offer*' (Blacketer 2000:40). Blacketer goes on to say that 'the position of Hoeksema and Danhof ... was precisely that the nature of the call was not that of an offer, particularly in the modern sense of the term. To use call and offer interchangeably, therefore begs the question' (Blacketer 2000:40). Homer Hoeksema points out this same confusion of terms in Berkouwer. He writes:

Berkouwer repeatedly confuses the concepts universal preaching and universal offer. The former Hoeksema steadfastly maintained; the latter he steadfastly denied. Indeed Hoeksema subscribed (with more than lip service) to Canons II, 5, but he always pointed out that Canons II, 5 does not speak of a general, conditional offer, but of the general proclamation of a particular promise. What Hoeksema denied was that the nature of the promiscuous proclamation of the gospel was that of a general, well-meant offer of grace. (Hoeksema 1975:44.)

By way of contrast, Hoeksema believed that the message of the gospel is a command and not an offer, and, hence, is to be preached promiscuously to all. Naturally, only those whom God has already regenerated will be able to obey the command.

G.C. Berkouwer was truly an eminent theologian in his own right, but to take up a further analysis of his theology in comparison with Hoeksema's would take us beyond the confines of our topic.

7.9 Raymond Blacketer's Assessment

The proof adduced for the first point of the Kalamazoo points is problematic. In the first place, Reformed theology has generally been reticent to connect any common or universal grace with the process of salvation, particularly since the Remonstrant party, the Arminians, conceived of common grace as a factor that made all individuals capable of responding to the gospel call. The first point, however, considers the universality of the call of the gospel to be evidence for the existence of common grace. More significant, however, is the introduction of the concept of the universal, well-meant offer of salvation. A historical examination of the issue will demonstrate that at this point the synod introduced a quite debatable doctrine into the church, and in doing so misinterpreted the confessions and prominent Reformed theologians. The result was that the ministers Hoeksema and Danhof were condemned, in part, for defending the proper interpretation of the Reformed confessions. Even if one considers their sweeping rejection of common grace to be dubious and extreme, their repudiation of the well-meant offer is much more defensible from a historical and confessional perspective. A further result was that the Christian Reformed Church was left with a doctrine that is of doubtful logical coherence, given the soteriological framework confessed in the Canons of Dort, and that does not find support among leading theological figures of the sixteenth and seventeenth centuries. The cause of this unfortunate state of affairs, moreover, appears to be a lamentable lack of careful historical and theological study of the issue by the 1924 synod and its defenders, as well as extreme and uncharitable recriminations on both sides. (Blacketer 2000:39.)

7.10 Conclusion

In this chapter, I have endeavored to show Hoeksema's response to the First Point of Common Grace as outlined in the decisions of 1924. To do this I have relied to a good degree on the thesis by A. C. De Jong which purports to discuss these views. Along the way I have pointed out some of the deficiencies inherent in De Jong, and by implication in Professor Heyns as well. The main thing, above all else, which I have sought to bring out in this chapter, simply because of its importance for the Reformed faith, is the total lack of conditionality in Hoeksema's theology. Whether it presents itself under the guise of the free offer of the Gospel, or presents itself in the demands by which you must keep yourself in the covenant, Hoeksema repudiated it all. God saves those whom He as chosen from before the foundation of the world. It is not up to them to save themselves, or to somehow keep that salvation once it is given them. Human nature can not effect salvation, nor add to it. All is dependent upon the sovereign, particular grace of God. There is no conditionality here.

I have also proven that in his repudiation of the free offer of the Gospel, Hoeksema did not depart from the path blazed by Calvin. Calvin did not hold to the theology of the free offer and, therefore, Hoeksema did not go beyond him in denying it. Hoeksema was no hyper-Calvinist.

In his stand for sovereign, particular grace; a grace with no strings or conditions, Hoeksema, contra what some may say, was a direct theological descendent of Calvin. A genealogy to which, I might add, the free offer of the Gospel and the conditional covenant are foreign.

Chapter 8

Point Two: The Restraint of Sin in the Heart of Man

Relative to the second point, which is concerned with *the restraint of sin in the life of the individual and in the community*, the synod declares that there is such a restraint of sin according to Scripture and the Confessions. This is evident from the citations from Scripture and the Netherlands Confession. Articles 13, 36 which teach that God, by the general operation of the Spirit, without renewing the heart of man, restrains the unimpeded breaking out of sin, by which human life in society remained possible; while it is also evident from the quotations from Reformed writers of the most flourishing period of Reformed theology, that from ancient times our Reformed fathers were of the same opinion.

The second and third points of common grace that were adopted by the Synod of the Christian Reformed Church in 1924, exclusive of the well-meant offer of the Gospel delineated in point one, are, as David Engelsma says: 'the theory of common grace that was taught by Abraham Kuyper and Herman Bavinck' (Engelsma 2003:2). This common grace teaches a non-saving operation, or activity, by the Holy Spirit in the hearts of all human beings in order to restrain sin. One result, according to Engelsma, is a partial rather than a total depravity of the human nature (Engelsma 2003:2), even, according to Hoeksema, 'preparing the entire creation for glory' (Danhof & Hoeksema [1923] 2003:129). Another result is that all of humanity, Christians and non-Christians alike, are given the ability to perform good works. These works, though not meant to have any bearing upon the spiritual state, or disposition, of the one performing them, are in themselves good, particularly in the civic or social sphere. The point I wish to address in this chapter only concerns the operation of the Holy Spirit in the lives of all humanity. Since there has never been any question regarding the operation of the Holy Spirit in the lives of Christians, we can dismiss this portion of the argument. The only point of contention, then, is the idea that there is an operation of the Holy Spirit in the lives of non-Christians, or the reprobate, if you will.

8.1 The Image of God as a Point of Contact

The non-saving work of the Holy Spirit in the unregenerate, or unbeliever or non-Christian requires a point of contact within the person. Hoeksema terms it 'a receptivity' (Hoeksema 1942:50). All the proponents of common grace that posit this work of the Holy Spirit within an individual attempt to identify a point of contact within the person, but many are not really explicit in their identification of such a point. This point of contact, irrespective of the various points of reference alluded to in different writers, Harry Boer concludes, lies in the *imago Dei*. For it is in this *imago Dei*, some of which is purportedly gone and some of which remains, that a cogent point of contact can be sought. As Harry Boer states: 'As unfallen Man was thus qualified in the direction of ever increasing enrichment of his gifts, so fallen Man retains both a certain goodness and a capacity for the development of his gifts. But these qualities are residual, remnants of the image in which he was created' (Boer 1990:68). Hoeksema agrees with Boer that traditional Reformed theology has indeed identified such qualities as remaining in fallen man and agrees that traditionally 'they are called the remnants of the image of God in man' (Hoeksema 1942:52). Boer, however, goes further. Boer writes that, 'Reformed theology, while acknowledging Man as continuing to be *imago Dei*, has failed to regard the imago aspect of Man's being as the basis of all restraint of sin in his life' (Boer 1990:70). Reformed theology has, instead, been too preoccupied with 'total depravity' (Boer 1990:70). Using this view of the image as his basis, Boer proceeds to take issue with the concept with the 'antithesis' as it is set forth in traditional Reformed thought. Boer writes;

The Reformed doctrine of predestination did not merely split the numerical mass of individual human beings into two absolutely disparate parts. It bifurcated the human *race*, dividing the *imago Dei* into two eternally irreconcilable segments: the elect and the reprobate. (Boer 1990:161.)

Boer is not the only one to link 'common grace' and the 'image of God' in the unregenerate. But the image of God remaining in fallen humanity is not one specific thing. It encompasses the remains of those excellent gifts, or qualities, given to humanity by God in the creation prior to the fall. Since no one has lived from before the fall until the present, it is difficult to categorize exactly which gifts were lost and which were retained, historically referred to as in the 'wider' and in the 'narrower' sense. Louis Berkhof, in his *Systematic Theology* mentions, first and foremost, the 'total depravity' of the human nature, the loss of communion with God, a change in human consciousness to reflect the now prevailing guilt, physical death, and, finally, a change of residence as our first parents were driven from the garden (Berkhof 1986:225-226). While Berkhof takes the traditional view of the fall and its effects on the image, he does not really specify in what way what is left to humanity differs from what humanity originally had. Although Berkhof, as well as many other Reformed theologians before him, tries to distinguish between 'total' and 'absolute' depravity (Berkhof 1986:226), Harry Boer sees this as completely the wrong way to go because of the deleterious effect it has on the image. Boer writes:

> Some have tried to take the sharpest sting out of "total depravity" by positing an even lower form of sinfulness called "absolute depravity." But this is inherently impossible. The state of "absolute" depravity would deprive a person of participation in the image of God, so that the category of humanity would cease to apply. Where the image of God exists, there cannot fail to be some manifestation of goodness, however small. There can be degrees of totality—greater or lesser, broader or narrower pervasiveness of evil. But "absolute" knows no degrees. (Boer 1990:61-62.)

Cornelius van Til, an undeniable exponent of traditional Reformed theology and an ardent supporter of the doctrine of common grace as espoused by the synod of 1924, speaks of the 'pre-redemptive state,' in which 'all men in Adam (elect and reprobate) have a unified understanding and interpretation of the revelation of God and His creation' (Dennison 1993:241). But Van Til also speaks of a 'point of contact' with the unbeliever. Using the measurement of a fish as an example, Van Til believes that 'in the metaphysical realm, both parties [believer and unbeliever-PB] deal with the same God, who alone exists, and the same universe which is created by God (common point of contact). Moreover, both parties are created in the image of God. For this reason, the believer and the unbeliever can agree that the bass is sixteen inches long and weighs three pounds' (Dennison 1993:238). 'For this reason,' writes Dennison,

> Van Til maintained that the antithesis between believer and unbeliever was never metaphysical and psychological, but always epistemological and ethical. Metaphysically and psychologically, mankind can never be anything but the image of God, nor can mankind ever escape the imprint of God upon every inch of the universe and the constitution of his own being. All men, even presently, are responsible for the original pre-redemptive revelation of God to mankind. (Dennison 1993:245.)

It seems Van Til believes that the image of God in humanity is corrupted, but aside from mentioning 'thinking' and 'behavior' without any concrete examples and one of which he explicitly contradicts in the story of the fish, he is at a loss as to how.

William Masselink speaks of the human heart specifically in referring to the restraining power of the Holy Spirit on sin. He writes: 'So the restraining power of sin is increased after the deluge, not because of any improvement in man's heart, but because of God's sovereign common grace. The beastlike heart of man shall be somewhat more caged by common grace than was the case before the flood' (Masselink 1953:201). It is interest that, quoting Isaiah, Harry Boer assigns both the head and the heart to the 'image' as component parts (Boer 1990:65).

As long as even part of the image of God remains in fallen humanity, a certain amount of good remains there as well. And, it is but a short step to enhance, or augment, this good by means of a further operation of the Holy Spirit to restrain sin. The point of contact is there. Due to what I perceive to be an important consideration in the doctrine of common grace, I would like to explore the concept of the *imago Dei* a bit further, along with Hoeksema's reworking of the concept to avoid any point of contact.

Afterwards, in place of a special operation of the Holy Spirit in the hearts of the unregenerate to restrain sin, Hoeksema posits his concept of 'organic development.' Hoeksema's idea of organic development covers the outworking, or unfolding, of total depravity in the lives of unbelievers, even giving place to 'good works.'

8.2 The Image of God in Man

Early on in his ministry Hoeksema adopted Abraham Kuyper's view of the image of God in man. In an early sermon on Lord's Day III, he said:

> Now, what does it imply that man is created in the image of God? Here we must clearly distinguish. Most generally the distinction is made between the image of God in a wider sense of the word, and in a narrower sense. And then it is said that the image of God in the narrower sense has been lost, but in the wider sense it has been retained by man. And we have no objection to such a distinction, if only we bear clearly in mind that they are not two images, nor two parts of the same image, but the image of God from a twofold point of view. See, friends, we must clearly understand that man, so to speak, was stamped by the impress of God's own image. He could never loose that image again. (Hoeksema 1969:97.)

However, immediately after bringing this to the attention of his listeners, Hoeksema injected a certain amount of confusion into his own argument by saying: 'And since our Heidelberger in this connection only speaks about the image of God from the point of view of its loss through sin, it refers to this image in the narrower sense only' (Hoeksema 1969:97). Hoeksema's more mature thought on the matter, as he set out in his *Reformed Dogmatics* (Hoeksema 1966), presents a decidedly different picture of the present state of fallen humanity. After dismissing any possible distinction between the 'image' and 'likeness' found in Genesis 1:26-27 as 'rather arbitrary' (Hoeksema 1966:204), he goes on to say that this view:

> led to the Roman Catholic theory of the image of God as *donum superadditum*. Man is *naturally* good; and man with the additional gift of the likeness of God, according to which he is able to seek the higher spiritual things of God, was spiritually perfect. Man, therefore, can loose the image of God and still be naturally good, although he is no longer able to perform spiritual works. That this theory is very closely related to the theory of common grace goes without saying. (Hoeksema 1966:204-205.)

Later Reformed theologians, however, made the distinction between the image of God in a 'wider' and a 'narrower' sense (Hoeksema 1966:206), a concept, as we saw above, Hoeksema inherited most directly from Abraham Kuyper. After demonstrating to his satisfaction that the confessions, specifically article 14 of the *Belgic Confession* and the *Canons of Dort* III, IV, 1, do not admit such a distinction, Hoeksema contended that such a distinction is, in effect, dangerous 'because it prepares room for the further philosophy that there are remnants of the image of God left in fallen man, and that therefore the natural man cannot be wholly depraved' (Hoeksema 1966:207).

Because the majority of opinion on the image of God in man left the depravity of the natural man an open question, Hoeksema sought an explanation that was satisfactory from a Biblical perspective, consistent with the Confessions of the Reformed churches, and not detrimental to the sovereignty of God in the salvation of man. Taking his cue from Ephesians 4:23-24 in which Paul encourages believers to 'be renewed in the spirit of your mind; and that ye put on the new man, which after God is created in righteous and holiness' (Bible 1983:1218), and from Colossians 3:10, in which Paul commends the Colossians for having 'put on the new man, which is renewed in knowledge after the image of him that created him' (Bible 1983:1226), Hoeksema tried a different distinction altogether. He wrote at some length:

> If a distinction is to be made in the image of God after which man was created, we prefer to make the distinction between the image in a formal sense and in a material sense. By the former is meant the fact that man's nature is adapted to bear the image of God. Not every nature of the creature is capable of bearing God's image, of showing forth the reflection of God's own ethical perfections of knowledge, righteousness, and holiness. It is evident that it requires a rational, moral nature to bear that image of God. And by the image of God in a material sense is meant that spiritual, ethical soundness of the human nature according to which man actually shows forth the virtues of knowledge of God, righteousness, and holiness. If you will, we may distinguish between man as the image *bearer*, that is, as being capable of bearing the image of God, and man as *actually bearing* God's image. By virtue of his creation, God breathing into his nostrils the breath of life, man's whole nature became adapted to be the bearer of God's image. This, however, is not the same as saying that he *is* the image of God. But it means that he is a personal being with a rational, moral nature, capable of standing in a conscious, personal relation to God, capable of knowledge of God, of righteousness, and of holiness. And his capability of being endowed with God's image we would prefer to call God's image in a formal sense. No matter what becomes of man, whether he actually shows forth the beauty and glory of the image of God, or whether he turns into the very opposite and reveals the image of the devil, always you can distinguish him as a creature that ought to show forth God's image, always he remains the living soul that was formed by God's fingers out of the dust of the ground and into whose nostrils God breathed the breath of life originally. Always he remains a personal, rational, and moral being, who ought to live in covenant fellowship with the living God. However, man was originally created so that he actually possessed the image of God. He was not only

formally adapted to bear God's image; but he was also materially endowed with the spiritual, ethical virtues of that image. These virtues are usually distinguished as true knowledge of God, righteousness, and holiness. And all three are often expressed in the one term, *man's original righteousness*. It is that original goodness of man's nature, according to which it was wholly motivated by the love of God and with all its faculties and powers moved in the direction of God, so that the operation of his heart and soul and mind and will and all his strength were in accord with the will of God. And this one virtue of complete integrity is distinguished as true knowledge, righteousness, and holiness. (Hoeksema 1966:208-209.)

After the fall, while humanity still retains its humanness, that specific adaptation of the human nature designed to bear the image of God, humanity no longer bears that image itself in any material way. Hoeksema would go even further still. He contended that 'it is not enough to say that man merely lost this image of God' (Hoeksema 1966:213), which he most certainly did. Hoeksema further contended:

The spiritual, ethical operation of his heart and mind and will and strength was put into reverse, so that his knowledge became darkness and love of the lie, his righteousness became rebellion and iniquity, his holiness became aversion to God and impurity in all his affections. The being that was designed to be the image of God changed into the image of the devil. (Hoeksema 1966:213.)

Only through the sacrifice of Christ and by His grace is this image restored, and indeed 'raised to a higher, to a heavenly level and glory that can be lost nevermore' (Hoeksema 1966:213).

This view of Hoeksema concerning the loss of the image of God in man might be considered, in some circles, novel at best. That there are truly a wide range of opinions regarding this image is amply demonstrated by Anthony Hoekema in his book, *Created in*

God's Image (Hoekema 1986). The majority of scholars chronicled in Hoekema's book would certainly not agree with Hoeksema. Herman Bavinck, for example, believed that 'man does not simply bear or have the image of God; he is the image of God' (Hoekema 1986:65), and, thus, it is hardly something he or she could loose. In contrast to Bavinck, Karl Barth argued that 'man and woman together are the image of God' (Hoekema 1986:97). Elsewhere Barth adds:

> We might easily discuss which of these and many other similar explanations is the finest and deepest and most serious. What we cannot discuss is which of them is the true explanation of Gen. 1:26. For it is obvious that their authors merely found the concept [of image] in the text and then proceeded to pure invention in accordance with the requirements of contemporary anthropology. (Boer 1990:8.)

Barth's view equally does not admit the possibility of loss of the image. However, Hoeksema does seem to have an ally in the Zurich reformer Heinrich Bullinger. Bullinger wrote that:

> For because all men of their own nature are destitute of the glory of God, that is, since they are without the true image of God, to these the likeness whereof they were created in the beginning: therefore all men verilie are unrighteous and sinners: whereupon it followeth, that in them there is no righteousness, and that they have nothing wherin to boast before the righteous God. (Bullinger 1587:551.)

For Bullinger, the image of God in humanity is lost in its totality, and this loss of the image is both a cause and a consequence of the unrighteousness inherent in the present human condition, i.e. depravity. Whether or not Hoeksema would agree with Bullinger as to exactly what constituted the image of God in man is certainly open to debate, but he most surely would agree with Bullinger on the material loss of that image and its consequences.

8.3 The Restraint of Sin

The Second Point of Common Grace as espoused by the Synod of 1924 speaks specifically about the restraint of sin in the heart of the unregenerate by the Holy Spirit. We have dealt at some length with the point of contact for this work of the Holy Spirit in fallen humanity. Now, I would have us look briefly at synod's justification for this assertion regarding the work of the Holy Spirit in the hearts of the unregenerate and Hoeksema's unique response.

The synod of the Christian Reformed Church in 1924 believed that articles 13 and 36 of the *Belgic Confession* were justification sufficient for their conclusions on the work of restraint of sin by the Holy Spirit. The specific passage from article 13 is: 'without the will of our Father, in whom we do entirely trust; being persuaded that he so restrains the devil and all our enemies that, without his will and permission, they cannot hurt us' (Schaff: 1985:397). Likewise, the specific passage from article 36 reads as follows:

> We believe that our gracious God, because of the depravity of mankind, hath appointed kings, princes, and magistrates, willing that the world should be governed by certain laws and policies; to the end that the dissoluteness of men might be restrained, and all things carried on among them with good order and decency. For this purpose he has invested the magistracy with the sword, *for the punishment of evil doers, and for the praise of them that do well.* (Schaff 1985:432.)

In his book *The Triple Breach*, after commenting briefly that any operation of the Holy Spirit in the hearts of the unregenerate keeps the person 'from a total corruption of his nature' so that that person 'is not as ungodly in his outward life as might otherwise be expected' (Hoeksema 1942:21), Hoeksema proceeds to criticize the foundation in the *Belgic Confession* upon which the Christian Reformed Synod rested this point. Speaking specifically with respect to article 13 of the *Belgic Confession* as used by the synod, Hoeksema contends that article has nothing to do with any operation of common grace by the Holy Spirit. Instead, he writes: 'It speaks of God's providence, and in connection with this blessed truth of God's power and dominion even over the instruments and agents of darkness' (Hoeksema 1942:21). The fact that this article speaks of 'devils' and the 'ungodly' 'in the same breath,' writes Hoeksema, should have warned the synod that if their 'so called interpretation' was correct that this article would also teach 'that there is a reforming influence of the Holy Spirit upon the devils' (Hoeksema 1942:21). Hoeksema agrees that this interpretation is absurd, but, he maintains, that if synod does not want an operation of common grace on devils than it cannot maintain that this article speaks of a 'gracious operation of the Holy Spirit at all, but simply God's almighty dominion, whereby He rules over and governs all things according to His eternal counsel' (Hoeksema 1942:22).

Continuing his criticism, Hoeksema now turns his attention to article 36. He writes:

> It is well-known, that this article does not speak of a certain restraint of the power and corruption of sin in the heart of the natural man by a certain general operation of the Holy Spirit, but of an external restraint of certain public sins by the power of the law supported by police-power. The plain teaching of this article is even, that without the power of the magistrates men are not restrained at all but are dissolute. If there were such an operation of the Spirit as is taught in the second point, the police, the sword-power of the magistrates would not be necessary. But now it is different. Article 36 does not proceed from the assumption of such an operation of grace upon the heart of natural man at all, and, therefore, professes the need for laws and police. (Hoeksema 1942:22.)

It was regarding article 36 and its use by the Christian Reformed Church, as I quoted in the biography, that Hoeksema, years later, quipped 'that the CRC Kalamazoo Synod of 1924 could not tell the difference between the Holy Spirit and a policeman' (Engelsma 2001:294).

8.4 Further Criticism of Point Two

In addition to his disagreement with traditional Reformed theology on the image of God in man, Hoeksema also took exception to Abraham Kuyper's teaching on common grace that was adopted by the synod of 1924 and enshrined in point two. Hoeksema states that he wants to 'call attention to certain fundamental principles that have been adopted in this second point, and that are in direct conflict with the entire presentation of the truth in the Word of God and with the fundamental line of Reformed thinking' (Hoeksema 1942:54-55).

The first of these principles, writes Hoeksema, involves the idea of God's sovereignty 'over the powers of sin and death and corruption' (Hoeksema 1942:55). Common grace as it is stated in point two, Hoeksema observes, offers a dualistic conception of God and the creation, 'more particularly God and the power of darkness' (Hoeksema 1942:55). It gives a representation to sin, death, and corruption that allows them to work outside the sovereign control of God. Hence, this point of common grace teaches God's restraint of these powers, which 'exists and works outside and apart of Him' (Hoeksema 1942:55). 'But this is dualism,' writes Hoeksema,

> and contrary to the fundamental conception of the Word of God. ...The corruption of the sinner is death, spiritual death. ...God inflicts the punishment of death upon the guilty sinner in Paradise. Also death and corruption are powers that can work only through God. But if this is maintained, one can no longer speak of a restraining power of the Spirit, for how could God check a power that operates only by His will and through Him? The theory of a restraining grace is fundamentally a denial of God's absolute sovereignty. (Hoeksema 1942:55.)

Secondly, Hoeksema sees this idea of a restraining grace as a denial of God's justice. Those who maintain the view of a restraining grace conceive of the light, the remnants of good that remain in humanity since the fall, and the semblance of outward righteousness, which all the proponents of common grace are seeking to come to terms with (Engelsma 2003:12-17), as 'unmerited grace of God' i.e. 'common grace' (Hoeksema 1942:55). 'Very well,' Hoeksema inquires, 'but on what basis of God's unchangeable justice does fallen man receive this light and life and goodness, this common grace?' (Hoeksema 1942:55). If the threat of God in the garden to Adam and Eve was, if you eat you will die, and God did not carry out the sentence, where is the justice? Hoeksema is quick to distinguish between this scenario and the remission of sins merited by the work of Christ available to the elect. 'But,' Hoeksema concludes, 'to what basis of justice can they point who maintain that natural man, outside of Christ, receives blessings of unmerited grace? (Hoeksema 1942:55-56).

Thirdly, Hoeksema maintains that point two is based on what he terms 'the serious error of resistible grace' (Hoeksema 1942:56). That is to say that the restraint of sin in the unregenerate, as outlined by the proponents of common grace, is resistible grace. As proof of this assertion Hoeksema states 'that corruption and sin are not actually checked, they make progress and develop continually. This was evident in the history of the pre-deluvian world. This becomes very evident in all history, also in the new dispensation, for the entire development of the world tends towards the realization of Antichrist' (Hoeksema 1942:56). On this point Hoeksema quotes Professor Louis Berkhof to the effect that 'the Spirit strives in vain. He attempts to check the power of sin and lead men to repentance, but He strives in vain, He fails' (Hoeksema 1942:56). Cornelius Van Till seems to concede this very point when he was guest lecturer at Calvin Seminary at approximately the same time point two was adopted. According to Van Til, writes James Bratt:

> Common Grace...was no continuing and renewing work of God but a fund given to mankind in general before the Fall that had been diminishing ever since. "Civic righteousness" was but a weak memory of ancestral blessings. Humanity was divided ever more sharply into two religious camps as the mist of common grace lifted from human consciousness, revealing to the reprobate their true enmity with God and thus triggering ever more thorough, forceful enmity towards the elect. (Bratt 1984:191.)

Even with all he wrote on the subject, Hoeksema considered his chief objection to point two was that it effectively denied total depravity. As I said at the outset of this chapter, points two and three of common grace are related. Point two gives a rationale to point three. While point three repeats some of point two, it would really cease to exist without it. Point two is the foundation and point three builds on that foundation. Hoeksema says that two and three relate as cause and effect. Without the restraint of sin in point two, there would be no 'civic righteousness' as outlined in point three. As Hoeksema writes:

> And fact is, that this second point simply teaches that the human nature since the fall is not wholly corrupt and totally depraved; it implies that it would have been totally corrupt if the restraining power of common grace had not intervened. ...Consider it how you will, the second point always presupposes that some of the original righteousness of Paradise is left in man, some moral integrity remained in him, some element of good, which may be preserved, some love of the neighbor, some receptivity for the truth is still discovered in him. If this is not presupposed there is nothing to keep, to preserve, to check. And for that reason the second point, in which the theory of common grace as expounded by Dr. A. Kuyper, Sr., was fully adopted, implies a denial of the total depravity of fallen man. (Hoeksema 1942:56-57.)

8.5 Organic Development

To counter his opponent's view of the restraint of sin in the heart of the unregenerate as a work of the Holy Spirit, Hoeksema posited his own concept of 'organic development' in order to explain the progress and development of sin in the world. This concept of 'organic development' would eventually become one of the dominant themes in Hoeksema's later theology, especially his view of the covenant. As to how Hoeksema came to adopt this perspective is not at all certain, although a good deal of influence from the great Dutch theologian, Herman Bavinck, can be discerned. The perspective itself, according to Leonard Peikoff, comes from the 'German historical school' (Peikoff 1982:259). Following this school of thought, sociologist Henry Pratt Fairchild, writing on modern life in the May 1932 issue of *Harper's Magazine*, said that it has become 'so definitely organic, that the very concept of the individual is becoming obsolete' (Peikoff 1982:268). Herman Hanko, in his recent doctrinal history of the Protestant Reformed Churches, also sets the idea of 'organic' over against that of 'individuality' (Hanko 2000:232-233). Hanko believes that this was Hoeksema's opinion also; pitting individualistic Arminianism against a Reformed 'organic conception of things' (Hanko 2000:232). Hanko also believes that when Kuyper and Bavinck followed the 'siren's song' of common grace, they also adopted this individualism, leaving behind their original, 'organic' outlook (Hanko 2000:232-233). My own studies reveal that this was hardly the case, at least for Herman Bavinck. Herman Bavinck was already a mature, seasoned theologian when he penned his enormously popular *Magnalia Dei* (translated as *Our Reasonable Faith*) in 1909. This volume was to serve as an abridgement, or compendium of his larger four-volume dogmatics, which was issued some ten years earlier. Writing on the covenant of grace in *Our Reasonable Faith*, Bavinck says that

> The second peculiarity or remarkable characteristic of the covenant of grace is that in all of its dispensations it has an organic character. ...The elect, accordingly, do not stand loosely alongside each other, but are one in Christ. ...It is one communion or fellowship, endeavoring to keep the unity of the Spirit in the bond of peace. ...Thus election cannot have been an arbitrary or accidental deed. If it was governed by the purpose of constituting Christ as Head of the church His body, then it has an organic character and already includes the idea of a covenant. (Bavinck 1956:276.)

Bavinck's view of the covenant, as demonstrated above, is most obviously organic in nature. Additionally, Bavinck previously investigated the idea of 'common grace' thoroughly in his rectoral address at Kampen in December 1894. Hence, to say that Bavinck's later studies on common grace altered, or transformed his former 'organic' outlook to one of individualism, does not seem to be the case. In fact, the whole enterprise of pitting 'organic' against 'individual' seems dubious at best. There are some things that are of an individual nature and there are some things that can best be explained from an organic perspective. Adopting the one need not demand precluding the other. I would like to suggest that this was also the case with Hoeksema. While he held to an organic view of the covenant, the elect in Christ, and even of the development of sin in the world, he did not hold to this perspective in areas such as ecclesiology where he lauded Kuyper for again giving respectability once again to the autonomy of the local church (see Englesma 1998:30), or in civil government where rights such as 'to keep and bear arms' is an individual one.

For all this discussion of 'organic' versus 'individual' one might consider a definition to be essential. Unfortunately, however, Hoeksema never really provided one. Herman Hanko, in his discussion of 'organic' admits just this:

> One would be hard pressed to find in all the writings of the ministers of the Protestant Reformed Churches a word used more commonly and in a more widely-diversified way than the word "organic." ...(Yet) the rather striking fact is, however, that one can search in vain for a definition of this word. Passages can be found in which some clear things are said about the term, and in which the writer made clear why the term could be applied to a given doctrine; but a definition cannot be found. (Hanko 2000:230-231.)

Earlier, quoting Gertrude Hoeksema, I said that one of Herman Hoeksema's theological mentors was Abraham Kuyper; Professor David Engelsma, current professor of dogmatics at the Protestant Reformed Seminary concurs in this regard (Engelsma 1998:29). However, Reverend Bernard Woudenberg, minister emeritus in the Protestant Reformed Churches, thinks otherwise. Having studied directly under Herman Hoeksema in the 1950s, Reverend Woudenberg has, what appears to me, to be a deep, abiding understanding and love for Hoeksema's theology. Hence, in contrast to Gertrude Hoeksema and David Engelsma, Reverend Woudenberg sees more of a general Secession influence in Hoeksema's thought on this subject, such as is seen in the theology of both Herman Bavinck (1854-1921) and Hoeksema's own teacher at Calvin Seminary, Foppe M. ten Hoor (1855-1934) (Woudenberg 2000:97). This would be in direct contrast to one of Hoeksema's other teachers, William Heyns (1856-1933) which I considered at some length in the biography of Hoeksema. Reverend Woudenberg said all this in conjunction with an article he wrote for *The Standard Bearer* analyzing 'The Covenant View of Herman Bavinck,' in the course of which he commented upon an article by Dr. Jelle Faber of the Canadian Reformed Church. He wrote:

> In this paper Dr. Faber examines the positions of seven early professors of Calvin Seminary, at least six of whom he proposes formed a consistent line of theological thought—essentially the same as that now held by the Liberated Churches (suggesting, no doubt, that those who would remain loyal to the historical teachings of the Christian Reformed can now best ally themselves with the Canadian Reformed). As I read this, however, something struck me as extremely strange. Faber deals with the last of these men, William Heyns and Foppe M. ten Hoor, as though they were of one theological cut, while I recall distinctly how Herman Hoeksema, who studied under both of them, took strong exception to the teaching of Heyns, while he was quite fond of ten Hoor and in a certain way looked upon him as his own theological mentor. ...Faber points outs that he (ten Hoor) had been a classmate of the great Dutch theologian, Dr. Herman Bavinck, and a correspondent with him in later life, leading to the likelihood that their theological positions were essentially similar. This sent me quickly to the shelf for Bavinck's great book, *Our Reasonable Faith*, and in it to the chapter on *The Covenant*. I was amazed. Here in most concise form are all the essential elements of Herman Hoeksema's covenant view—at almost every point precisely opposite to that of Heyns, Schilder and the Liberated Churches. (Woudenberg 2000:97.)

The specific characteristic that allied Hoeksema's covenant view with that of both Bavinck and Ten Hoor was, according to Reverend Woudenberg, that elusive quality of 'organic development' (Woudenberg 2001). Again we find ourselves pressed into a quest for a definition. Reverend Woudenberg frankly admitted that Herman Hoeksema never defined the term in any abstract or objective sense. Yet, Reverend Woudenberg did say that the key quality of 'organic,' for Hoeksema, was the idea of 'living.' Hence, 'organic' refers to a living relationship; a relationship of like kinds, a sort of symbiosis. This living relationship is between Christ and the Church, His Body, and, by logical extension, a union of the whole church with the individual. A definition, which, at least to my mind, is far different than Hanko's definition in which the individual is pitted against the collective.

It is of particular interest then that James Daane, minister and teacher in the Christian Reformed Church and an ardent exponent of common grace, criticizes Hoeksema' 'individualism,' for focusing exclusively on the individual in his covenant concept to the exclusion of the whole. He writes:

> Rev. Hoeksema claims to believe in the Covenant of Grace. Nevertheless, in common with the Fundamentalist and the Liberal, he believes essentially that God deals with mankind as individuals. For, in Hoeksema's thought, God does not *first of all* deal with elect and reprobate together, *in their covenantal historical relatedness.* God has no *common* attitude towards *both* elect and reprobate. Consequently, Hoeksema denies both common grace and common wrath. God *only loves* the elect and *only hates* the reprobate. (Daane 1951:11.)

On the next page of the same article, in the course of expounding his conception of 'man, both one and many,' Daane says that the 'individual is, indeed, superior to the state' because the state is 'a thing,' while at the same time saying that the individual is not superior to the 'social community' because it is 'a community of persons' (Daane 1951:12). Nowhere does he define 'social community' apart from saying it is a community of persons. Is not the state also a community of persons? Daane does not seem to understand clearly, if he does he is unable to communicate it, what an individual is in himself or herself and, in turn, what is the relationship of that individual to the organic whole. For Hoeksema, humanity is indeed organically related, but not in the 'covenantal historical relatedness' that Daane imagines. Using Biblical imagery, Hoeksema believed that the relatedness of the different individuals that make up the human race is that of 'kernel' to 'husk' or of 'chaff' to 'wheat.' (Hoeksema 1966:214-226). They grow together in the world as they grow together on the plant, and in the end they will be separated. The 'wheat,' however, is not the 'chaff,' and vice versa. They grow together organically, but they are not related spiritually. The 'wheat' and 'chaff,' as in the Scriptures, signify the elect and the reprobate and they grow separately from a spiritual perspective along different lines.

Commenting on the covenantal aspect from the perspective of the elect, Reverend Woudenberg says that this living relationship is that in which we receive our life from Christ, and he used the figure of the vine and the branches as detailed in John 15 to illustrate his meaning. This concept of 'organic,' i.e. 'living,' broadens out into the line of human generations also (Bavinck held to this view also, see Van Genderen 1995:58). As a physical vine produces further new growth so the spiritual branch produces further new branches, which would, in turn, rightly be called spiritual growth. All of which occurs under the rubric of organic development.

Hoeksema, as we have seen in the biography, was a follower of Secession theology as well as that of Abraham Kuyper. Both strains figure strongly in his theological development. Still, it was from Herman Bavinck and F. M. ten Hoor that Hoeksema inherited most of his ideas on the nature of the covenant, with the idea of an organic or living relationship as paramount. Concerning this organic conception of the covenant and its influence on Hoeksema, over against the more judicial categories of Abraham Kuyper, Reverend Woudenberg writes:

> This perhaps more basically than anything separates his (Hoeksema's) views from that of Schilder, who, like Abraham Kuyper before him "had a preference for judicial categories and for terms like statute, obligation and legal status, defined by the *speaking God*, the God of the *Word*, both for those who will respond positively, and for those whose response will be negative." Meanwhile, however, the Rev's H. Danhof and H. Hoeksema had followed Bavinck's suggestion and focused on the organic relationship of friendship as the heart of their covenantal

thought. To them the idea of the covenant as a living relationship was far more Biblical and far richer in thought than that of a legal right to something that might not even be realized in the end. (Woudenberg 2000:99.)

In speaking of the 'organic' Hoeksema everywhere begins in the book of Genesis with the 'moederbelofte' of Genesis 3:15, and, while we have elements of the 'individual' there are also elements of the 'organism.' Also known as the 'protevangel,' this is the promise 'that God will put enmity in the heart of man against Satan and his seed' (Hoeksema 1966:261). Hoeksema gives this perspective:

> All the rest of the history of God's people in the world is plainly the realization of this prophecy. This prophecy is called the protevangel (in Dutch: moederbelofte). It is called thus because it is the beginning of the gospel of salvation; and all the rest of the revelation of the gospel in Christ may be conceived as only a further unfolding and expansion of this promise. …Only, in the course of history it is gradually revealed in all its implications. By the seed of the serpent, although also the serpent brood is meant, is indicating principally the seed of the devil, that is, the children of the devil among men in the line of generations of the reprobate, culminating in the Antichrist, the Man of Sin. On the other hand, by the seed of the woman is meant: The spiritual children of the covenant, the holy seed in the line of the generations of the elect. (Hoeksema 1966:260.)

We have already examined the development of this 'holy seed' in the lines of generations of the elect. This is the covenant, both in its individual and corporate (organism) manifestations. In the next chapter, in connection with the third point of common grace, I will look at the darker side of the 'moederbelofte,' which, according to Hoeksema, is the organic development of sin, and those associated with it.

8.6 Conclusion

As I said at the outset of this chapter, the second and third points of common function together. The second point speaks specifically of a work of the Holy Spirit in the hearts of the unregenerate to restrain sin so that, point three, they are able to perform good works. This work of the Holy Spirit is termed common grace because it teaches a restraint of sin in the hearts of unbelievers—no one has ever argued against the Holy Spirit working in the hearts of believers, at least as far as common grace is concerned. In conjunction with the second point, we have also looked at Hoeksema's analysis of the support from the *Belgic Confession* given to this point by the Christian Reformed Synod of 1924. Hoeksema effectively showed that the proof adduced by the synod for the second point from the confession, really had nothing to do with the point they were trying to prove. In fact, as Hoeksema retorted, they were confusing the Holy Spirit with a policeman.

For common grace to work there has to be a point of contact in the person in whom it is to work. While most specify various points of contact, the image of God, or various facets thereof, usually seems to be in view. Traditional Reformed theology, with its description of the image as partially gone and partially remaining, gives support to this view. After all, if part of the image remains, there remains something good in unregenerate, and the function of the Holy Spirit expounded in point two simply works in conjunction with what is already in the person. For this reason, Hoeksema repudiated the notion any vestiges of the image of God in fallen humanity. His view was that the image in any material sense was lost in the fall, although human beings still retained the capacity as image bearers; it is simply their humanity.

While Hoeksema may have not believed in any work of the Holy Spirit in the unregenerate from outside the creation, he believed in organic development within the creation. We have discussed this organic, living development in conjunction with the covenant. In the next chapter, we will look at the other side of organic development, the darker side, the development of sin.

Chapter 9

Point Three: The Development of Culture

Relative to the third point which is concerned with the question of *civil righteousness as performed by the unregenerate*, synod declares that, according to Scripture and the Confessions, the unregenerate, though incapable of doing saving good, can do civil good. This is evident from the quotations from Scripture and from the Canons of Dordrecht, III, IV, 4, and the Netherlands Confession Art. 36, which teach that God without renewing the heart so influences man, that he is able to perform civil good; while it also appears from the citations from Reformed writers of the most flourishing period of Reformed Theology, that our Reformed Fathers from ancient times were of the same opinion.

In this chapter we will investigate the Third Point of Common Grace as adopted by the synod of the Christian Reformed Church in 1924. This points states emphatically that unregenerate humanity is able to do good works, more specifically civic good, and that this is possible because of the direct influence of God. The point also states that any good that a person may do because of this specific work of God, while of civic good, which has been understood as cultural good as well, is not of saving good. That is to say, that while these works may be of merit in this world, they are not of merit in the next.

Hoeksema denied the truth of this point as well as of the other two. His reason primarily was that this point as well as its predecessor denied the Reformed truth of total depravity. In doing so it also denied the truth of the antithesis. Many of the same arguments used against point two are used against point three as well since both points speak of a non-saving work of God in the unbeliever. I have tried not to overlap the arguments, but to keep each to the point against which they were made. There will nevertheless be some overlap in concepts, it was simply unavoidable.

In the next few pages we will be looking at the concept of culture and whether, from Hoeksema's perspective, this is possible at all. In analyzing the teaching of this point and Hoeksema's response to it, I will also be presenting a positive statement of Hoeksema's teaching on the antithesis, total depravity, and organic development. This is not to say that everything I write in this chapter will be positive. Not everything Hoeksema had to say on these matters was positive. But I do hope to present a faithful representation of Hoeksema's thoughts on these matters and to show in the process that Hoeksema's position was not just a reactionary one as De Jong believed, but rather a well thought out statement of what he believed to be the truth of the matter.

Some may lament the lack of references to Abraham Kuyper and Herman Bavinck. My purpose in analyzing this point, although the thinking of Kuyper and Bavinck looms large in the background, is simply to deal with the third point as framed by the Synod of 1924 and, hence, as Hoeksema encountered it.

9.1 Synod's Confessional Proof

As proof for their decision in adopting this point, synod referred to article 36 of the *Belgic Confession* and the *Canons of Dordrecht*, III and IV, 4. Article 36 of the *Belgic Confession* was given as proof for the second point as well. This article says: 'We believe that our gracious God, because of the depravity of mankind, hath appointed kings, princes, and magistrates, willing that the world should be governed by certain laws and policies; to the end that the dissoluteness of men might be restrained, and all things carried on among them with good order and decency' (Schaff 1985:432). This article, as Hoeksema seeks to demonstrate, proves the opposite of what the synod adduced from it in the third point. Article 36 article proceeds from the assumption of the 'depravity of mankind' and the need for external restraint (the magistrate with the sword) to curb that depravity. But, Hoeksema concludes, 'If the declaration of synod were true, that an influence of God urges the natural man to do good, the police might be abolished. But since that declaration is untrue the sword-power is peremptory in society' (Hoeksema 1942:24).

The confessional basis for point three also seems a bit confusing. The *Acts of Synod* for 1924 in one place lists the confessional proof for the third point as being the Third and Fourth Heads of Doctrine, article 4 (*Acta der Synode* 1924:132), and in another place is added another article from the same Heads of Doctrine (*Acta der Synode* 1924:146). Article 3 from the Third and Fourth Heads of Doctrine reads: 'Therefore all men are conceived in sin, and are by nature children of wrath, incapable of any saving good, prone to evil, dead in sin, and in bondage thereto; and, without the regenerating grace of the Holy Spirit, they are neither able nor willing to return to God, to reform the depravity of their nature, nor dispose themselves to reformation' (Schaff 1985:588). Since this article from Dort does not appear as a proof in the final version of the Three Points of Common Grace, Hoeksema did not comment on it in regard to its usage here. But I have enlisted Hoeksema's son, Homer Hoeksema, in order to ascertain what this article from Dort would have meant to Hoeksema. Homer Hoeksema's comments run approximately four pages, concentrating on total depravity and the need for the regenerating grace of God. He ends by saying: 'Only through the grace of regeneration can he be delivered from his corruption. This leaves him in the hand of God: for the grace of regeneration is of the Holy Spirit. That grace is the indispensable prerequisite of all correction of a depraved nature and of any disposition to such correction' (Hoeksema1980:451). Herman Hoeksema was a bit more ruffled by synod's use of article 4 of the *Canons of Dort*, Third and Fourth Heads of Doctrine, because, in so doing, they quote only the first half of the article. From the Acts of Synod for 1924, this article is quoted as follows: 'There is, to be sure, a certain light of nature remaining in man after the fall, by virtue of which he retains some notions about God, natural things, and the difference between what is moral and immoral, and demonstrates a certain eagerness for virtue and good behavior' (*Acta der Synode* 1924:132). The second part of article 4 of the Third and Fourth Heads of Doctrine, the part which the Synod of 1924 omitted, reads: 'But so far is this light of nature from being sufficient to bring him to a saving knowledge of God, and to true conversion, that he is incapable of using it aright even in things natural and civil. Nay farther, this light, such as it is, man in various ways renders wholly polluted, and holds it [back] in unrighteousness; by doing which he becomes inexcusable before God' (Schaff 1985:588). Hoeksema considered synod guilty of deceptive practices in the framing of the Third Point of Common Grace because of its misuse of the confessions. He wrote that synod's use of this article 4 from the Third and Fourth Heads of Doctrine was 'very deceiving, because it contains only half of the article to which it refers, a fact which is all the more deplorable because the second half of the same article makes it evident that synod by its partial quotation is corrupting its meaning and changing it into the very opposite from what it actually teaches' (Hoeksema 1942:24).

It is interesting to note in this connection that James Daane in his book on common grace uses article 4 of the Third and Fourth Heads of Doctrine in the very same manner as the Synod of 1924, quoting only the first part of the article, in the course of his discussion of the 'Restraint of Sin and Civic Righteousness' (Daane 1954:88). In a further attempt to bolster his case for the production of 'civic righteousness' by the unregenerate, Daane cites 'the traditional manner in which Reformed theology accounted for this difference between total and absolute depravity was by reference to a general, gracious operation of the Holy Spirit upon unregenerate human hearts' (Daane 1954:88). Nowhere does Danne offer any proof for this assertion, he just assumes its truth. However, as I shown before, Harry Boer strongly disagrees; believing instead that any attempt to distinguish between 'total depravity' and an 'absolute depravity…is inherently impossible' (Boer 1990:62).

9.2 Culture

The civic righteousness that both the third point of common grace and James Daane make reference to can also be referred to under the title of 'culture.' Hoeksema does this in his small book *The Christian and Culture*, as does Henry van Til in his persuasive work *The Calvinistic Concept of Culture* and more recently Richard Mouw in his book, which was based on the Stob Lectures delivered in 2000 on the campus of Calvin College and Calvin Theological Seminary, entitled *He Shines in all that's Fair: Culture and Common Grace*. All these men are keenly aware of the inherent difficulty in defining the word 'culture.' Additionally, David Engelsma of the Protestant Reformed Churches, in his response to Mouw's offering, has much to say on this matter as well. The allusiveness that attaches to this concept seems to be felt by all who attempt to write on it. The term itself, Engelsma writes, is both 'ambiguous' and 'unhelpful' (Engelsma 2003:53). By contrast, Henry van Til expends a great deal of space attempting to give satisfactory definition to the word 'culture.' He understands the concept 'culture' as conceived by some as too narrow and by others as too broad (Van Til 1959:25-35). In chapter two he says that 'religion cannot be subsumed under culture' (Van Til 1959:25), and in chapter three commenting on the chief end of man as outlined in the Westminster Confession of Faith, Van Til writes: 'This service cannot be expressed except through man's cultural activity, which gives expression to his religious faith' (Van Til 1959:37). On the same page Van Til quotes Paul Tillich with approval when the latter states that 'Religion is the substance of culture and culture the form of religion' (Van Til 1959:37). Later, quoting Emil Brunner, Van Til admits that 'The meaning of life does not lie in culture as such, but culture derives its meaning from man's faith in God; it is never an end in itself, but always a means of expressing one's religious faith' (Van Til 1959:28), hence, 'religion and culture are inseparable. Every culture is animated by religion' (Van Til 1959:44).

Van Til is very helpful when he comments on the etymology of the word 'culture.' Deriving from the Latin *'colere,'* it originally signified 'the tilling or cultivation of the ground. This is the idea of Scripture when we read that God placed Adam in the garden to "dress" it' (Van Til 1959:29). However, 'today,' writes Van Til, 'we use the word "culture" of any human labor bestowed on God's creation in the widest sense...by which it receives historical forms and is refined to a higher level of productivity for the enjoyment of man' (Van Til 1959:29). With a measure of finality, Van Til finally says that culture 'is any and all human effort and labor expended upon the cosmos, to unearth its treasures and its riches and bring them into the service of man for the enrichment of human existence unto the glory of God' (Van Til 1959:29-30).

Hoeksema is in agreement with Van Til on the etymology of the word, but insists that since the eighteenth-century it has acquired a much wider meaning (Hoeksema 1946:5). On this wider meaning Hoeksema writes:

> The whole man, with all his powers and in all his relationships, belabors the whole kosmos. He works upon it with his mind and discovers its laws and relations, its motion and force, its hidden laws and treasures, and the culture of the natural sciences is the result, biology and physics, astronomy and chemistry, etc. He exerts his physical power and mental ingenuity upon the world, to subdue it and to press it into his service, in agriculture and mining, in navigation and aeronautics, in all the various modern industries and inventions. He cleaves the depth of the sea and soars through the height of the heavens, he chains the very lightening and rides on it; he knows how to swallow up distance and speaks to his neighbor a thousand miles away. All these belong to modern culture in the comprehensive sense of the term. Then, too, he discovers the laws of harmony and beauty, and gives expression to it in the culture of fine arts; on the canvas and in the symphony, in sculpture and architecture he reproduces what his soul perceives and experiences of the beautiful in the world about him. And the same attention he devotes to himself. He examines his own physical organism, discovers its laws of operation, and finds the causes of disease and death; and then sets himself the task to develop the powers and the form of that organism in physical culture, athletics and sports of various sorts; and to fight sickness and pain, corruption and death by the culture of the medical and surgical sciences and arts. He investigates the workings of his own soul, his sensations and perceptions, his imaginations and reason, his emotions and aesthetic feelings, and devotes himself to psychic culture, the development of the intellect and will, and the building of moral character. And he studies the various relationships in human life, in the home in the school, in society and in the state, and develops the sciences of eugenics, pedagogy, sociology, economics and politics, in order to set himself the task of improving and perfecting all these relations between individuals, groups

and nations. All these, and the products of these efforts must be regarded as belonging to what is known as modern culture. (Hoeksema 1946:6-7.)

But, according to Hoeksema, rather than simply investigating the things of the world and subduing them to its use, humanity is driven to aim higher still; humanity is looking for perfection (Hoeksema 1946:7). Recounting the belief of the ancient Greeks 'of the beautiful soul in the beautiful body as the aim of human culture' (Hoeksema 1946:7), Hoeksema writes:

> And so modern culture, whether it is always conscious of this ultimate aim or not, cannot rest satisfied until it has attained to the perfect soul of the perfect body, the perfect man in the perfect society, in which all strife and disruption, war and unrest is found no more, from which suffering and even death are banished; and the perfect society in the perfect world, in which everything is subjected to man and serves him as its lord and sovereign! Such is the inevitable urge and purpose of modern culture! (Hoeksema 1946:7.)

Van Til brings up this same striving for perfection in connection with the views of Matthew Arnold, but believes that 'with respect to culture, which indeed seeks perfection in the sense of fulfillment, Arnold is too naïve when he speaks of sweetness and light. For culture is not the opposite of depravity' (Van Til 1959:25-26). Hoeksema refers to this 'striving' in man as a 'cultural urge,' or 'cultural mandate' from which man can never rid himself (Hoeksema 1946:9). Van Til sees the same effects of this 'cultural urge' or 'cultural mandate,' 'as man strives to be master of the world, ruler of all that he surveys, king of the universe; he would be lord and sovereign over all that exists under the sun' (Van Til 1959:34).

9.3 The Cultural Aspirations of Humanity

If Van Til is correct when he concluded that culture is derived from, even an expression of one's faith (Van Til 1959:28), then humanity's 'urge' to subdue everything to itself as lord and sovereign makes humanity the object of their own faith. Humanity, it seems, wants nothing less than to be God. It would seem to me that this desire on the part of humanity, if indeed anything, is the result of total depravity. But how, then, can Van Til speak in such positive terms of culture deriving from this sort of faith? Maybe, Van Til is speaking of Christians, the elect, developing culture. He does not speak with any particular approval of the cultural activities of the Medieval Roman Catholic Church (Van Til 1959:15-19). He does not mention the fact that government offices in a good many European countries are referred to as 'ministries,' reflecting a time when Christian ideas permeated the institutions of society. But, we are really not talking about Christian cultural activities, but the cultural activities that naturally flow from one's faith.

Hoeksema succinctly dissects the civic righteousness or cultural aspirations of the 'natural man' as they flow from naturally from his faith. In a book originally published prior to the events of 1924 entitled *Langs Zuivere Banen (Along Straight Paths)*, Hoeksema writes:

> And what, then, is civil righteousness? According to our view, the natural man discerns the relationships, laws, rules of life and fellowship, etc., as they are ordained by God. He sees their propriety and utility. And he adapts himself to them for his own sake. If in this attempt he succeeds the result is an act that shows an outward and formal resemblance to the laws of God. Then we have civil righteousness, a regard for virtue and external deportment. And if this attempt fails, as is frequently the case, civil righteousness disappears and the result is exactly the opposite. His fundamental error, however, is that he does not seek after God, nor aim at Him and His glory, even in this regard for virtue and external deportment. On the contrary, he seeks himself, both individually and in fellowship with other sinners and with the whole world, and it is his purpose to maintain himself even in his sin over against God. And this is sin. And in reality his work also has evil effects upon himself and his fellow creatures. For, his actions with relation to men and fellow creatures are performed according to the same rule and with similar results. And thus it happens, that sin develops constantly

and corruption increases, while still there remains a formal adaptation to the laws ordained of God for the present life. Yet the natural man never attains to any ethical good. That is our view. (Hoeksema 1942:75-76.)

There is another component to the cultural activities of the unregenerate that, according to Hoeksema, no one seems to be taking into account. This has to do with the curse that God placed upon Adam and Eve before their expulsion from the garden. Hoeksema admonishes us that, we must, in any discussion of culture, take account of the effects of this curse. He writes:

> The possibility of "culture" is frequently deduced from paradise and the original state of righteousness and perfection, as if the terrible fact of the curse upon creation and of death, even in the natural, physical sense of the word, need not enter into the discussion. This, however, is a fundamental error. The ground is cursed, and the creature is in the bondage of corruption and made subject to vanity. The result is that creation gets nowhere. Vanity of vanities, all is vanity, saith the preacher. (Hoeksema 1946:10.)

Hoeksema's stance with respect to culture and its development is not a popular position. But French Reformed theologian Jacques Ellul seems to be in agreement when he writes that 'we are forced to assert that beneath all this apparent movement, and apparent development, actually we are not moving at all. It is true, of course, that there is great deal of disorder and violence, that there is progress in technics, that there are social and political experiences, but in reality our world is standing still' (Ellul 1967:33).

While it is possible for humanity to discover some of God's laws, as was previously said, and based upon these discoveries to come up with new advances in medicine and technology that are of benefit, according to Hoeksema it is still vanity. These inventions may indeed be considered good gifts of God, but they are 'slippery places' to the unregenerate. This concept of 'slippery places' quoted throughout Hoeksema's writings, comes from Psalm 73, in which the good gifts of God are for the purpose of making the way to destruction for the unregenerate sure. The gifts God gives are always and truly good even though the recipient is not. Additionally, good gifts are given to the regenerate and unregenerate alike; to the regenerate for their good, to the reprobate to further their condemnation. Regarding good gifts and their purpose for the reprobate Hoeksema writes:

> And while God in his providence and by the Word of His power sustains his nature as man, and sustains his relation to the universe, thus providing him with means to develop and realize his life in the organism of all things, with these things man is always the sinner, the ungodly, the object of the wrath of God, gathering for himself treasures of wrath in the day of final judgment. (Hoeksema 1947:315.)

But what about the more noble and higher aspirations of humanity; those closer to God, if you will? Hoeksema posits a hierarchy or taxonomy on what are considered the components of culture. Technology and the mathematical sciences are relegated to the periphery because 'the spiritual-ethical attitude of man hardly comes to expression in them' (Hoeksema 1946:11). However, Hoeksema teaches, 'the closer we approach to those branches and departments of modern culture in which man's ethical nature finds its expression, the more it becomes evident that modern culture is corrupt' (Hoeksema 1946:11-12). It is at this point that Hoeksema takes issue with Abraham Kuyper, whom he believes made art, because of common grace, central to his world of cultural pursuits. Kuyper writes:

> But if you confess that the world once *was* beautiful, but by the curse has become *undone*, and by a final catastrophe is to pass to its full state of glory, excelling even the beautiful of paradise, then art has the mystical task of reminding us in its productions of the beautiful that was lost and of anticipating its perfect coming luster. Now this last-mentioned instance is the Calvinistic confession. It realized, more clearly than Rome, the hideous, corrupting influences of sin; this led to a higher estimation of the nature of paradise in the beauty of

original righteousness; and guided by this enchanting remembrance, Calvinism prophesied a redemption of outward nature also, to be realized in the reign of celestial glory. From this standpoint, Calvinism honored art as a gift of the Holy Ghost and as a consolidation in our present life, enabling us to discover in and behind this sinful life a richer and more glorious background. Standing by the ruins of this once so wonderfully beautiful creation, art points out to the Calvinist both the still visible lines of the original plan, and what is even more, the splendid restoration by which the Supreme Artist and Master-Builder will one day renew and enhance even the beauty of His original creation. (Kuyper 1987:155.)

Van Til believes that art is the object of a 'sensitivity in the natural man's cultural striving, a sense of deity, even a yearning for the things of the spirit' (Van Til 1959:33). And furthermore, because of this yearning for the things of the spirit, natural man 'longs for truth, beauty, and goodness and expresses this longing in music, poetry, painting, and gives expression to his spiritual aspirations by building cathedrals, mosques, or pagodas' (Van Til 1959:33). Responding specifically to Kuyper's words above, but in words equally critical of Van Til, Hoeksema writes:

> Flighty words and high sounding phrases I consider these words of Dr. Kuyper's, that are rather the expression of unrestrained imagination than historical truth and sober thought. It is quite impossible for the artist to reconstruct the original world of perfection. What painter, for instance, could ever produce a picture of man in his first state, without sin and suffering and death, in righteousness, holiness and truth, with his original power and royal majesty in the midst of creation? The little halo that is painted around the head of some saints in old paintings is a confession of the artist's incompetence to produce on his canvas a true representation of a righteous man. Neither original righteousness nor regeneration and its life of perfection can be put on the canvas. And the perfect world that is to come can so little be construed by art that even Scripture always speaks of that world in earthly terms. It belongs to those things which "eye hath

not seen, ear has not heard, and never arose in the heart of man." And what is true of art is true of science and of culture in general. It must needs move within the scope of the vicious circle of corruption and death, of the curse and vanity. Culture cannot make the perfect man, not build the perfect world. (Hoeksema 1946:13.)

9.4 General Revelation

Even so, for Hoeksema, the ungodly never learn anything of God in the gifts He gives to them. While Hoeksema never really developed his ideas on what is commonly called 'general revelation,' he saw the concept as it stood in need of work. The Christian Reformed Church has of late taken the step of making an understanding of general revelation dependent upon common grace (Committee on Creation and Science 1988:7-9). They are of the opinion that 'if God reveals himself in nature, then this means that we know him in our experience of nature' (Committee on Creation and Science 1988:9). This report further concludes that we must 'think of general revelation as the manifestation of God's wisdom in the world and of science as the discovery of that wisdom' (Committee on Creation and Science 1988:9). In the thinking of the Christian Reformed Church, it seems that science has taken a major role in the development of culture. In fact, it could be said that culture in general at the beginning of the twenty-first century is increasingly defined by science in all quarters. This was the thesis of French Reformed theologian and law professor, Jacques Ellul, forty years ago in *The Technological Society* (Ellul 1964); a book as radical in its day as it is strangely prophetic in ours.

In Hoeksema's estimation, for general revelation, or rather the revelation of God as revealed in nature, to be understood humanity would have to have retained the image of God, which, for Hoeksema, they did not. Since he denied common grace, Hoeksema also reconsidered what was available to the understanding of humanity in the creation. In his *Dogmatics* he concluded:

> We are accustomed to distinguish two forms of revelation, a "general" revelation in "nature," and a "special" revelation in Scripture. And frequently these two

forms of revelation are presented as if they were two wholly different revelations, not only distinct, but separated from each other. The one is adapted to reason as its subjective principle of knowledge, the other to faith. The one is a revelation of God to man in general, the other to His people in Christ. The one provides man with the necessary material for the structure of a "natural theology;" the other is the source of Christian dogmatics. But this is plainly erroneous. It speaks about general revelation, natural theology, and natural religion as if the original condition of the first paradise still existed. And it completely fails to take into account the important change that was brought about in his "general revelation" through the fall of man and the curse of God. Yet, on the one hand, through this fall the recipient of God's revelation was so changed and corrupted that he can no longer truly hear the Word of God. For he lost the image of God, and all his light was changed into darkness. And although the light still shines in the darkness, the darkness comprehendeth it not. But, on the other hand, it dare not be overlooked that also the medium of revelation, the speech of God through the things that are made, is changed. For the creature is made to bear the curse of God and is subjected to vanity; and man himself pines and dies through the fierce wrath of God upon him. (Hoeksema 1966:41-42.)

What Hoeksema is saying, essentially, is that at the point of the fall the lights went out in creation. Prior to this, Adam named the animals according to their essence, which he could clearly see in each of them. Now humanity stumbles about in darkness, never really knowing what things mean. There is only one recipient of God's revelation and that is 'the new man in Christ Jesus. In His light do we see the light' (Hoeksema 1966:42). In an unpublished paper on Romans chapter one, Herman Hanko quotes a letter from his father Cornelius Hanko who probably knew Herman Hoeksema better than anyone, at least he knew him longer than anyone did. In the letter, the elder Hanko lends some interesting insight into Hoeksema's understanding of general revelation, he writes:

I recall that in H.H.'s notes on Genesis, he makes a point of it that God saw the light, that it was good. He spoke of the fact that light "carries" the object into our vision and thus to our minds. I often tell the catechumens that when we speak of ἀποκάλυψις, this implies an object that is capable of "seeing" receiving the revelation. Just as a beam of light hits an object and thus becomes light for us, so God's revelation finds its object in our souls. We reflect the light. And just as our natural eyes see what the light reveals, so our spiritual eyes see what God reveals. Manifestation is something quite different. Seeing they see but believe not; hearing they hear but perceive not. God manifests His power and divinity to the wicked. They know it; can never escape it, but suppress that knowledge in unbelief and unrighteousness. Herein the wrath of God is revealed to God's people, who have eyes to see even that in paganism. An idolater bowing before his idol is a revelation to us of the wrath of God. An evolutionist is no less a revelation of that wrath. ...And thus even in the pagan it becomes evident that before God no flesh is justified, but that justification is only by faith through the Spirit in our hearts. I think that is the point H.H. tried to make in his repeated references to Romans 1 in school. (Hanko [s.a.]: viii.)

This paragraph from Cornelius Hanko identifies the only knowledge of God available to humanity in general as 'manifestation' as oppose to 'revelation.' The difference, from my perspective, is that revelation is the communication of a father to his children in a language understood by both, while manifestation, lacking any emotional or endearing quality, is simply an in-your-face proclamation or announcement which may or may not be comprehended. Hanko is explicit in that God manifests both His power and divinity to the wicked. Hoeksema says the same in numerous places. It is this manifestation that leaves the reprobate without excuse, as Hanko understands Romans 1 to say. In other places Hoeksema denies any knowledge at all to the reprobate. This may seem like a contradiction, and maybe some will see it that way, but having read Hoeksema at length I think he is just saying the same thing as Cornelius Hanko. On this matter of knowledge to the reprobate, Herman Hanko writes: 'Hence, they have no subjective knowledge of God at all. Not because God does not give it to them. But because they hate it. There is therefore, no "revelation." There is constant manifestation, but no revelation of God. Revelation always presupposes a person who can see it, understand it, appropriate it and come, through it to a knowledge of God. This they do not have' (Hanko [s.a.]:x.). This knowledge, according to Hanko, is not saving knowledge, simply because it is not meant to save. Neither is it a knowledge that puts the unbeliever on some higher spiritual plane simply for having it, as the purveyors of point one of common grace would have it. It is knowledge that is suppressed. But, is this knowledge suppressed consciously? Hanko concludes that:

> The point is therefore, that the wicked refuse to keep this manifestation of God even in their consciousness. They not only reject it, they will not even allow it to come before their mind's eye. They drive it out. They bury it beneath the level of their thinking. They will not admit they possess it. In fact, they will not even admit this to themselves. They refuse it room within their consciousness continuously so that it never appears there. This is their awful sin. Not for a moment will they tolerate any thought of God whatsoever. This does not deny that it is there. God sees to it that it is. But they bury it continuously and drive it from them whenever they come face to face with it. (Hanko [s.a.]:x.)

I see the knowledge available to the unbeliever as knowledge that is never really known. It is knowledge, according to Hanko and I think Hoeksema as well, that is not even consciously acknowledged. Because of the totally depraved nature of the unbeliever any knowledge of God in general revelation is automatically and unconsciously suppressed or rejected. It is a natural or involuntary reflex stemming from the depraved nature of the unbelievers mind to do this. Like breathing, it is a simple unconscious reaction. It is also, in this regard, an organic reaction that occurs naturally along the lines of the antithesis. I am convinced by what I have read of Hoeksema that this was indeed his position, although he probably would have phrased it differently.

9.5 Anabaptism and the Antithesis

Because of his distinctive and unpopular position on common grace, Hoeksema and those who stood by him were given the label 'Anabaptists.' Right after the expulsion of Professor Janssen from the Christian Reformed Church, Jan Karel van Baalen, Christian Reformed minister in Munster, Indiana entered the fray to take up Janssen's cause. In his 1922 book '*De Loochening der Gemeene Gratie: Gereformeerd of Doopersch*' (*The Denial of Common Grace: Reformed or Anabaptist*), Van Baalen argued that the struggle for and against common grace is 'de strijd tusschen Calvinisme en Anabaptisme' (the struggle between Calvinism and Anabaptism) (Van Baalen 1922:9). In so doing he gave Hoeksema a label that has outlived its subject. The Protestant Reformed Churches to this day bear the same stigma. Between his 1922 book and another that followed in 1923 entitled 'Nieuwigheid en Dwaling' (Innovation and Error), Van Baalen did no more than repeat his original charge. Taking the two books together, his argument is simply that we need common grace in order to make the world, culture if you will, both accessible and relevant to the Christian. Christians need the non-Christians and vice versa and common grace is the only thing that gives legitimacy to any cooperative effort, which there must be if the church is to have a world view and, in turn, communicate this world view to the unregenerate and gain adherents. By contrast, according to Van Baalen, Hoeksema's denial of common grace drove a sharp distinction between the church and the world that did not belong. What Hoeksema was really advocating was world-flight; withdrawal from a depraved and sinful world where only sin reigned and in which the believer could therefore have no positive effect.

Much of what Van Baalen said was true. Hoeksema did indeed believe that the world was a place where sin reigned and the curse had controlling interest. Hoeksema also believed that the regenerate and the unregenerate had little to nothing in common. This lack of commonality was inherent in the organism of the race as a whole because of the 'antithesis.' The antithesis was, in the providence of God, a line of demarcation separating the human race into the elect and reprobate. Harry Boer is of the opinion that it was predestination that split the race into elect and reprobate (Boer

1990:161). In a sense, Boer is right. It is God, in His decree that determines the eternal disposition of each individual that comprise the human race. But it was this predestinating activity of God in eternity that found expression in time in the antithesis. As we have seen before, the 'moederbelofte,' mother promise given in Genesis 3:15 put enmity between the seed of the serpent and the seed of the woman (Hoeksema 1966:260). This early promise of redemption constitutes the creation of the antithesis. The antithesis is the complete disjunction between the elect part of the race and the reprobate part. The disjunction begins in Genesis 3:15 and continues along spiritual/ethical lines. Hoeksema also sees this separate development as organic development as well. The elect remnant develops along the lines of the covenant in history 'with believers and their children, in their generations (Hoeksema 1981:8). Hence, in Genesis 3:15, 'by the seed of the woman is meant,' Hoeksema concludes: 'The spiritual children of the covenant, the holy seed in the line of the generation of the elect. In the highest sense it is Christ, the Son of Mary, David, Judah, Israel, Abraham, Shem, Noah, Seth, Adam, born of a virgin without the will of man. And the positive meaning of the enmity against Satan which is here announced by God is the covenant fellowship of the Most High' (Hoeksema 1966:261). The reprobate also develop along organic lines, according to Hoeksema, lines which reflect their enmity with God, that is, along the lines of sin (Hoeksema 1966:260-261).

This organic development of sin, as a component part of the antithesis, depends for its outworking on the connectedness of the human race. This connectedness of the race, for Hoeksema, is found in its organic head, Adam. In fact, Adam's relation to the race in a corporate sense is three-fold:

> (first) he was the first father, the bearer of the entire human nature, so that organically the entire human race was in him; secondly, he was the head of all mankind, so that he legally represented them; and finally, he was the root of the race, so that, figuratively speaking, all nations, tribes, families, and individuals are branches of the tree of which Adam is the root. (Hoeksema 1966:223.)

Hoeksema is at pains to point out that the historic confessions of the church emphasize the 'organic rather than the legal relation of Adam to his posterity' (Hoeksema 1966:223), as it is on this organic relation that the legal relation rests (Hanko 2000:240).

The organic nature of the race, for Hoeksema is divided along the lines of election and reprobation. As Hoeksema explains it, the significance of this is that:

> (God) created a church from the beginning of the world organically, that is, within the organism of the human race, which, of course, included the reprobate element of humanity. …That this reprobate shell in time lives under God's providence in natural organic relationship, as chaff with the grain, with the elect organism. Elect and reprobate are in a natural, organic sense of the word temporarily one. The reprobate shell serves the organism of the elect, of the church. The two are separated along the line of election and reprobation by an ever-continuing process, and in the end of the world the organism of the elect church will be finally and completely separated from the reprobate shell. …According to our conception, God from eternity proposed to create a church in Christ. That church was created in the loins of Adam organically, together with the reprobate shell of the human race. And in the line of election and reprobation God separates the pith from the shell and brings His elect church to glory. Nothing is lost. Sin and Satan must simply serve the purpose of realizing the church of Christ. (Hoeksema 1966:574-575.)

Elsewhere, Hoeksema, in the book he co-authored with Henry Danhof in 1923, describes this organic development along the lines of election and reprobation, of sin and grace, as the 'antithesis.' Speaking first of grace, Hoeksema wrote that,

> This is the positive line. With an eternal, unchangeable purpose of irresistible love in Christ His Beloved, and through His work of reconciliation and reunion by the Holy Spirit of regeneration and qualification, He turns to His elect people. He brings that people to faith in Christ, makes them worthy of suffering for Christ, and allows them to experience in Christ the

covenant of His friendship. The end-result is that the tabernacle of God is with men, and God shows forth gloriously in Zion in the perfection of beauty. The grace of God has triumphed. But parallel to that runs the negative line. At the same time and in the same manner as the work of God's elective love that delivers, saves, and exalts to a fellowship of friendship, there is a separating, banishing, rejecting, humiliating action of God's aversion, hate, wrath, anger, and great displeasure in regard to the non-elect, along the line of reprobation. This also takes place according to the immutability of God's will. ...Emphasis must be laid upon the twofold operation of God's will: from the will of God's eternal good pleasure proceeds the operation of love, election, saving grace; but also the operation of hate, rejection, wretchedness, banishment. Scripture speaks of life and death, of blessing and curse, of light and darkness, struggle, victory, rest, salvation, and the joy of the Lord, but also of increase in unrighteousness, hardening in that which is evil, perishing, condemnation, suffering, and everlasting fire. Living out of the principles of sin and grace, humanity is divided into friendship and enmity toward God and toward one another. The development of all things takes place along antithetical lines. (Danhof & Hoeksema [1923] 2003:169-170.)

Hence, as Hanko says, 'the line of reprobation is the line of the organic development of sin' (Hanko 2000:252). Hanko further relates this organic development of sin to both the cultural mandate depicted in Genesis and the sovereignty of God in the outworking of His counsel. In a well written passage, Hanko develops this theme of the organic development of sin thoroughly.

The human race itself develops, It develops socially, economically, politically, culturally. All this development is, however, in connection with the carrying out of the cultural mandate. God gave His command to Adam as king to subdue the earth. After the fall, man continued to perform that original cultural mandate. But he did so totally in the service of sin rather than in the service of God. The result is that sin develops as the cultural mandate is carried out and man subdues the earth. He invents many wonderful inventions and puts more and more of the marvelous powers of the creation to use so that they can be subordinate to his purposes and serve his goals. And so sin manifests itself in more and more ways. All is used to demonstrate fully and completely man's disobedience of God's commands. Adam could not sin with television; modern twenty-first century man can and does. Cain could not sin with an automobile; today's generation can. Nimrod could not sin with an atomic bomb; America does. God wills that throughout history all the powers which He has put within the creation are uncovered by man and subjected to man's nefarious and God-dishonoring purpose. When the creation is completely subdued, then men will have sinned as much as it is possible to sin and will have expressed the root sin of disobedience in every possible way. ... This one root sin develops in such a way, therefore, that each generation builds upon the generation that precedes it, both by making use of past inventions and perfecting them, but also by different ways in which to use them to sin. And as new inventions are added to the list, they are incorporated into the life of the human race and become part and parcel of the cultural life of mankind. Through it all, God's purpose is accomplished. It is in the way of this organic development of sin, although under the sovereign control and direction of God's providence, that man becomes ripe for judgment. He shows in all his life that he will do nothing but sin—even when God gives him such great gifts as are to be found in the creation. The greater the gifts, the more man sins and the more terrible do his sins become. ...Hence, in this sense, there is "organic" development of sin because it takes place along with and is inseparable from that organic development of the world of reprobate men. (Hanko 2000:254-255.)

There is, however, no common grace here either. This development is again another example of the unfolding of God's providence in history. As David Engelsma explains:

The power of providence is directed by the counsel of providence, which is the wise plan of God decreeing that and how all things will glorify Him in the day of Jesus Christ. The power of grace originates in and is controlled by the counsel of predestination, which purposes the salvation of the elect church (Eph. 1:3-12). The power of providence is all-comprehensive, extending to devils as well as to angels and including the wicked deeds of the reprobate as well as the good works of the elect. The power of grace is particular, extending exclusively to the elect church in Jesus Christ. Providence serves grace. God's upholding and governing of all things accomplish the spiritual and eternal good of the elect believers. ...but providence *is not* grace. (Engelsma 2003:59.)

9.6 Was Van Baalen Correct?

Having discussed Hoeksema's ideas on organic development, as relating to both election and reprobation, which, in turn, determined his view of the antithesis, I think the following question is in order. Was Jan Karel van Baalen correct in branding Hoeksema an 'Anabaptist;' one who was guilty of world flight?

Some believe that when used of Hoeksema and those, who, with him, were embroiled in the events of 1924, Anabaptist is nothing but a term of opprobrium. As Engelsma observes, it is often the case that when one denies common grace 'the defenders of common grace make him out to be an anti-cultural barbarian or, what seemingly is worse, an Anabaptist' (Engelsma 2003:54). I believe Engelsma is correct here. Hoeksema always, in all his works, portrays the Christian as one who is in the world but not of it, as a pilgrim and sojourner here, whose affections are set on heavenly things. I do not see this as Anabaptism. Nowhere, for example, does Hoeksema spurn governmental authority, which was so characteristic of Anabaptism (Troeltsch 1986:36). Ernst Troeltsch sees Anabaptists as guilty of a 'wholly individualistic, subjectivistic Spiritualism' (Troeltsch 1986:36). For all the epithets that have been hurled a Hoeksema, no one has ever accused him of holding a subjective spiritualism. If anything, because of his insistence of the use of logic and reason in theological construction, his error would be in the opposite direction. But what about other possible similarities? In his recent book on common grace, Richard Mouw provides an answer to this as well as uncovering a pertinent piece of history surrounding Van Baalen's use of the Anabaptist epithet. He writes:

> As the Christian Reformed pastor-theologian Leonard Verduin has argued in a number of writings, it is no accident that Anabaptist-type themes keep making their presence known within the Calvinist community. They are not alien thoughts that keep forcing their way from the outside; they emerge from home-grown convictions. Calvin Seminary professor William Heyns made a similar point—albeit without Verduin's Anabaptist sympathies—in a 1922 letter to Christian Reformed minister J. K. Van Baalen, who had just written a rather inflammatory pamphlet depicting Hoeksema and his associates as Anabaptists. Heyns endorsed the general thrust of Van Baalen's critique, but he chided him for his rhetoric, instructing Van Baalen that he "would have done better to leave out that epithet 'Anabaptist,' which here can serve only as a scornful word." Surely, Heyns wrote, Van Baalen was not ignorant of the fact "that all of the same things" he found in Hoeksema's thinking could "also be said of the old theologians of Reformed scholasticism." (Mouw 2001:23.)

9.7 Christ against Culture

'Professor Henri Bergson has described religion,' writes H. Richard Niebuhr, 'as "the crystallization, brought about by a scientific process of cooling, of what mysticism had poured, while hot, into the soul of man"' (Niebuhr 1988:1656). Professor Niebuhr goes on to say that this quote from Bergson 'is subject to many criticisms' (Niebuhr 1988:1656). In this I agree, but I think it has much to say if we take the concept and apply it, which is essentially what Niebuhr did in his book *The Kingdom of God in America*, in which he also makes pertinent use of the terms 'dynamic' and 'static.' In his other book, *Christ and Culture*, Niebuhr speaks of five ways of relating Christ to culture, one of which is the title of this section.

I think it safe to say that Hoeksema pitted Christ against culture (Hoeksema 1966:261). To him culture was the result of the organic outworking in history of reprobation. That is to say, the development of culture followed in the lines of the generations of the unbelieving. Christians, while in the world, are not of it; they are strangers and sojourners. Hence, the bulk of what might be considered culture is a result of the activity of the unbelieving. And, while all this culture building proceeds according to the dictates of God's providence, it is still not a result of grace nor pleasing in His sight. You might even say that, from Hoeksema's perspective, the mother promise contained in Genesis 3:15 promises nothing but enmity between Christ and culture, i.e. the world throughout history; further still, it is the stuff of which history is made. David Engelsma makes this exact point citing John 2:15-17 as evidence: 'Love not the world, neither the things that are in the world. If any man love the world, the love of the Father is not in him. For all that is in the world, the lust of the flesh, the lust of the eyes, and the pride of life, is not of the Father, but is of the world. And the world passeth away, and the lust thereof: but he that doeth the will of God abideth for ever' (Engelsma 2003:54). Niebuhr also reviews this and similar verses concluding that they are integral to the Christ against culture position (Niebuhr 1956:48). But, given Hoeksema's very detailed definition of culture, cited earlier, can one really divorce one's self from the surrounding culture entirely?

Speaking of the 'radical Christian,' the one who pits Christ against culture, the one who feels the need to choose Christ as opposed to man's culture, Professor Niebuhr understands their quest as an impossible one. It is possible to separate one's self from the world to a certain extent; to become a hermit or a monastic. Even striving to be a recluse is possible, but not usually with a following. No matter the degree to which one thinks he or she has separated themselves from the world, the culture, they still must use the tools culture has provided, as there are no others. As Niebuhr writes:

It is so with all the members of the radical Christian group. When they meet Christ they do so as heirs of a culture which they cannot reject because it is part of them. They can withdraw from its more obvious institutions and expressions; but for the most part they can only select—and modify under Christ's authority—something they have received through the mediation of society. (Niebuhr 1956:70.)

One must work within the culture that prevails. It can be railed against as the prophets of old, but there is simply no substitute. Hoeksema railed against some of the more flagrant and flamboyant demonstrations of culture, but this the church has always done. Hoeksema did not seek to become a monastic, although there were many cultural activities, especially amusements, from which he abstained. Hoeksema was in the world and he did not seek escape from it, but he was not of the world in that the world was not his focus.

Many who followed Hoeksema in the Protestant Reformed Churches, however, lacked his balance. Some have adopted a cultural variant and labeled it Dutch culture or 'Dutchness,' because of the Dutch overtures contained in it whether real or imagined. Others in the Protestant Reformed Churches have tried to separate themselves from the things of the world as much as possible both physically and mentally. This tendency has produced some interesting, and at times amusing, cultural anomalies. For instance: I remember my first encounter with the Protestant Reformed Churches, I was not greeted with a 'hello' or a 'nice to meet you,' rather the first words spoken by a Protestant Reformed minister to me was 'why are you here?' I have already mentioned in the biography that union membership is prohibited; so are movies and dancing. In many households having insurance is seen as circumventing God's sovereignty. Anesthesia for women in childbirth is frowned upon because it somehow mitigates the curse. Women's suffrage is repudiated. But the main staple of Protestant Reformed dogma is the denial to any marriage after a divorce, irrespective of who is at fault or the circumstances. I could mention many more examples, but I think this is sufficient to get a proper understanding of what defines the Protestant Reformed Churches culturally.

These cultural oddities are, however, only a symptom, and I believe there is an explanation. Let us return again to our quote from Henri Bergson. I would like to change the quote a bit to reflect what I believe has happened in the Protestant Reformed Churches. What constitutes the Protestant Reformed Churches today is, in fact, the crystallization, brought about by time, of what Hoeksema poured, while hot, into his church. Hoeksema was original, creative, and equally dynamic. Additionally, Hoeksema was not conservative. He was orthodox, but he was not a conservative. He did not seek to conserve for conservation sake. Hoeksema's own definition of the theological task is that 'in which the dogmatician, in organic connection with the church in the past as well as in the present, purposes to elicit from the Scriptures the true knowledge of God, to set forth the same in systematic form, and, after comparison of the existing dogmas with Scripture, to bring the knowledge of God to a higher state of development' (Hoeksema 1966:5). There is nothing in this definition about conserving the doctrines of the past just because they are from some glorious past. No, Hoeksema believed that conserving for conserving sake was not the job of the theologian. Hence, Hoeksema never had the 'wagon train' mentality that characterizes much of what the current Protestant Reformed Church stands for.

Still, what Niebuhr had to say about men and movements is as true today as when he said it, and I think it captures well the relationship of Hoeksema to the church he founded.

> Yet, institutions can never conserve without betraying the movements from which they proceed. The institution is static whereas its parent movement had been dynamic; it confines men within its limits while the movement had liberated them from the bondage of institutions; it looks to the past, the movement had pointed forward. Though in content the institution resembles the dynamic epoch whence it proceeded, in spirit it is much like the state before the revolution. …Institutions, however, differ not only in spirit from their parent movements; they tend also to change the content which they are trying to conserve. When the great insights of a creative time are put into the symbolic form of words, formulas and creeds, much must always be omitted. The symbol is never the reality and it is

subject to progressive loss of meaning; in time it often comes to take the place of the experience to which it originally pointed. (Niebuhr 1988:168-169.)

What Niebuhr says here is true of all religious movements in one way or another, and this is no less true of Hoeksema and his church. As the institution tries to conserve for posterity advances made by the dynamic individual or movement, the result is 'only to have these cool off into crystallized codes, solidified institutions' (Niebuhr 1988:167) and an unhealthy preoccupation with the law. The conservation process brings about conservatism, which, in and of itself, precludes the dynamic at all costs. Hence, while the conservative mind seeks to conserve the advances of the dynamic time, laws, rules and regulations become the norm. As dynamic moves to conservative, understanding yields to practice, explicit faith to implicit faith and the orientation of this faith also changes from what God has done to what man must do. When the leader's vision is reduced to codes of conduct he never stressed, this 'emphasis on conduct may lead to the definition of precise rules, concern for one's conformity to such rules, and concentration on one's own will rather than on the gracious work of God' (Niebuhr 1956:79).

Herman Hoeksema broke with the Puritan legalism he found in the Christian Reformed Church (Goris 1932), only now to have the Protestant Reformed Churches which he founded return full circle. Admittedly, on paper their theology is still that of Hoeksema, but for all intents and purposes, the understanding is gone and only the rules remain. In 1995 Cornelius Hanko wrote an article for the *Standard Bearer* entitled 'Where We Stand Today.' One might have expected a glowing assessment of the current state of the Protestant Reformed Churches, but this was not to be. He starts with the question: Is there a difference between the preaching in our churches now and the preaching in our early years? Out of obvious loyalty to a church in which he ministered for seventy years, Hanko's criticism is mild and unabrasive. Still, he puts his finger on the problem straight away. He writes:

> Yet it must also be admitted that there has been a shift in emphasis in the preaching. Anyone who will listen to a tape or read a sermon or the *Standard Bearer* of fifty or

more years ago will immediately recognize the strong emphasis on doctrine. An example of that can be found in the sermons of Rev. Herman Hoeksema in *God's Eternal Good Pleasure*. We were advised in the seminary: "When the truth is preached, God's people can and do apply it to their own lives." Or again, "Preach to the most intelligent in your audience; the others will be edified." Today the preaching often emphasizes the problems we face as believers in an evil world, especially problems related to family. And a more serious effort is made to reach the young people and the children of the congregation. The question, however, may well be raised, "Has the pendulum swung too far the other way? Are our people being as thoroughly indoctrinated as they should be?" We must maintain the one, but not at the cost of the other. (Hanko 1995:45.)

Niebuhr is hopeful that the 'the same institutionalism which represents the death of an old movement can be, as history amply illustrates, the pregnant source of a new aggression' (Niebuhr 1988:198). That is to say, the destruction of one movement lays the seeds for the rise of the next. This has been happening throughout church history, but rarely do two dynamic men or movements come from the same source.

9.8 Conclusion

In this chapter we have looked at the last of the *Three Points of Common Grace* as adopted by the Christian Reformed Synod of 1924 and Hoeksema's objections to it. We began by analyzing, through Hoeksema's eyes, the confessional proof cited by the synod for its justification in adopting this point. The significant feature regarding this confessional proof revolves around the Third and Fourth Heads of Doctrine of the Canons of Dort, article 4, in which synod quotes only the first half of the article to prove their point. The second half of the same article, as Hoeksema pointed out, proves exactly the opposite of what synod was attempting to prove.

While point three mentions 'civic righteousness' specifically, most writers take this in the wider sense of culture as did Hoeksema. Hence, we have dealt with the cultural aspirations of humanity and inquired into their motivation. Humanity sees their cultural mandate to subdue the all things to themselves, as they are their own lord. Hoeksema is at pains to show that this cultural activity is not a grace from God. Good gifts from God are definitely given, but these are with the sole purpose to further the condemnation of the unbelieving. To Hoeksema, this is simply not grace.

What is usually called 'general revelation' is equally not a grace of God to the unregenerate. Hoeksema maintains that there is no revelation to the reprobate whatsoever. God manifests himself to them, but revelation presupposes a capacity to receive it. This the reprobate do not have. This capacity, if you will, is a gracious gift of God for the elect alone.

For his ideas Hoeksema was branded an Anabaptist, one guilty of world flight. Upon examination this label also falls to the ground. Hoeksema did, however, teach the antithesis between the elect and the reprobate; an antithesis that continues throughout history along the organic lines of the generations of each. This antithesis, this enmity, will continue until God in His time brings it to an end. Even this does not prove Anabaptism. Although Hoeksema did pit Christ against culture, he never sought a monastic existence. He always saw himself as one who is in the world but not of it, it was simply not his focus.

Not so for the denomination which he founded. The Protestant Reformed Churches have sought to preserve the gains and insights made by Hoeksema who was not really a conservator of the past himself. In doing so, they have taken that which was dynamic and reduced it to what is static. They have taken understanding and reduced it to rules, regulations and practices. In so doing they have, in theory, created their own distinct culture, one that bears little similarity to the teachings of the founder.

Conclusion

In the preceding pages I have tried to give due consideration to Herman Hoeksema as a man, a pastor and a theologian. In a sense these roles cannot be separated from the man because Hoeksema lived and breathed theology, it was in his veins and it was his life's blood. We have looked primarily at Hoeksema's spiritual/intellectual development in the biographical portion, because it is in this spiritual/intellectual development that we gain the insight needed to understand the mature theologian.

In many ways Hoeksema was a product of his early years in the Netherlands. Essentially, he grew up on the streets of Groningen with little to no parental supervision. He learned to fight for what he wanted and he seemed to like it. This liking for a good fight, indeed not being able to resist a good fight, would not suit him well, however, in an ecclesiastical confrontation. This bellicosity was also combined with a confidence bordering on cockiness; Hoeksema just assumed he was right and it was everyone's duty to see this and acquiesce. Unfortunately, when he encountered Professor Janssen, who was well versed in church politics, Hoeksema did not really know what to do. In the end, because of this same church politics, Hoeksema, and others of like mind, found themselves out of their own denomination wondering what happened.

Hoeksema's theology began to take shape in the Netherlands as well. While his parents were divorced while he was still a boy, Hoeksema's mother, Johanna, was a pious *Afscheiding* woman who instilled in her son a religious heritage he never forgot. It was from the *Afscheiding* that Hoeksema took the rudiments of what eventually became his view of the covenant as a bond of friendship and love between God and man. Additionally, his stress on the 'organic' nature of things can also be traced to the church of his youth. Later, because of a childhood friend, Hoeksema migrated to a church with a background in the *Doleantie*. Later in his life, he would read the writings of the leader of the *Doleantie*, Abraham Kuyper, and in the process made many of Kuyper's ideas his own. While there is debate in certain circles as to whether the *Afscheiding*

(Bernard Woudenberg) or the *Doleantie* (David Engelsma) had more influence on Hoeksema's theology, I have tried to demonstrate that Hoeksema learned from both but copied neither. That is to say, both movements are reflected in Hoeksema's mature thought, but not in their original form. Hoeksema was original and creative; he took what was available and worked with it until it was unrecognizable. He then put these unrecognizable elements together into a coherent whole; a whole that bore little resemblance to its constituent parts.

In addition to being creative and original, Hoeksema was also dynamic. His capacity for work was breathtaking. His charisma was felt by all who met him. He was the kind of man who initiates movements. And this is what he did; he founded the Protestant Reformed Churches after being expelled from the Christian Reformed Church over the issue of common grace. He taught for many years in the seminary of the Protestant Reformed Churches, training others to follow in his footsteps. In many ways, however, this was simply not to be. As the Protestant Reformed Churches tried to conserve for posterity the gains Hoeksema had made, a dynamic understanding of the truth gave way to a myriad of rules and regulations, and the leader's vision was reduced to codes of conduct he never stressed.

The dynamic of Hoeksema's theology, however, was the sovereignty of God. It is God who wills to do His good pleasure and it is given to us, i.e. Christians, to understand what God does. God does not hide Himself from the elect, those whom He has chosen in love from before the foundation of the world. No, God reveals Himself in everything He does. His decrees, according to Hoeksema, are a mirror image of the historical process. It is nothing less than God's counsel being worked out in time; this is the stuff of history. This history, also according to the plan of God, unfolds organically along the lines of election and reprobation. The line of election is the visible unfolding of the covenant in history and the line of reprobation is the organic development of sin. Revelation is, therefore, for those who have been given the capacity to receive it, i.e. the elect. For the rest, the reprobate, God manifests Himself, but because of total depravity this manifestation is never acknowledged, much less understood.

This dynamic reveals, at least from my perspective, the most important aspect of Hoeksema's theology; its thoroughly unconditional nature. The centerpiece of Hoeksema's thought was a covenant which was absolutely unconditional from the perspective of the believer. This covenant was defined as a relationship of friendship and love between God and His elect. And this friendship and love was initiated and maintained by God alone. That is to say, for Hoeksema, the covenant was both established and maintained by God apart from anything the creature would do. Hence, God was seen to be faithful even when the creature was not. Or, as I heard a young lady in church put it: we constantly think we have to hold on to Him when, in reality, it is He who always has hold of us.

In addition to his being dynamic, Hoeksema was also bold. Many of his theological constructs were radical in nature. As I said, he was not a conservative. His views of the covenant, the image of God in humanity, election and reprobation, general revelation and more, were breakthroughs in new directions. He broke new ground. Much of this has gone unnoticed because, even in the church he founded, the implications of many of his original insights have yet to be worked out. In other areas, Hoeksema, with a sentence from a book, or a line in a sermon points the way to a line of thought he himself never investigated. Hoeksema's boldness, however, did not go unchallenged. He has been labeled a 'Hyper-Calvinist,' a 'rationalist,' and a 'theological reactionary.' I have dispelled the cavil of 'Hyper-Calvinist' by showing that Hoeksema never went beyond Calvin in the direction his detractors claim he did. Hoeksema has been labeled a 'rationalist,' a notion which I have also sought to dispel. Rationalism is a philosophy; a philosophy to which Hoeksema did not subscribe. While not subscribing to rationalist philosophy, at the same time Hoeksema was thoroughly rational. He firmly believed that either the logic of revelation is our logic, or there is no revelation. Therefore, I am convinced that those who persist in calling Hoeksema a rationalist simply confuse rationalism with rationality. Additionally, Hoeksema's theology is also not a theology of reaction as some have claimed; either in reaction to common grace or anything else. It is true that some, not all, of Hoeksema's doctrinal formulations were given impetus by doctrines or beliefs he saw as untenable, but this in no way proves his theology is reactionary. If it were true, much of his theology would be characterized by the negative, this is simply not the case and I cite his doctrine of the covenant as the embodiment of friendship and love as an example. In the course of the thesis, even when dealing with Hoeksema's conflicts, such as the events surrounding 1924, I have tried to present a positive statement of Hoeksema's theology. In fact, given all the misrepresentations his theology has endured over the years, I felt that a positive statement of Hoeksema's theology was definitely in order.

The theory of Common Grace as adopted by the Synod of the Christian Reformed Church in 1924 became the source of Hoeksema's greatest theological battle. This doctrine with its three points was seen by Hoeksema as a rejection of those theological tenets which he held dear. After his meddling in the Janssen case, where Professor Janssen was dismissed from his post in part because of Hoeksema's efforts, many wanted Hoeksema gone as well and it seems that the doctrine of common grace was well suited to accomplish just that. After the Three Points of Common Grace were adopted in 1924, along with his subsequent refusal to abide by synod's decision in adopting them, Hoeksema was removed from the ministry of the Christian Reformed Church and immediately went about constructing a new church to replace the one that was now lost. His writings on the Three Points of Common Grace show clearly their innovative character. The proof adduced by the Synod of 1924 for their adoption falls to the ground under Hoeksema's pen. Contrariwise, Hoeksema maintained the grace is never common but always particular; it is always for the elect alone. God gives good gifts to the reprobate, but this is to further their condemnation, not to bless them in any way. Equally, there is no free offer of the Gospel in which God sincerely desires the salvation of those whom he has chosen not to save. No, for Hoeksema, the Gospel is always a command which can only be obeyed by those whom God has regenerated. But, just because the Gospel is seen as a command that can only be obeyed by those whom God has regenerated in no way nullifies the need for the promiscuous preaching of the Gospel, i.e. external call, to all humanity without distinction. Hoeksema also maintained that there is no work of the Holy Spirit in the hearts of the unbeliever to restrain sin. This is what we have the police for. And since there is no work of the Holy Spirit in the hearts of the unbeliever, the unbeliever produces no civic good, or culture or anything else that might be considered good in the sight of God.

Throughout this thesis I have tried to portray the issues as seen through Hoeksema's eyes. I wanted the reader to get to know Herman Hoeksema intimately. This does not mean that I agree with Hoeksema in all he said. As a man, Hoeksema could be aloof, brusque and arrogant. I am not so sure that he was all that likable, and this is what family members have told me. But, Hoeksema is significant nonetheless. Many of his insights were truly inspiring. I consider this study foundational and I hope that others will be motivated by what they read here to develop further the theological legacy Herman Hoeksema has left us. As a historical study, I know I have left many doctrinal questions unanswered. This, however, was unavoidable, as I did not want to go beyond my subject.

Bibliography

Acta der Synode 1922. Acta der Synode 1922 van de Christelijke Gereformeerde Kerk. Gehouden van 21 Juni tot 5 Juli, 1922 te Orange City, Iowa. Grand Rapids, MI: Grand Rapids Printing Co.

Acta der Synode 1924. Acta der Synode 1924 van de Christelijke Gereformeerde Kerk. Gehouden van 18 Juni tot 8 Juli, 1924 te Kalamazoo. Michigan. Grand Rapids, MI: Grand Rapids Printing Co.

Acta der Synode 1928. Acta der Synode 1928 van de Christelijke Gereformeerde Kerk. 13-29 Juni, 1928, Holland, Michigan. Grand Rapids, MI: Office of the Stated Clerk.

Algra, H 1966. *Het wonder van de 19e eeuw, van vrije kerken en kleine luyden*. Zesde Druk, Franeker: T. Wever.

Bangs, C 1971. *Arminius: A Study in the Dutch Reformation*. Nashville & New York: Abington.

Bavinck, H 1883. *De Wetenschap der Heilige Godgeleerdheid*. Kampen: G. Ph. Zalsman.

--- 1929. *Gereformeerde Dogmatiek*. Derde Deel, Vierde onveranderde druk.. Kampen: J.H. Kok.

--- 1956. *Our Reasonable Faith*. Grand Rapids, MI: Eerdmans.

--- 1977. *The Doctrine of God*. Edinburgh, Scotland: The Banner of Truth Trust.

--- 1989. Common Grace. Translated by Raymond C. Van Leeuwen, in *Calvin Theological Journa*l Volume 24, Number 1 (April 1989): 38-65.

Beets, H 1946. *The Christian Reformed Church: Its Roots, History, Schools and Mission Work, A.D. 1857 to 1946*. Grand Rapids, MI: Baker.

Benoît, JD 1966. Calvin the Letter-writer, in *John Calvin: A Collection of Distinguished Essays*. Edited by G. E. Duffield. Grand Rapids, MI: Eerdmans: 67-101.

Berkhof, L 1925. *De Drie Punten in Alle Deelen Gereformeerd*. Grand Rapids, MI: Eerdmans.

--- 1948. *Riches of Divine Grace (Ten Expository Sermons)*. Grand Rapids, MI: Eerdmans.

--- 1986. *Systematic Theology*. Grand Rapids, MI: Eerdmans.

Berkouwer, GC 1977. *A Half Century of Theology*. Translated and Edited by Lewis B. Smedes. Grand Rapids, MI: Eerdmans.

Beza, T 1982. *The Main Predestination Writings of Theodore Beza*. Translated by Philip C. Holtrop. Grand Rapids, MI: Philip C. Holtrop.

Bible. Authorized King James Version. 1983. *The Holy Bible: Containing the Old and New Testaments*. (S. l.): National Publishing Co.

Blacketer, RA 2000. The Three Points in Most Parts Reformed: A Reexamination of the So-Called Well-Meant Offer of Salvation, in *Calvin Theological Journal* Volume 35, Number 1 (April 2000): 37-65.

Boer, HR 1972. Ralph Janssen After Fifty Years, in *The Reformed Journal* Volume 22 (December 1972): 17-22.

--- 1973. The Janssen Case: Aftermath, in *The Reformed Journal* Volume 23 (November 1973): 21-24.

--- 1983. *The Doctrine of Reprobation in the Christian Reformed Church*. Grand Rapids, MI: Eerdmans

--- 1990. *An Ember Still Glowing: Humankind as the Image of God*. Grand Rapids, MI: Eerdmans.

Bolt, J 1984. *Christian and Reformed Today*. Jordan Station, Ontario, Canada: Paideia Press.

--- 2000a. Common Grace and the Christian Reformed Synod of Kalamazoo (1924): A Seventy-Fifth Anniversary Perspective, in *Calvin Theological Journal* Volume 35, Number 1 (April 2000): 7-36.

--- 2000b. Common Grace, Theonomy, and Civic Good: The Temptations of Calvinist Politics (Reflections on the third Point of the CRC Kalamazoo Synod, 1924), in *Calvin Theological Journal* Volume 35, Number 2 (November 2000): 205-237.

Boonstra, H 2000. Calvin College School Life in the Early 1900s, in *Origins: Historical Magazine of the Archives*, Volume XVIII, Number 2. Grand Rapids, MI: The Hekman Library, Calvin College and Calvin Theological Seminary: 36-43.

--- 2001. An anniversary revisited, in the *Christian Courier* (17 September, 2001): 16 and 23.

Bouma, H 1995. *Secession, Doleantie, and Union: 1934-1892*. Neerlandia, Alberta, Canada: Inheritance Publications.

Bratt, JD 1984. *Dutch Calvinism in Modern America. A History of a Conservative Subculture*. Grand Rapids, MI: Eerdmans.

--- 1996. Abraham Kuyper, American History, and the Tensions of Neo-Calvinism, in *Sharing the Reformed Tradition: The Dutch-North American Exchange, 1846-1996*. VU Studies on Protestant History 2, Edited by George Harinck & Hans Krabbendam, Amsterdam: VU Uitgeverij: 97-114.

Bronkema, F 1928. The Doctrine of Common Grace in Reformed Theology or New Calvinism and the Doctrine of Common Grace. Th.D. Thesis. Cambridge, MA: Harvard University.

Bruins, E 1996. "An American Moses": Albertus C. van Raalte as Immigrant Leader, in *Sharing the Reformed Tradition: The Dutch-North American Exchange, 1846-1996*. VU Studies on Protestant History 2, Edited by George Harinck & Hans Krabbendam, Amsterdam: VU Uitgeverij: 19-34.

Buck, C (ed.) 1826. *A Theological Dictionary Containing Definitions of all Religious Terms.* Philadelphia, PA: Joseph J. Woodward.

Bullinger, H 1587. *Fifty Godlie and Learned Sermons, Divided into Five Decades.* London: Ralph Newberie of Flete Street.

Calvin J 1950. The Eternal Predestination of God, in *Calvin's Calvinism.* Grand Rapids, MI: Eerdmans: 25-206.

--- 1960. *Institutes of the Christian Religion*, Vol. II: *Books III.XX to IV.XX.* The Library of Christian Classics, Volume XXI. Edited by John T. McNeill. Philadelphia, PA: Westminster Press.

Campbell-Jack, WC 1992. Grace Without Christ? The Doctrine of Common Grace in Dutch-American Neo-Calvinism. Ph.D. Thesis. Edinburgh, Scotland: University of Edinburgh.

Cassell's Latin Dictionary 1959. Revised by Marchant, JRV and Charles, JF. New York: Funk & Wagnalls.

Committee on Creation and Science 1988. *Report to the Christian Reformed Church of the Committee on Creation and Science.* Grand Rapids, MI: Committee on Creation and Science of the Christian Reformed Church.

Cunningham, W 1979. *The Reformers and the Theology of Reformation.* Edinburgh, Scotland: The Banner of Truth Trust.

Daane, J 1951. Common Grace Versus Individualism, in *The Reformed Journal* (April 1951): 11-12.

--- 1954. *A Theology of Grace: An Inquiry into and Evaluation of Dr. C. Van Til's Doctrine of Common Grace*. Grand Rapids, MI: Eerdmans.

--- 1971. Therefore Have I Spoken, A Biography of Herman Hoeksema, by Gertrude Hoeksema, Reviewed by James Daane, in *The Reformed Journal* (July-August 1971): 20-22.

Danhof, H & Hoeksema H [S.A.]. *Om Recht en Waarheid, een Woord van Toelichting en Leiding*. Kalamazoo, MI: Dalm.

--- 1922. *Niet Doopersch maar Gereformeerd, Voorloopig Bescheid aan Ds. Jan Karel van Baalen Betreffende De Loochening der Gemeene Gratie*. Grand Rapids, MI: [S.N.].

--- [1923] 2003. *Sin and Grace*. Grandville, MI: Reformed Free Publishing Association.

Daniel, CD 1983. Hyper-Calvinism and John Gill. Ph.D. Thesis. Edinburgh, Scotland: University of Edinburgh.

Dee, JJC 1990. *Picturalia: fotobiografie K. Schilder*. Goes, The Netherlands: Oosterbaan & Le Cointre.

Deist, F 1990. *A Concise Dictionary of Theological and Related Terms*. Second Revised and Enlarged Edition. Pretoria, RSA: Van Schaik.

De Jong, AC 1954. *The Well-Meant Gospel Offer: The Views of H. Hoeksema and K. Schilder*. Franeker: T. Wever.

--- 1963. "God Loves All Men"—Continuing the Discussion, in the *Reformed Journal* Volume 13, Number 4 (May-June 1963): 14-17.

De Jong GD 1926. The History and Development of the Theological School, in *Semi-Centennial Volume, Theological School and Calvin College*. Grand Rapids, MI: The Semi-Centennial Committee of the Theological School and Calvin College: 20-48.

De Jong, GF 1978. *The Dutch Reformed Church in the American Colonies*. Grand Rapids, MI: Eerdmans.

De Jong, PY 1984a. A darkness over the land, in *The Reformation of 1834. Essays in Commemoration of the Act of Secession and Return*. Edited by Peter Y. De Jong and Nelson D. Kloosterman. Orange City, IA: Pluim Publishing Inc: 9-20.

--- 1984b. The dawn of a new day, in *The Reformation of 1834. Essays in Commemoration of the Act of Secession and Return*. Edited by Peter Y. De Jong and Nelson D. Kloosterman. Orange City, IA: Pluim Publishing Inc: 21-34.

--- 1986. 1886—A Year to Remember, in *Mid-America Journal of Theology*, Volume 2, Number 1 (Spring 1986): 7-52.

De Klerk, P 1990. Klaas Schilder, The Man, a paper delivered at the conference on Suffering and Survival: The Netherlands, 1940-1945, held at Dort College, Sioux Center, Iowa on 28 September 1990.

De Moor, JC 1980. *Towards a Biblically Theo-Logical Method: A Structural Analysis and a Further Elaboration of Dr. G. C. Berkouwer's Hermeneutic-Dogmatic Method*. Kampen: J. H. Kok.

Dennison, WD 1993. Van Til and Common Grace, in *Mid-America Journal of Theology*, Volume 9, Number 2 (Fall 1993): 225-247.

Dijk, K 1912. *De strijd over Infra- en Supralapsarisme in de Gereformeerde Kerken van Nederland.* Kampen: J. H. Kok.

Douma J 1966. *Algemeene Genade. Uiteenzetting, vergelijking en beoordeling van de opvattingen van A. Kuyper, K. Schilder en Joh. Calvin over 'algemeene genade.'* Goes: Oosterbaan & Le Cointre.

Dykstra, RJ 1998. Abraham Kuyper and the Union of 1890, in *The Standard Bearer*, Volume 75, Number 2 (October 15, 1998): 36-38.

Eaton, M 1995. *No Condemnation: A New Theology of Assurance.* Downers Grove, IL: InterVarsity Press.

Ellul, J 1964. *The Technological Society.* New York: Alfred A. Knopf.

--- 1967. *The Presence of the Kingdom.* New York: Seabury.

Engelsma, DJ 1980. *Hyper-Calvinism and the Call of the Gospel.* Grand Rapids, MI: Reformed Free Publishing Association.

--- 1998. "Father" Abraham or The Indebtedness of the PRC to Abraham Kuyper, in *The Standard Bearer*, Volume 75, Number 2 (October 15, 1998): 28-30.

--- 2000. A Notable Meeting on Behalf of the reunion of the CRC and the PRC, in *The Standard Bearer*, Volume 77, Number 1 (October 1, 2000): 4-7.

--- 2000b. Hoeksema's Romans Sermons, in *The Standard Bearer*, Volume 76, Number 13 (April 1, 2000): 293-296.

--- 2001. A Proposed Reformulation of the Third Point of Common Grace, in *The Standard Bearer*, Volume 77, Number 13 (April 1, 2001): 292-294.

--- 2002. A Word about Martin Swart, the Transcriber, in Hoeksema, H, *Righteous by Faith Alone: A Devotional Commentary on Romans*. Edited by David J. Engelsma. Grandville, MI: Reformed Free Publishing Association.

--- 2003. *Common Grace Revisited: A Response to Richard J. Mouw's He Shines in All That's Fair*. Grandville, MI: Reformed Free Publishing Association.

Faber, J 1996. *American Secession Theologians on Covenant and Baptism*. Neerlandia, Alberta, Canada: Inheritance Publications.

--- 1997. William Heyns as Covenant Theologian, in *Calvin's Books: Festschrift Dedicated to Peter de Klerk on the Occasion of his Seventieth Birthday*. Edited by Wilhelm H. Neuser, Herman J. Selderhuis and Willem van `t Spijker, Heerenveen, The Netherlands: J.J. Groen en Zoon.

Frame, J 1976. *Van Til: The Theologian*. Chattanooga, TN: Pilgrim Publishing Company.

Frost, WL 1985. 356 Years of Formal Education in New York City: The Origins of the First Dutch School in New Amsterdam in 1628, in *Education in New Netherland and the Middle Colonies: Papers of the 7th Rensselaerswyck Seminar of the New Netherland Project.* Edited by Charles T. Gehring & Nancy Anne McClure Zeller. Albany, New York: New Netherland Project, New York State library: 1-4.

González, JL 1987. *A History of Christian Thought,* Vol. III: *From the Protestant Reformation to the Twentieth Century.* Revised edition. Nashville, TN: Abington Press.

Goris, G 1932. Puritan Legalism as a Method of Moral and Religious Reform in the Christian Reformed Church. Doctor of Theology Thesis. New York: Union Theological Seminary.

Grosheide, FW & van Itterzon, GP (eds.) 1957. *Christelijke Encyclopedie*, Volume II: *Bovarysme – Ezra.* Kampen: J. H. Kok.

Grotenhuis, E 2000. Interview by telephone. From Byron Center, Michigan.

Gritters, BL 1988. *Grace Uncommon: A Protestant Reformed Look at the Doctrine of Common Grace.* Byron Center, MI: The Evangelism Society of the Byron Center Protestant Reformed Church.

Hanko, C 1995. Where We Stand Today, in *The Standard Bearer*, Volume 72, Number 2 (October 15, 1995): 44-46.

--- 2000b. Interview by telephone. From Jenison, Michigan.

Hanko, H [S.A.]. "Revelation" in Romans 1. Unpublished Paper.

--- 1970. *The Christian's Social Calling and the Second Coming of Christ.* South Holland, IL: Evangelism Committee, South Holland Protestant Reformed Church.

--- 1976. *The Development of the Reformed Faith: From Dort to Today.* Grandville, MI: Theological School of the Protestant Reformed Churches.

--- 1988. A Study of the Relation between the Views of Prof. R. Janssen and Common Grace. Master of Theology Thesis. Grand Rapids, MI: Calvin Theological Seminary.

--- 1989. *The History of the Free Offer.* Grandville, MI: Theological School of the Protestant Reformed Churches.

--- 2000. *For Thy Truth's Sake: A Doctrinal History of the Protestant Reformed Churches.* Grandville, MI: Reformed Free Publishing Association.

--- 2002. The Publication of *Van Zonde en Genade* (3), in *The Standard Bearer*, Volume 79, Number 5 (December 1, 2002): 104-106.

Harinck, G 1996. Valentijn Hepp in America: Attempts at International Exchange in the 1920s, in *Sharing the Reformed Tradition: The Dutch-North American Exchange, 1846-1996.* VU Studies on Protestant History 2, Edited by George Harinck & Hans Krabbendam, Amsterdam: VU Uitgeverij: 115-138.

Heerema, E 1986. *R. B. A Prophet in the Land: Rienk Bouke Kuiper, Preacher – Theologian – Churchman*. Jordan Station, Ontario, Canada: Paideia Press.

--- 1990. *Letter to My Mother: Reflections on the Christian Reformed Church in North America*. Cape Coral, FL: Rev. Edward Heerema.

Hepp, V 1923. *Het Misverstand in Zake De Leer Der Algemeene Genade*. Grand Rapids, MI: Eerdmans.

Heppe, H 1950. *Reformed Dogmatics, Set Out and Illustrated from the Sources*. London, UK: George Allen & Unwin LTD.

Heslam, PS 1998. *Creating a Christian Worldview: Abraham Kuyper's Lectures on Calvinism*. Grand Rapids, MI: Eerdmans.

Hesselink, J 1973. Contemporary Protestant Dutch Theology, in *Reformed Review*, Volume 26, Number 2 (Winter 1973): 67-89.

Heyns, W 1903. *Liturgiek. Ten dienste van de studenten aan de Theologische School der Christelijke Gereformeerde Kerk te Grand Rapids, Michigan*. Holland, MI: H. Holkeboer.

--- 1906. *Kybernetiek voor de Christelijke Gereformeerde Kerk in Amerika*. Grand Rapids, MI: Calvin Theological Seminary.

--- 1907. *Handboek voor de Catechetiek*. Grand Rapids, MI: Eerdmans-Sevensma.

--- 1914. *Verhandelingen over het Genade-Verbond.* Grand Rapids, MI: s.n.

--- 1916. *Gereformeerde Geloofsleer.* Grand Rapids, MI: Eerdmans-Sevensma.

--- 1926. *Manual of Reformed Doctrine.* Grand Rapids, MI: Eerdmans.

Hoekema, AA 1953. Herman Bavinck's Doctrine of the Covenant. Th.D. Thesis. Princeton, NJ: Princeton Theological Seminary.

--- 1986. *Created in God's Image.* Grand Rapids, MI: Eerdmans.

Hoeks, HJ 2000. Interview by telephone. From Grand Rapids, Michigan.

Hoeksema, G 1969. *Therefore Have I Spoken: A Biography of Herman Hoeksema.* Grand Rapids, MI: Reformed Free Publishing Association.

--- 1992. *A Watered Garden: A Brief History of the Protestant Reformed Churches in America.* Grand Rapids, MI: Reformed Free Publishing Association.

Hoeksema, H [S.A.]. *The Reunion of the Christian Reformed and Protestant Reformed Churches.* Grand Rapids, MI: Reformed Free Publishing Association.

--- 1912. Rousseau and Education. Senior Paper at Calvin Preparatory School. Grand Rapids, MI: Archives, Hekman Library, Calvin College.

--- 1930. Unpublished sermon on Lord's Day 2 of the Heidelberg Catechism. Swart transcription.

--- 1930b. Unpublished sermon on Lord's Day 21 of the Heidelberg Catechism. Swart transcription.

--- 1935. Unpublished sermon on Romans 2: 17-21a. Swart transcription.

--- 1939. *God's Goodness Always Particular.* Grand Rapids, MI: Reformed Free Publishing Association.

--- 1939b. Dr. Schilder's Lecture on Common Grace, in *The Standard Bearer*, Volume 15, Number 11 (February 15, 1939): 243-246.

--- 1942. *A Triple Breach in the Foundation of Reformed Truth: A Critical Treatise on the "Three Points", Adopted by the Synod of the Christian Reformed Churches in 1924.* Reprint Edition. Grand Rapids, MI: First Protestant Reformed Church.

--- 1946. *The Christian and Culture.* Reprint Edition. Grand Rapids, MI: Sunday School Mission Publishing Association.

--- 1947. *The Protestant Reformed Churches in America, Their Early History and Doctrine.* Second Edition. Grand Rapids, MI: Reformed Free Publishing Association.

--- 1954. Book Review: The well-Meant Offer. By Dr. A. C. De Jong, in *The Standard Bearer*, Volume 30, Number 19 (August 1, 1954): 439.

--- 1966. *Reformed Dogmatics*. Grand Rapids, MI: Reformed Free Publishing Association.

--- 1971 *Believers and Their Seed*. Grand Rapids, MI: Reformed Free Publishing Association.

--- 1979. *God's Eternal Good Pleasure*. Grand Rapids, MI: Reformed Free Publishing Association.

--- 1981. *The Covenant: God's Tabernacle with Men*. Reprint Edition. Grand Rapids, MI: Reformed Free Publishing Association.

--- 1993. *The Place of Reprobation in the Preaching of the Gospel*. Reprint Edition, Grandville, MI: Evangelism Committee, Southwest Protestant Reformed Church.

--- 1995. *The Clark – Van Til Controversy*. Hobbs, NM: The Trinity Foundation.

--- 1996. *A Power of God unto Salvation or Grace Not an Offer*. Grandville, MI: Theological School of the Protestant Reformed Churches.

--- 2002. *Righteous by Faith Alone: A Devotional Commentary on Romans*. Edited by David J. Engelsma. Grandville, MI: Reformed Free Publishing Association.

Hoeksema, H 2001. Interview with Herman Hoeksema Jr. From Colonna, Michigan.

Hoeksema, HC 1977. A Critique of Dr. G. C. Berkouwer's Een Halve Eeuw Theologie, in the *Protestant Reformed Theological Journal*, Volume VIII, Number 2 (April 1975): 38-45.

--- 1980. *The Voice of Our Fathers: An Exposition of the Canons of Dordrecht.* Grand Rapids, MI: Reformed Free Publishing Association.

Hoeksema, HC & Hanko, H 1982. *History of Dogma.* Grandville, MI: Theological School of the Protestant Reformed Churches.

Hoeksema, J 1929. Death Certificate #5823, supplied by the Cook County Coroner, Chicago, Illinois.

Hulse, E 1973. *The Free Offer of the Gospel.* Worthington and Haywards Heath, Sussex, UK: Carey Publications.

Holwerda, DE 1989. Hermeneutical Issues Then and Now: The Janssen Case Revisited, in *Calvin Theological Journal*, Volume 24, Number 1 (April 1989): 7-34.

Hylkema, CB 1911. *Oud-en Nieuw-Calvinisme: een vergelijkende geschiedkundige studie.* Haarlem, Nederland: H. D. Tjeenk Willink & Zoon.

Hyma, A 1947. *Albertus C. Van Raalte and His Dutch Settlements in the United States.* Grand Rapids, MI: Eerdmans.

Janssen, R 1922. *De Crisis in de Christelijke Gereformeerde Kerk in America*, Grand Rapids, MI: Grand Rapids Printing Co.

Kamps, M 1998. The Son of God Eternally our Mediator, in *The Standard Bearer*, Volume 75, Number 2 (October 15, 1998): 38-40.

--- 2001. Appendix: Abraham Kuyper's Distinction between Grace and *Gratie*, in Kuyper, A, *Particular Grace: A Defense of God's Sovereignty in Salvation*. Grandville, MI: Reformed Free Publishing Association: 353-356.

Kendall, RT 1979. *Calvin and English Calvinism to 1649*. Oxford: Oxford University Press.

Klooster, FH 1951. *The Incomprehensibility of God in the Orthodox Presbyterian Conflict*. Franeker: T. Wever.

Knappert, L 1911. *Geschiedenis der Nederlandsche Hervormde Kerk gedurende de 16e en 17e Eeuw*. Amsterdam: Meulenhoff & Co.

Knight, J 2000. Klaas Schilder and the 1944 Secession, in *Origins: Historical Magazine of the Archives*, Volume XVIII, Number 2. Grand Rapids, MI: The Hekman Library, Calvin College and Calvin Theological Seminary: 24-28.

Kossman, EH 1978. *The Low Countries 1780-1940*. Oxford: Clarendon Press.

Kregel, L 2000. Interview by telephone. From Grand Rapids, Michigan.

Kromminga, DH 1943. *The Christian Reformed Tradition, from the Reformation till the Present.* Grand Rapids, MI: Eerdmans.

Kromminga, J 1949. *The Christian Reformed Church: A Study in Orthodoxy.* Grand Rapids, MI: Baker.

Kuiper, HJ 1925 *The Three Points of Common Grace, Three Sermons with Footnotes.* Grand Rapids, MI: Eerdmans.

Kuiper, RB 1922. The Janssen Trial, in *Religion and Culture*, Volume 4 (August 1922): 35-36.

Kuiper, E 2000. Interview with Herman Hoeksema's granddaughter. Byron Center, Michigan.

Kuyper A [S.A.]. *Uit Het Woord*, Tweede Serie, Eerste Bundel: *Dat Genade Particulier Is.* Amsterdam & Pretoria: Höveker & Wormser.

--- 1931. *Lectures on Calvinism: Six Lectures Delivered at Princeton University under the Auspices of the L. P. Stone Foundation (1898).* Grand Rapids, MI: Eerdmans.

--- 1998. Common Grace, in *Abraham Kuyper: A Centennial Reader.* Edited by James Bratt. Grand Rapids, MI: Eerdmans.

--- 2001. *Particular Grace: A Defense of God's Sovereignty in Salvation.* Grandville, MI: Reformed Free Publishing Association.

Lagerwey, W 1964. The History of Calvinism in the Netherlands, in *The Rise and Development of Calvinism*. Second Edition, Edited by John H. Bratt, Grand Rapids, MI: Eerdmans: 63-102.

Lucas, HS [1955] 1989. *Netherlanders in America: Dutch Immigration to the United States and Canada, 1789-1950*. Grand Rapids, MI: Eerdmans.

Masselink, W 1953. *General Revelation and Common Grace: A Defense of the Historic Reformed Faith Over Against the Theology and Philosophy of the So-Called "Reconstructionist" Movement*. Grand Rapids, MI: Eerdmans.

McGoldrick, JE 2000. *God's Renaissance Man: The Life and Work of Abraham Kuyper*. Auburn, MA: Evangelical Press.

McWilliams, DB 2000. Herman Hoeksema's Theological Method. Ph.D. Thesis. Wales, UK: University of Wales, Lampeter.

Mouw, RJ 2001. *He Shines in all that's Fair: Culture and Common Grace: the 2000 Stob Lectures*. Grand Rapids, MI: Eerdmans.

Mulder, MS 2001. Letter to PJ Baskwell.

Muller, RA 1985. *Dictionary of Latin and Greek Theological Terms Drawn Principally from Protestant Scholastic Theology*. Grand Rapids, MI: Baker.

--- 1991. *God, Creation, and Providence in the Thought of Jacob Arminius: Sources and Directions of Early Scholastic Protestantism in the Era of Early Orthodoxy*. Grand Rapids, MI: Baker.

--- 1995. Grace, Election, and Contingent Choice: Arminius's Gambit and the Reformed Response, in *The Grace of God, The Bondage of the Will*, Vol. 2: *Theological and Historical Perspectives on Calvinism*. Edited by Thomas R. Schreinder & Bruce A. Ware. Grand Rapids, MI: Baker: 251-278.

Murrray, J & Stonehouse, NB 1948. *The Free Offer of the Gospel*. Phillipsburg, NJ: Lewis J. Grotenhuis.

Niebuhr, HR 1956. *Christ and Culture*. Torchbook Edition. New York: Harper & Row.

--- 1988. *The Kingdom of God in America*. Middletown, CT: Wesleyan University Press.

Phillips, N 2001. Interview by telephone. From Michigan.

Piekoff, L 1982. *The Ominous Parallels*. New York & Denver: Mentor Books.

Piersma, J 2002. Interview by telephone. From Pella, Iowa.

Pieters, KJ 1865. *Het Baptisme*. Franeker: T. Telenga.

Pieters, KJ & Kreulen, JR 1861. *De Kinderdoop vologens de beginselen der Gereformeerde Kerk*. Franeker: T. Telenga.

Plantinga, T 1995. Appendix I: The Dissenters of 1892, in Bouma, H 1995.

Praamsma, L 1985. *Let Christ Be King: Reflections on the Life and Times of Abraham Kuyper.* Jordan Station, Ontario, Canada: Paideia Press.

Pronk, C 1987. F. M. Ten Hoor: Defender of Secession Principles Against Abraham Kuyper's Doleantie Views. Master of Theology Thesis. Grand Rapids, MI: Calvin Theological Seminary.

--- 2005. Interview with Rev. Cornelis Pronk. From Brantford, Ontario, Canada.

Rasker, AJ 1981. *De Nederlandse Hervormde Kerk Vanaf 1795: Haar geschiedenis en theologie in de negentiende en twintigste eeuw.* Kampen: J. H. Kok.

Reitsma, J 1933. *Geschiedenis van de Hervorming en de Hervormde Kerk der Nederlanden.* Utrecht: Kemink & Zoon.

Ridderbos, SJ 1947. *De Theologische Cultuurbeschouwing van Abraham Kuyper.* Kampen: J. H. Kok.

Robbins, JW 1986. *Cornelius Van Til: The Man and the Myth.* Jefferson, MD: The Trinity Foundation.

Rouwendal, P 2001. Herman Hoeksema. Leven en opvattingen van een controversieel theoloog, in *Tijdschrift voor Nederlandse kerkgeschiedenis.* IV, 3 (September 2001): 70-82.

Runciman, S 1968. *The Great Church in Captivity: A Study of the Patriarchate of Constantinople from the Eve of the Turkish Conquest to the Greek War of Independence.* Cambridge: Cambridge University Press.

Ryskamp, H 2000. *Offering Hearts, Shaping Lives: A History of Calvin College 1876-1966*. Edited by Harry Boonstra. Grand Rapids, MI: Calvin Alumni Association.

Schaff P (ed.) 1985. *The Creeds of Christendom, With a History and Critical Notes*, Vol. III: *The Evangelical Protestant Creeds with Translations*. Sixth Edition. Grand Rapids, MI: Baker.

Schilder, K 1933. *Zur Begriffsgeschichte des "Paradoxon" mit besonderer Berücksichtigung Calvins und des nach-Kierkegaardschen "Paradoxon."* Kampen: J. H. Kok.

--- 1996. *Extra-Scriptural Binding—A New Danger*. Neerlandia, Alberta, Canada: Inheritance Publications.

Schilling, H 1991. *Civic Calvinism in Northwestern Germany and The Netherlands: Sixteenth to Nineteenth Centuries*. Volume XVII, Sixteenth Century Essays & Studies. Kirksville, MO: Sixteenth Century Journal Publishers.

Schuringa, HD 1985. The Preaching of the Word as a Means of Grace: The Views of Herman Hoeksema and R. B. Kuiper. Master of Theology Thesis. Grand Rapids, MI: Calvin Theological Seminary.

Stebbins, KW 1978. *Christ Freely Offered: A Discussion of the General Offer of Salvation in the Light of Particular Atonement*. Lithgow, NSW, Australia: Covenanter Press.

Stob, G 1955. The Christian Reformed Church and Her Schools. Th.D. Thesis. Princeton NJ: Princeton Theological Seminary.

Ten Hoor, FM [s.a.]. *Compendium der Gereformeerde Dogmatiek.* Holland, MI: A. ten Hoor.

Ten Hoor, FM; Heyns, W; Berkhof, L; & Volbeda, S [s.a.]. *Nadere Toelichting omtrent de Zaak Janssen.* Holland, MI: Holland Printing Co.

Terpstra, C 1998. A. Kuyper, Developer and Promoter of Common Grace, in *The Standard Bearer*, Volume 75, Number 2 (October 15, 1998): 40-43.

Toon, P 1967. *The Emergence of Hyper-Calvinism in English Nonconformity 1689-1765.* London, UK: The Olive Tree.

Troeltsch, E 1986. *Protestantism and Progress: The Significance of Protestantism for the Rise of the Modern World.* Philadelphia, PA: Fortress Press.

Tuininga, J 1966. The Christological Basis of Common Grace. Master of Theology Thesis. Philadelphia, PA: Westminster Theological Seminary.

Van Baalen, JK 1922. *De Loochening der Gemeene Gratie, Gerformeerd of Doopersch?* Grand Rapids, MI: Eerdmans-Sevensma.

--- 1923. *Nieuwigheid en Dwaaling, De Loochening der Gemeene Gratie.* Grand Rapids, MI: Eerdmans.

Vander Hart, M 1984. The influence of 1834 west of the Mississippi, in *Essays in Commemoration of the Act of Secession and Return.* Edited by Peter Y. De Jong and Nelson D. Kloosterman. Orange City, IA: Pluim Publishing Inc: 67-74.

Vander Kam, H 1986. Some Comments on Kuyper and Common Grace, in *Mid-America Journal of Theology*, Volume 2, Number 1 (Spring 1986): 53-62.

--- 1996. *Schilder: Preserver of the Faith*. New York: Vantage Books.

Van Eyck, WO 1950. *The Union of 1850: A Collection of Papers by the Late Wm. O. van Eyck, Esq. on the Union of the Classis of Holland with the Reformed Church in America, in June 1850*. Grand Rapids, MI: Eerdmans.

Van Genderen, J 1995. *Covenant and Election*. Neerlandia, Alberta, Canada: Inheritance Publications.

Van Leeuwen, RC 1989. Herman Bavinck's "Common Grace," in *Calvin Theological Journal*, Volume 24, Number 1 (April 1989): 35-37.

Van Reest, R 1990. *Schilder's Struggle for the Unity of the Church*. Neerlandia, Alberta, Canada: Inheritance Publications.

Van Til, C 1947. *Common Grace*. Philadelphia. PA: Presbyterian and Reformed Publishing Company.

--- 1967. *The Defense of the Faith*. Third Revised Edition. Phillipsburg, NJ: Presbyterian and Reformed Publishing Company.

--- 1968. Herman Hoeksema: Reformed Dogmatics, A Review, in *Westminster Theological Journal*, Volume 31, Number 1 (November 1968): 83-94.

--- 1977. *Common Grace and the Gospel.* Nutley, NJ: Presbyterian & Reformed.

Van Til, HR 1959. *The Calvinistic Concept of Culture.* Grand Rapids, MI: Baker.

Van 't Spijker, W 1984. Theologie en spiritualiteit van de afgescheidenen, in *De Afscheiding van 1834 en haar geschiedenis.* Redaktie: W. Bakker, O. J. De Jong, W. van 't Spijker and L. J. Wolthuis, Kampen, The Netherlands: J. H. Kok.

Veenhof, J 1968. *Revelatie en Inspiratie: De Openbarings- en Schriftbeschouwing van Herman Bavinck in vergelijking met die der ethische theologie.* Amsterdam: Buijten & Schipperheijn.

Veldman, E 2000. Interview by telephone. From Jenison, Michigan.

Vogelaar, L 1996. Hoeksema was verbaasd over Schilder, in *De Hoeksteen.* Volume 25 (December 1996): afl. 5-6, pg. 210-213.

Vree, J 1984. De Nederlandse Hervormde Kerk in de jaren voor de Afscheiding, in *De Afscheiding van 1834 en haar geschiedenis.* Redaktie: W. Bakker, O. J. De Jong, W. van 't Spijker and L. J. Wolthuis, Kampen, The Netherlands: J. H. Kok.

Wielenga, B 2000. Interview by telephone. From Pietermaritzburg, South Africa.

Wintle, M 1987. *Pillars of Piety: Religion in the Netherlands in the Nineteenth Century 1813-1901.* Hull, UK: Hull University Press.

Woudenberg, B 2000. *Hoeksema/Schilder: An Analysis of the Split of '53*. Grandville, MI: B. Woudenberg.

--- 2001. Several interviews by telephone. From Jennison, Michigan.

Zwaanstra, H 1973. *Reformed Thought and Experience in a New World: A Study of the Christian Reformed Church and its American Environment 1890-1918*. Kampen, The Netherlands: J. H. Kok.

www.ingramcontent.com/pod-product-compliance
Lightning Source LLC
Chambersburg PA
CBHW031614160426
43196CB00006B/132